Fotoğraf: Cemal Işıksel

© Dante Publishing, 2019

Mustafa Kemal Atatürk
The Speech For Young Readers

T.C Kültür Bakanlığı
Sertifika No: 23858
ISBN: 978-605-80926-3-1

Dante: 24

First Edition: May 2019

Edited and translated by: Derman Kızılay
Cover Design: Barış Şehri

As Dante Publishing, we would like to thank Işıksel Family for their permission to use the original photos taken by Cemal Işıksel, who was Mustafa Kemal Atatürk's personal photographer.

Print: Şenyıldız Yay. Matbaacılık Ltd. Şti.
Topkapı /İstanbul (Sertifika No: 11964)

Şişli Merkez Mah. Hanımefendi Sk. No:144/12 Şişli/İstanbul
Tel: +90 212 513 03 43 • www.danteyayincilik.com
twitter.com/danteyayin instagram.com/danteyayin

MUSTAFA KEMAL ATATÜRK

THE SPEECH
For Young Readers

Dante

Fotoğraf: Cemal Işıksel

PREFACE

"THE SPEECH" - THE LEGENDARY SIX DAYS IN ATATÜRK'S LIFE

This book is a very historical statement authored by doubtlessly one of the most important leaders of the 20th century. It is the real-life story written and read by Mustafa Kemal Atatürk, "the Father of the Turks" in the Turkish Parliament during a continuous session that lasted six days between October the 15th and 20th, 1927. It is a detailed account of the great military victory as well as the diplomatic and political successes of Atatürk.

The world's most important leaders have never hidden their great admiration and respect for this legendary founder of the Turkish Republic who has been acclaimed worldwide by historians as having the most complete profile for a leader versed with such diverse attributes: From strategy to courage, from creative perspectives to revolutionary spirit, from intelligence to pragmatic contextual discipline, from the power of convincing and giving a sense of belonging to the masses, to becoming a role model for so many other leaders around the world, in the west as well as the east... We can keep going on with these praises that are underpinned with sound content... The Cuban revolutionaries led by Castro and Che Guevara had always kept his example alive during their journey. While Fidel chose to go to Cuba with his 82 revolutionaries on his boat the "Granma", he was inspired by the epic journey of Atatürk from İstanbul to Samsun onboard his boat "Bandırma" in 1919. Castro, most likely had also been inspired by the great Turkish leader for much of his achievements and anti-imperialistic stand. When he came to Turkey for the Habitat Conference in 1997, he never ceased to repeat his own admiration for Atatürk in front of the Turkish youth, praising his revolutionary spirit. Only two weeks before his assassination in November 1963 John F. Kennedy, during a filmed interview at the White House, was eloquently acclaiming Atatürk on the occasion of the 25th anniversary of his passing away.

In the Speech, you will go through a thriller-like text on life and political history, full of lessons and inspirations for whoever is eager to learn from one of the most striking corner stones of human history; indeed, the elevating leadership of Atatürk served as an example not only to Fidel, Che and their fellow comrades, but all weaker nations that succumbed to the pressures of Imperialism, including India with Gandhi and Nehru, Egypt with Nasser, China with Mao, Tunisia with Habib Bourguiba and to a lesser extent Iran with father Shah Reza Pahlavi.

"The Speech", is a breathtaking account of a series of facts that we cannot unveil in its entirety.

The long thin road that led first to the Erzurum and Sivas Congresses, opened the path for Atatürk to leave his own titles and powers, while struggling at the time with his own "Pashas" who could not follow his pace and created serious internal turmoil. "The Speech" also goes on to giving an account of the impressive military field victories of

İnönü as well as the astonishing diplomatic maneuvers at Lausanne... Those days were followed by structural reconstructions such as the founding of the first political party (CHP – Peoples' Republican Party) that was going to set up the Republic, the ending of the Khalifate, the negotiations for the peace treaties, his exemplary solidarity and teamwork with his right hand İsmet İnönü, the struggles against the traitors that created continuous obstacles to his huge lifetime project, the secular Turkish Republic, his most important goal since his passage to adulthood as a young officer.

Reading the Speech, more than 80 years after the death of Atatürk, one should also be aware that his legacy and political path are still more than alive, as his political discourse, is still a fresh and valid one... Today Lenin's socialism, Franco's fascism, religious fundamentalism or wild capitalism represented by the imperialist west, are not actual political paths that have the capacity to move deeply hundreds of millions of young world citizens in the third millennium. Unfortunately, our era is marked by hatred motivated by race-religion and ethnic conflicts. Atatürk, not only had saved the citizens of a whole sinking Empire from being thrust on unknown and unfriendly shores, but also managed to place them on the raising journey of a new nation following the paths of democracy, secular education, science, art, peace and universal friendship. No other world leader before World War II had the chance to see those "contemporary rights" that seem to be so basic but yet were so evasive for all these other world statesmen. Believe it or not, for those who can understand it without prejudice, "Kemalism" is still a valid political theory as well, and can be one of the last surprisingly healthy "exits" for reaching world peace for the future of our planet. Who could be against secularism, democracy or a free spirited republic? Or against a revolution that has placed art and culture on its central point, alongside science and technology? Who would be against a society were women and men are equal *(reaching their rights long before many European countries)* where no gender, race or ethnicity differences are brought up? Who could think of being against a world speaking of peace in universal terms of brotherhood/sisterhood?

It is now time to read the historical "Speech" of a unique man whose motto in life has been "Peace at home, peace abroad".

Bedri Baykam

Gentlemen,

The 19th day of the May 1919, I arrived at Samsun. Situation and general view:

The group of Powers had been defeated in the World War and the Ottoman Government was in that group. The Ottoman Army had been damaged in every ground and a treaty to end the war had been signed and it had very hard conditions. During the long Great War years, the people had become very tired and poor. Some people had pushed the country and its people into the World War, then they had started to worry about their own life and run away from the country. Vahdettin occupies the throne and the Caliphate. He was an immoral man and looking for a shameful way to guaranty only himself and his throne. Damat Ferit Pasha directed The Cabinet and the members of the Cabinet were all impotent, inglorious, and coward. The members only obeyed the Sultan and they could accept everything which would protect themselves and the Sultan.

The enemy had taken the weapons and the guns of the army, they were still taking them away...

The Entente Powers did not respect the laws of war. For some reasons, the Entente navy and soldiers stayed in Istanbul. The French army occupied Adana. The English occupied Urfa, Maraş, Antep. The Italian soldiers were in Antalya and Konya. The English soldiers were in Merzifon and Samsun. Foreign officers, officials and special agents were active around the country. The Entente Powers allowed the Greeks and finally their army was sent to Izmir on 15th May 1919.

Morever, small Christian groups were trying to achieve their secret or clear, specific plans to destroy the state.

Mavri Mira band, the establishment of the Istanbul Greek Patriarchate, was busy in organizing groups. They were going to make demonstrations and propaganda within the cities. The Greek Red Cross and the official emigrants were making the work of "Mavri Mira" easier. The "Mavri Mira" was directing The Boy Scouts of the Greek schools and they were getting stronger everywhere.

The Armenian Patriarch, Zaven Efendi, was also working with the "Mavri Mira." Armenians were working hard like the Greeks.

The Pontus Community, whose headquarter was in Istanbul, was working easily and successfully.

The situation was very hard everywhere and several people had started to look for a solution for rescue. Around Edirne, there was an association called Trakya – Pashaeli. In the East, in Erzurum and Elazig, there was Association for Defence of the National Rights of Eastern Provinces and their headquarters were in Istanbul. There was also 'Conservation of Rights in Trabzon' and Association for Decentralization of Trabzon and its District.

Some of the young patriots in Izmir had noticed that Izmir was going to be occupied. They had made a meeting at the 14th of May and they had agreed to prevent the Greek occupation. They had decided to refuse the rule of the Greeks. At the same night a protest was made to announce this decision. Some people had gathered at the Jewish cemetery in Izmir. The protest couldn't achieve its expected aim. The Greek troops were at the pier the next day,

I will give a short information about these communities.

I had already met in Istanbul some of the leaders of the "Trakya Pashaeli" Association. They thought the Ottoman State was about to fall apart. If the Ottoman country fell apart, they were thinking of controlling Thrace. However, they thought they could only achieve it if England or France helped them.

They tried to have interviews with foreign high officials. They wanted to establish a Thracian Republic.

The Association for Defence of the National Rights of Eastern Provinces wanted to find the useful way to be free in the practice of the religious and political rights of the small groups of people living in the east. They were ready to defend the historical and national rights of the Muslim people in the region. They wanted to investigate the reasons of troubles and murders in the eastern provinces. They wanted to heal the wounds that the war caused in the eastern provinces.

The Erzurum Branch decided to maintain the rights of the Turks in the eastern provinces. They wanted to convince the world that the Turkish people did not treat badly to Armenians and the Armenian properties were preserved until the Russian invasion. On the other hand, the Muslim people were harmed cruelly, even some Armenians who were saved from the deportation were treating bad to the ones protecting them.

The members of the first Erzurum Branch of the Association for Defence of the National Rights of Eastern Provinces had determined their future work as these three points: [Printed report of the Erzurum branch]

1. Never to emigrate;
2. Form scientific, economic and religious organizations immediately;
3. To unite in the defence of even the smallest district of the Eastern Provinces that might be attacked.

To defend the rights of Muslims living in the Eastern Provinces the Association for Defence of the National Rights of Eastern Provinces published a newspaper in French and its name was "Le Pays." They had the publication rights of the newspaper "Hadisat". In the meantime, they presented notes to the prime ministers and representatives in Istanbul of the Entente Powers. They attempted to send a delegation to Europe.

The most important reason and concern that created Association for Defence of the National Rights of Eastern Provinces was the possible cession of eastern provinces to Armenia. They thought if the Armenians were shown as the majority and priority in the eastern provinces, the ones who planned to mislead the world public opinion could achieve their aim and the false idea that the Muslim people are savages who slaughter Armenians would be accepted as a fact. The Society tried to defend the national and historical rights.

There was also a fear that a Greek Pontic State might be founded on the district at the Black Sea shore. Another association was formed in Trabzon. They aimed at preventing Muslim people from being controlled by the Greeks. They wished to secure their rights and existence.

Obviously, The Association for Decentralization of Trabzon and its Districts intended to separate the area from the Central Government.

In addition to these associations, there were more communities and enterprises existing all around the country. There was the Society for the Rise of Kurdistan in the Diyarbakır, Bitlis and Elazig provinces which was controled from Istanbul. The aim of this community was to create a Kurdish State under protection of foreign countries.

At Konya and its surrounding, Revival of Islam Community Association was being created. Its head offices were in Istanbul. Around the country there were Unity and Freedom Association and Peace and Salvation Community Association.

In Istanbul there were a number of organizations, calling themselves parties or association and secretly or openly pursuing various aims.

The society of İngiliz Muhipleri [the Friends of English people] could be seen as an important organizations. In my opinion, these people were the ones who loved themselves and their personal interests and they wanted only to secure themselves and their interests under the protection of Lloyd George government.

The initiators of this society were the Ottoman Sultan and Caliph Vahdettin, Damat Ferit Pasha, Ali Kemal, the Minister of the Interior, Adil Bey, Mehmet Ali Bey and Sait Molla. And as it's understood from the information and activities, the head of this community was the Priest Frew.

The Society had two sides and natures. On the one hand, it openly directed towards the demand and obtaining of English protection by civil methods. And the other was its secret slant and its real activities. The community organized rebellions and revolts around the country. Sait Molla played an active role in secretly in the community. I will give further information about this later.

In Istanbul some important men and women were thinking that the real salvation depended on American protectorate. They insisted on this idea and tried hard to prove that their point of view was the only possibility. I will give further information also about this later on.

To show the general situation, I will explain in what condition the military units were. In Anatolia two Army Inspectorship were formed. As soon as the armistice was signed, combatant soldiers of the troops were destroyed, their weapons and guns were taken away. They had no fighting value.

I, as the head of the 3rd Army Inspectorate, arrived at Samsun with my Staff. I was going to command two Army Corps. One of them was the 3rd Amy Corps and it had its headquarters in Sivas [Its commander was Colonel Refet Bey, he came with me to Samsun]. The headquarters of one division of this Corps, [the 5th Caucasian Division], was in Amasya; and another other branch [the 15th Division], was in Samsun. The other one was 15th Army Corps. Its headquarters were in Erzurum. Its commander was Kazım Karabekir Pasha. Rüştü Bey commanded one of his divisions, [the 9th Division], and its headquarters was in Erzurum; the other [3rd Division] had its headquarters in Trabzon. Its commander was Lieutenant Colonel Halit Bey. Halit Bey had been invited to Istanbul and he quitted his command, he hid himself in Bayburt. So, an Agent commanded that division. The 12th Division was at the border at the east of Hasankale, and the other Division 2nd was in Beyazit. The 13th Army Corps, which had two divisions, was situated around Diyarbakır and was independent, as it was directly under the control of Istanbul. One of its divisions, [the 2nd], was in Siirt, and the other [the 5th], was in Mardin.

In addition to my authority in these two Army Corps, I could also give orders to other troops in the district of Inspection and also to the provinces that were in my area or neighboring it.

I had the authority to communicate and correspond with the 20th Army Corps at Ankara and its superior Army Inspection, with the Army Corps in Diyarbakir and with the heads of the Civil Administration in almost all of the Anatolia.

You might wonder how they gave me this authority while they sent me to Anatolia to drive me out of Istanbul. They didn't give me this authority by thinking much on it. They invented a reason to send me away and told me "go and see Samsun and its neighbourhood, take actions for the problems there".

I told them in order to do that I needed to have a special authority. They didn't see any harm in it. I met with some men on the General Staff and they could guess my intentions. They planned the inspectorship duty and I made the order issued. Şakir Pasha, the Minister of War, hesitated to sign the order and he sealed it roughly.

The Enemies were breaking in the Ottoman state and they had decided to destroy it and divide it into parts. The Padişah-Caliph was worried only about his own life and comfort. His Government were in the same situation. The nation lost their leaders. They were not aware of it and they were waiting for their destiny in darkness and uncertainty. Those who started to understand the terror and heaviness of the situation tried to take precautions. They thought those actions could be a solution in the area around them. The Army had no power. The commanders and officers were exhausted by the troubles and difficulties of the World

War, and they were in deep sorrow because their country was being destroyed. They were looking for a way for salvation, a dark abyss was getting deeper before their eyes.

The Nation and the Army were not aware of the Sultan-Caliph's betrayal. They were loyal to the throne and to the Sultan with the religious and traditional ties that were established in centuries. They primarily concerned about the salvation and security of the Caliphate and the Sultanate. They couldn't imagine a salvation without the Caliph and Padişah... Shame on the people who would protest this! They would immediately be the heretics, the traitors and dismissed.

Another important point is that while looking for a way for salvation, it was very important to avoid displeasing the great powers -England, France and Italy. People thought it was impossible to fight against even one of these states. It seemed totally irrational an unreasonable to have another war with the Entente Powers. They had defeated the Ottoman State with powerful Germany and Austria-Hungary all together after all.

The people who were seen as savior were thinking like the common people.

Therefore, while looking for a way for salvation, two things were out of question: Firstly, no hostility towards the Entente Powers and secondly full loyalty towards the Sultan-Caliph.

Under these circumstances, what kind of a decision could come to minds for salvation?

According to the information I have given and the witnessing I explained, there were three decisions:

First, to demand English protection,

Second, to demand mandatory of the America.

The people who made the two decisions above wanted to keep the Ottoman Stare as a whole under another state's protection. They did not want it to be shared among several States.

The third decision was about acting locally. Some districts wanted to find ways to stay as a part of the Ottoman State. Some others took it for granted that the State had already been torn apart, they tried to save themselves.

I did not think any of these decisions were allright. All of the evidences and considerations underlying were illogical and false. The Ottoman State was collapsed, expired. Ottoman lands were completely torn apart. We had only a piece of a fatherland with a few Turks living in it. It was going to be shared too. Ottoman State, its independence, Padişah, Caliph, Government—those were meaningless words.

They were asking for help from whom, for what? For whose inviolability they requested it?

What could be the serious and the real solution then?

In these circumstances, there was only one decision. And that was to found a new, independant Turkish State whose sovereignty unconditionally and solely belonged to the Nation.

It was our decision before we left Istanbul, we began to put it into practice when we arrived in Samsun.

The strongest judgement and logic was:

The main point is that the Turkish nation lives as an honorable and dignified nation. This could only be obtained by total independence. No matter how rich and prosperous a nation is, if it is deprived of its independence, that nation cannot have a higher position than a slave in the eyes of civilized humanity.

To accept the protection and help of a foreign State is nothing but confession of lack of human qualities, laziness and incapacity. In fact, it is not possible for people to accept a foreign master willingly if they have not fall to this degree of difficulty.

However, the the dignity, honour and talent of the Turk is huge. Such a nation would prefer to be ruined rather than living as a slave.

Therefore, Independence or Death!

This was the motto of all those who desired the real salvation.

Let's suppose for a moment that while applying this decision we had failed. What would happen? Slavery!

Well, would not it be the same consequence if we had bowed down before the other decisions?

A nation that takes the risk of death for its independence comforts itself that it had done all sacrifice that human honor and dignity require and it has a more respected position in the eyes of the friends and strangers unlike the dishonored one that accepted slavery itself.

To work for keeping the Ottoman dynasty would have been the greatest harm against the Turkish nation surely. Because even if the nation kept its independence by making every kind of sacrifice, this independence could not be certain as long as the sultanate existed. How could it be allright that many mad men, who are not mentally or faithfully attached to the motherland and nation, held a position as the protector of the independence and the dignity of the nation and the State?

And when it comes to Caliphate, isn't that everybody laughed at it in such a civilized world lightened by science?

As you see, to apply the decision we made, it was necessary to deal with the matters that the nation did not know anything about. It was totally necessary to discuss the matters which were seen dangerous.

Rebelling and making the whole nation and the army revolt against the Ottoman Government, the Sultan and the Caliph was essential.

It was necessary to respond and take up arms against everyone who attacked the Turkish fatherland and the Turkish independence. Of course it would not be allright to express everthing at once. It was necessary to move slowly. We had to make the nation's emotions and thoughts ready step by step. In fact this is what actually happened. If you look at our actions and success over nine years logically, you will see that we never departed from the road and the purpose shaped by our first decision.

Now, to get rid of any doubts, we must examine one fact. It was a natural and certain that, although saving the motherland from invasion was the only propose, it was a historical journey and getting success slowly made the basics and principles of national sovereignty ready step by step. The ruler of the dynasty had foreseen this historical journey and from the first moment he became the enemy of the national fight. From the first moment I also could examine and observe this historical progress. But we didn't reveal and express this examination completely at first. If we had talked too much about the future, it could be something like a dream. It could harm some people's resistance who were disturbed by the coming danger. Rhey could be scared because the possible changes would not fit in with their usual traditions, ideas and physchology. Taking each step at the right time was the practical and safe way to reach success. It was the safe way for the development and rising of the nation. So I acted in this way. However, this way sometimes caused both strong and minor disagreements, resentments and seperation between me and my co-workers in terms of principles, actions and practices. Some of those people opposed me, protested me in the effort of establising a national life, a republic with its laws when their mind could not apprehend anything anymore and their moral courage got weaker in this process.

To sum up, because I believed in the capacity of our nation for progression, it was obligatory for me to act slowly to turn that talent into reality by myself and I kept this belief to myself as a national secret.

I wrote to the commander of the 15th Army Corps in Erzurum on 21 May 1919 and I said that I was very unhappy and sad because of the desperate situation. That's why, I had accepted this last official duty because I thought that it would be possible to do our duty towards the nation and the country by working together. I said that I wanted to go to Erzurum. But I had to stay for a few more days in Samsun because of the public disorder, which might cause unpleasant events around there. I asked him to tell me if there were any issues I needed to get information about.

The situation had got worse in Samsun and around because while the Greek gangs were attacking the Muslims, the local government could not do anything to stop it due to the foreigners' intervention.

On 23 May 1919, I informed the commander of the 20th Army Corps at Ankara and told him that I had arrived at Samsun and I wanted to keep in touch with him to get information about Izmir because he could get it easily."

From Amasya on 18th June 1919, I sent an order to Cafer Tayyar Bey who was the commander of the 1st Army Corps in Edirne. I told him that "You see that the actions of the Entente Powers wipe out our national independence and create the danger of the disintegration of our country; and you are aware of the captive and weak situation of the Government."

"Leaving the fate of the nation to the hands of such a Government means you accept the collapse."

"We have decided to form a firm and strong committee at Sivas, a safe place where we can unite the national associations of Thrace and Anatolia, and make the world hear the voice of the nation."

"The Trakya Pashaeli Association may have a committee in Istanbul on the condition that it holds no authority."

"When I was in Istanbul I spoke with some of the members of the Thracian Society. Now it is the right time. Meet secretly with the right people and make the organization and send one or two honorable men to me as delegates. Until they arrive, declare by a coded telegram with their signatures on it that the members of the organization have chosen me as their representative for the protection of the rights of Edirne province."

"I swear that I will work devotedly with the nation until we gain our total independence. I have firmly decided not to leave Anatolia."

To give emotional support to the people of Thrace, I added the following information: "The people of Anatolia have banded together. All the command staff and our friends made the decisions altogether. The Valis and Mutasarrifs are on our side. The national organization in Anatolia expanded to every district and town. The propaganda for the establishment of an independent Kurdistan under English protection has been eliminated and its followers have been disbanded. The Kurds ally with the Turks."

Meanwhile I was informed that the Greek army had occupied Manisa and Aydın and their surroundings. However, I could not get any clear information about the situation of the troops of Izmir and Aydın. I wrote some orders directly to their commanders. Finally, on the 29th June, I received a coded telegram, dated two days ago, from Bekir Sami Bey, commander of the 56th Division.

According to this telegram someone called Hurrem Bey had commanded the 56th Division at Izmir. He and nearly all the survivors of the two regiments at Izmir with their officials had been taken prisoner. The Greeks had taken them to Mudanya by ship. Bekir Sami Bey had been sent to take over the command of those survivors.

In his telegram dated 27 June 1919, Bekir Sami Bey wrote that he could only receive my two orders -dated 22nd July 1919- when he arrived in Bursa on 27th July. He stated that: "Since I could not get the necessary means to fulfill the national aims, I thought that I could serve better if I could reorganize my division. That's why, I had to leave Kula and went to Bursa on the morning of the 21st June. Moreover, in spite of many difficulties, I still managed to spread the idea that a national struggle is absolutely necessary to save the country." He reported that he believed in my ideas and actions. He wrote that he had started to negotiate this subject, and he asked me to go on and send orders also to the 57th Division at Çine, and also keep sending orders to him.

The people had not been fully informed about the occupation of Izmir and, later, of Manisa and Aydın and about the attacks, consequently there had been no public reaction or protest against the attacks. In this case, the silence and the lack of interest of the nation could not be something favorable. Therefore, it was necessary to warn the people and make them take action. For this purpose, on 28 May 1919, I sent a circular to the Valis, the independent Mutasarrifs, the commanders of the 15th Army Corps in Erzurum, the 20th in Ankara, the 13th in Diyarbakir and the Army Inspection in Konya. I told them:

"The occupation of Izmir, Manisa and Aydın showed the approaching danger clearly. To protect the territorial integrity of the state, we must show our national enthusiasm more actively and persistently. Such events as occupation and annexation, which effects our lives and national independence, makes entire nation feel very depressed. Such a sorrow and pain cannot be relieved. This unacceptable and intolerable situation must reach an end immediately. All the just and civilized nations and the great Powers must act fairly. That is why, next week -starting from Monday to Wednesday- we must hold national demonstrations altogether with exciting protests. These demonstrations must extend to all of the towns and villages. We must send feverent telegrams to the representatives of the great Powers in Istanbul. We have to impress the foreigners and act in dignity and orderly while the demonstrations continue. We must avoid any harassment or hostile actions against the Christian people, I am sure that you will act carefully and efficiently, so everything will be alright and we will be successful. I kindly ask you to inform me about the results."

After these instructions meetings were immediately organized in every district.

There were doubtful people only in a few places. They had some kind of delusions. For example; we could see that delusion in the coded telegram dated 9 June 1919. The commander of the 15th Army Corps sent it to Trabzon district and said that: "Although we decided to hold a meeting, we didn't do it, because we were worried that Greeks might misbehave while we held that meeting. Unpleasant things might have happened for no reason. Strati and Politis were present when the meeting's organizing committee came together."

Since Trabzon was a very important place on the Black Sea coast, being indetermined about national initiatives and actions or allowing Strati, Politis Efendis to take part in meetings about national protests against Greeks could make the attempt seem like an undisciplined one. Surely these could be seen as a favourable sign by Istanbul and by the enemies.

There were also some people using my orders against us. For example, the new Mutasarrif of Sinop told that he led the manifestations in that town by himself. He wrote the meeting decisions on his own and made the people sign them. He sent us a copy of them. In this lengthy document, which he made the poor population sign in the middle of all the commotion, the following lines were hidden; "If the Turks could not made any progress and develop, if they could not accept and adapt the principles of European civilization, it is only because of the fact that they have never been under a good administration. The Turkish nation can only exist under a Government that is organized under the supervision and control of Europe— naturally, with the provision that it remains under the sovereignty of its Sultan."

When I glanced through the signatures under this memorandum that was given to the representatives of the Entente Powers, in the name of the population of Sinop on 3 June 1919, the signature following the signature of the deputy Mufti made me explore the spirit that had written these lines. It was the signature of the Vice-President of the party "Unity and Freedom."

Three days after I had ordered to organize protests everywhere — that is to say, on 31 May 1919—I received this telegram from the Minister of Defence:

"The copy of the note sent by the English Emergency Commissar to the Sublime Porte and the Ministry of Defence is attached herein.

1. I have recently received some extremely worrying news regarding the situation at Sivas and the things happening in Sivas as well as the safety of the Armenian refugees who are concentrating in this city and its vicinity.
2. Therefore I kindly request you to send an urgent telegram to the commander and instruct him to do every possible thing to protect the Armenians in the district under his command, and, inform him that, he will be held directly responsible if any killing or ill treatment happens there.
3. I also request you should send an order similar to this to the related civil officials.

4. As I know you are concerned about the disorder around the country, I am sure you will immediately do what is necessary.
5. I should state that I will be very happy when I get information about when these orders will be send out."

In a telegram I received from the Deputy Vali of Sivas on the 2 June 1919 stated that; "today in the telegram signed by Colonel Demange, warnings meaning following were stated ; "upon the occupation of Izmir, Christian people in Aziziye were threatened with death. This kind of behaviors are not right. I should warn you about the situation, because such occurrences might lead to the occupation of your province by the troops of the Allies"

In reality, there were neither any worrying situation in Sivas nor Christian people were threatened with death. The problem was that the Christian elements were affected negatively by the protests that the people had begun to organize and they regarded these protests as an obstacle on their way to their aims and therefore they intentionally spread these rumors abroad for the purpose of attracting the attention of foreign countries.

I sent a telegram to Minister of Defence and I wrote down the following:

There had been no incident in the Sivas and surroundings, that could scare the Armenians who existed there of old and the refugees that arrived later. There is, neither in Sivas nor in its surroundings, any worrisome situation. Everyone calmly deals with their usual works. I hereby certainly inform you and guarantee it. Therefore, I have to know the source of the news that were stated in the note of the English. It is possible that some people were frightened by the meetings that have been held by the Muslim population, following the news of the distressing occupation of Izmir and Manisa, and that had no hostile thought against the Christian elements. There is no reason for the non-Muslim elements to be scared as long as the Entente Powers stay respected to the rights and independence of our nation and as long as the nation trusts that the country will not be attacked and splitted. I take all responsibility in this subject and ask you to put full confidence in me. However, in face of the possibility of incidents that destroy and threat the national independence and national existence such as occupation, assassination and oppression that took place in Izmir and surroundings to repeat, neither I nor anyone else has the power and ability to prevent and suppress the jitter and indignation of the nation and national protests that can be held as a result of this feelings. I can neither imagine a single military commander, civil official, or any government that could accept responsibility for any events that could arise under such conditions.

I wrote down the following when Sadrazam Ferit Pasha was invited to Paris:

His Highness the Grand Vizier will undoubtedly do everything he can to protect the rights of the Ottoman at the Conference. Among these rights, there are two points that are really important: First; the complete and total independence of the State and the Nation. Second; in the homeland the majority shall not be sacrificed in favour of the minority. Otherwise, the nation might find itself in a very difficult position and face irreparable fait accomplish.

It had been one month since I arrived in Anatolia. During this period permanent communication with the divisions of all the Army Corps had been kept up; the nation, informed as far as possible about current events, had been aroused; the idea of forming a national organization was growing. It was no longer possible for me to control conduct the whole movement in my position as a military commander. Since I refused to obey the recall order and continued to lead the national movement and the national organizations there were no doubt that I was regarded as a rebel. Besides, it was not difficult to guess that the measures and procedure which I decided to carry out would be strong and severe. Therefore, these measures and actions had to lose their individual characters and they had to be conducted in the name of a corporation that represented the unity and solidarity of the whole nation.

As a result, it was time to carry out a point that I mentioned in the order I gave in Thrace on 18 June 1919. As you will remember, this point was to hold a general assembly in Sivas by compounding the associations of Anatolia and Rumelia, so that they could be represented as a single body and be controlled from one centre. The main points in the circular which I dictated at Amasya with this propose to Cevat Abbas Bey, my aide-de-camp, during the night of 21 June 1919, were these:

1. The integrity of the country and the independence of the nation are at great risk.
2. The Government in Istanbul is unable to fulfill their responsibilities. This results in our nation to be considered as extinct.
3. The independence of the nation will be saved by the determination and the decision of the nation.
4. It is absolutely necessary to form a National Committee which is free of restraint and inspection, in order to meet the requirements of the situation and

conditions that the nation is facing and defend its rights before the whole world.
5. It has been decided to immediately hold a national congress in Sivas, which from every point of view is the safest place in Anatolia.
6. For his propose, three delegates from every district of all the provinces, who gained the confidence of the people must be sent without delay so that they may arrive as soon as possible.
7. To avoid any danger, this must be kept a national secret and the delegates must travel without using their real identities, if necessary.
8. On 10th of July, a congress of the Eastern Provinces will be held at Erzurum. If the delegates of the other provinces can reach Sivas in time, the members of the congress at Erzurum will also depart for Sivas to attend the general meeting.

The invitation for the congress had been sent in a coded teelgram to the civil and military authorities. It had also been sent to certain people in Istanbul and I wrote an accompanying letter to them. Now I will summarize the main points in the letter:
1. Meetings and similar demonstrations can never attain the realization of great aims.
2. They can only have a healthy result when they are directly supported by the spiritual power emanating from the soul of the nation.
3. The most important factor that made the difficult situation extremely dangerous is the opposition in Istanbul, and the political and anti-national propaganda which harmed the national attempt. We suffer

from the consequences of this and they are disadvantageous to our country.
4. After now, Istanbul should not rule the Anatolia, but obey it.
5. You will make a sacrifice which has the utmost importance.

I stayed in Amasya until 25th of June. You must remember, Ali Kemal Bey, at that time Minister of the Interior, had issued a coded circular in which he announced that I had been discharged and all official correspondence with me should be ceased and my orders should not be obeyed.

Since this coded telegram dated 23 June 1919 and numbered 84 is a document showing a strange way of thinking, I will share it with you as it is:

"Mustafa Kemal Pasha is a great soldier, but in spite of his strong patriotism and efforts, since he doesn't know present politics well enough, he could never be successful in his new position. In accordance with the demand and insistence of the English Emergency Commissioner he has been discharged. What he has been doing and writing after this revealed this incompetence of him. He has aggravated his political mistakes by the telegrams he has continued to send in favour of certain disorganized, disrespectful and illegal organizations such as the Anti-annexation Association which does nothing but destroy the Muslim people in the districts of Balikesir and Aydin for no reason and extort money from them. It is the duty of the Ministry of Defence to bring this person to Istanbul. However, the strict order of the Ministry of the Interior is to know that this man has been discharged, not to enter into official correspondence with him and not to respond to any of his requests regarding administrative affairs.

I could only hear about this coded circular on my arrival in Sivas on June 27, 1919. On 26 June 1919, after making a great service to the enemies of our country and the Sultan by his circular on 23 June, Ali Kemal Pasha withdrew from the Government.

After giving orders to necessary people regarding the organization in Sivas and how to move, we departed from Sivas to the direction of Erzurum, on the morning of 26/27 June after a night without sleep.

On 3 July 1919, after a tiresome journey for a whole week, we arrived in Erzurum, where we were sincerely greeted by the population and the army. On 5 July 1919, I ordered all of the commanding officers to take measures in the important communication centers to take the control and prevent the Istanbul Government to send another circular against us.

I communicated with the commander, the Vali and the Erzurum Branch of the "Association for Defence of the National Rights of the Eastern Provinces."

The Istanbul government had dischared Münir Bey, the Vali. He was still at Erzurum because of the message I had sent him to remain there. Mazhar Müfit Bey, who had given up his position as Vali of Bitlis and had been on his way to Istanbul, was also waiting for me there.

I considered it appropriate to make a serious evaluation with my friends these two Valis; the commander of the 15th Army Corps Kazım Karabekir Pasha; Rauf Bey who was accompanying me; Süreyya Bey the former Mutasarrif of Izmit; Kazım Bey, the Chief of the Staff at my headquarters; Staff officer Husrev Bey, and Dr. Refik Bey. I explained them the general and particular situation, as well as the way we had to follow. At this occasion I went into the most adverse possibilities, the general and personal dangers and sacrifices to which we would all have to make in any case. And I also said: "Today only the Crown, the Government and the enemies think to destroy the ones who would come forward for the national propose. However, the possibility to deceive the entire nation and turn them against us must be considered. At beginning, the leaders must decide that they will never give up from the aim whatever happens and that they will continue making sacrifices for this propose until their last breath and in the last piece of the country. It would be better for those who don't feel this power in their hearts not to take part in this attempt. Because otherwise they would deceive both themselves and the nation.

Moreover, this duty is not one of those that could be undertaken in secret under the protection of the official authorities and the uniform. It can be carried in this way up to a certain level. But time for it has already passed. It is necessary to go out and raise our voices in the name of the rights of the nation and make the people join us.

There is no doubt that I have been discharged and I have to face with every kind of bad consequences. People's collaborating with me openly means that they already accept the same consequences with me. Besides, there is no such claim that I myself am certainly the man that can deal with the current situation. However, one of us had to take a step. It is possible that another fellow could also be preferable than me as long as that friend moves in accordance with the current situation's requirements."

As I thought it would not be appropriate to make a decision right after this speech and explanations, I notified that I ended meeting so as to have a little time to think and exchange opinions privately.

When we came together again, they expressed that they wish me to continue to be the leader of the movement and they would help and support me. One of them, Munir Bey, asked to be excused from taking an active duty for a while because of an important reason. Though I formally resigned from the Army I was still the Commander-in-Chief, just like until now, and I pointed out that they still had to obey my orders to succeed in. After this point was fully accepted and approved our meeting came to an end.

I had made agreements and meetings like I made here in Erzurum. Until I arrived Erzurum I met with every commander, officer and every kind of statesman and notable people that I communicated everywhere, in Istanbul I visited the Chief of the General Staff Cevat Pasha and his successor Fevzi Pasha, and even Ismet Bey, who worked in the Peace Preparation Commission and. The benefits of these visitings are obvious.

During the first few days of my arrival in Erzurum, we gave importance to make all the necessary steps for the congress to be held there.

The Erzurum branch of the Association for Defence of the National Rights of the Eastern Provinces, which had been founded on 3 March 1919 in Erzurum for the purpose of forming an executive committee, had agreed also with Trabzon province, attempted to hold a "congress of the Eastern Provinces" on 10th of July 1919. When I was still at Amasya in June, they also offered and invited eastern provinces to send delegates. From that time until my arrival, and afterwards, they made extraordinary effort to invite delegates from these provinces.

However, how hard it was to do these things in those days is quite obvious. Even though the 10th July was drawing on, it was the day that the congress would gather, the delegates were not chosen and sent.

As well as sending open notices to each of the provinces, necessary announcements were made to the Valis and the Commanders in code. Finally, after a delay of thirteen days, we held the congress with sufficient number of delegates.

In the meantime we were busy with other works, we were also losing time in answering the misleading telegrams from Ferit Pasha, the Minister of Defence in Istanbul, and the Sultan who were continually sending me those messages to make me return to Istanbul.

Minister of Defence said "Come to Istanbul!" Sultan at the beginning said; "Go on leave for some time, stay somewhere in Anatolia, and do not involve in anything." But then they both told: "You must come." I replied: "I cannot return." Finally, at night of 8/9 July, while the telegrams were still being exchanged with the Palace suddenly the curtain fell and the play came to an end and it had been going on for a month—from 8 June to 8 July. Istanbul cancelled my official duty at that moment. At the same moment — at 22:50 on 8 July 1919 — I sent a telegram to the Minister of Defence and at 23:00 to the Sultan himself. I announced them that I resigned both my official duties and my position in the Army.

I myself notified the situation to the troops and the people. After this I continued my conscientious duty without an official rank and authority. We were trusting only in the love and the commitment of the nation, inspired and empowered by the source of that endless strength and its abundance.

It is not difficult to guess that while we were talking to Istanbul via telegram at the night of 8/9 July, there were other people who listened to us and were interested in that talk.

I sent the following general notice telegram on 7 July 1919:

1. The national forces, which are formed and organized for the preservation of our independence, cannot be interfered or attacked. The national will is determinant and sovereign with regard to the fate of the State and the people. The Army is faithful to the national will and at its service.

2. If, for some reason, inspectors and commanders are removed from their command, they may transfer it to their successors provided that the successors have the necessary qualifications to collaborate; however, they should remain in their districts and continue to carry on their national duties. Otherwise, that is to say if men who might cause incidents like in Izmir are appointer as their successor, the command will never be handed over to them, and the all of the inspectors and commanders will refuse to recognize the appointments which is made because they were not trusted.

3. If, as a result of pressure exercised by the Entente Powers for the purpose of easily occupying our country, the Government orders to disband any Corps or any military or national organization, such order must be disregarded and not obeyed.

4. The Army will prevent any influence or interference which would weaken or dissolve anti-annexation association or association for the defence of national rights, the efforts of which are aimed at the

maintenance and preservation of national independence.

5. For the propose of maintaining the independence of the State and the Nation, like the army, all of the civil officers are the lawful assistants of the Association for the Defence of National Rights and Anti-annexation Association.

6. If any part of the country is attacked, since the entire nation is ready to stand up for its rights, each district will immediately inform each other for collaboration and provide cooperation in Defence.

In a letter, dated 10 July 1919, from the Erzurum Branch of the Association, they proposed me to be the leader of the association and accept the position of chairman of the Executive Committee. They also stated names of five other persons that they wanted me to work with.

This five people were; Raif Efendi; Süleyman Bey, a retired squadron leader, Kazım Bey, a retired squadron leader, Necati Bey, director of a newspaper called "Albayrak;" and Dursunbeyzade Cevat Bey. In the same letter it was also stated that Rauf Bey had been elected as the vice-chairman of the Executive Committee.

In a telegram which they tried to deliver to the headquarters in Istanbul, the Erzurum Branch requested them "to notify that the authority to express opinion and ideas in the name of headquarters was given to me."

Furthermore, to help me to join the congress the retired squadron leader Kazım Bey and Dursunbeyzade Cevat Bey, both of whom had been elected delegates to represent Erzurum at the congress, resigned from the position of delegates.

As you all know the Congress met at Erzurum on 23 July 1919 in a humble schoolroom. They elected me as chairman on the first day. In my opening speech, which I made to inform the members about the real state of affairs, at a certain level, and the aim we had in view I stated that it was impossible to consider a patriot who would not be able to see the bloody and the darkened threats that the history and the maneuvers of incidents made us fell into. I mentioned about the occupations and the attacks which had been carried out against the provisions of the armistice.

I told them that history can never fail to recognize the existence and the rights of a nation, and therefore the decisions pronounced against our country and the nation had no other choice than ending in failure.

I stated that; the power that would say the last word about the salvation, the preservation of the sacred existence of our country and nation along with applying the resolution is just the heroic spirit of the national movement which became like an electrical network all around the country.

To raise the morale, I summarized some information about the activities of the present time's downtrodden nations which manage to maintain their national rights.

And I explained that a national will that would have the control over the destiny of its own can only raise up from Anatolia. In order to point out the initial aims of the activities of Congress I suggested to establish the National Assembly, founded on the will of the nation, and form a Government that would derive its strength from this same will.

Gentlemen, Erzurum Congress lasted 14 days. The results of its activities are the regulations determined there and the articles of the manifesto which declared the provisions of those regulations.

If we examine the contents of these two documents by putting certain views and questions of minor importance that were necessary at that context aside, we can reach some essential and comprehensive principles and decisions.

With your permission, I will point out what these principles and decisions were consisted of:

1. The country's each and every piece inside of its national frontiers is an entirety and it is undivided.
2. In the event of any kind of foreign invasion and intervention and the Ottoman State's splitting up, the nation, as a whole, will defend itself and resist them.
3. If the Istanbul Government is incapable of preserving the integrity of the country and its independence, a provisional Government will be formed to safeguard these. The Government will be elected by the national congress. If the congress is not convened, then the Executive Committee will make the election.
4. We must make the national forces the determinant factor and the will of the nation the sovereign power.
5. No privileges that could impair our political sovereignty and our social equilibrium will be granted to the Christian elements.
6. Accepting a mandate or a protectorate is out of question.
7. We will ensure that National Assembly gathers immediately and the works of the Government are controlled by it.

Although they were put forward in different forms, these principles and decisions were applied without losing their main characteristics.

While we were working in the congress to determine these principles and the decisions, the Grand Vizier Ferit Pasha was publishing certain declarations via agencies. It would be right to call these declarations "denouncing of the nation by the grand vizier". With his declaration dated 23 July 1919, the Grand Vizier announced to the world that:

"Certain disturbances have occured in Anatolia. Meetings are being held under the name of the Chamber of Deputy even though it is against the Constitution. It is the duty of the military and civil authorities to prevent them."

We took the necessary measures against this and the Parliament was called to assemble.

On 7th August I declared to the members of the congress that; "quite serious resolutions were made, the existence and the unity of the our nation were declared to the whole world". And I added that; "History will remember our congress as an exceptional and a great work."

I believe that the time and the events have proved that I was right in what I said then.

In accordance with its constitution, the Erzurum Congress chose a Representative Committee.

There had been some discussions about my taking a part in Erzurum Congress. There were also some people who showed hesitation about me being the Chairman after I joined the congress. While it would be appropriate to attribute the hesitation of some of these people to their goodfaith and sincerity, I, even in that time, had no doubt that some others were following insincere and despicable purposes. For instance, even though Omer Fevzi Bey was a spy of the enemy together with his friends, he had somehow managed to be elected for the congress from some place in the province of Trabzon. The betrayal of this man became obvious with the things he did in Trabzon and Istanbul, where he fled to later on.

Two or three days before the Congress came to an end, there was another discussion. Some of my close friends thought that it might be unfavorable if I would join the Representative Committee and work publicly. Their ideas might be summarized as; "It is necessary to show that the national attempts and the works are born out of the nation itself and they are national in the fullest meaning of the word. Then these attempts will become stronger and will not let anyone denigrate them or yield to any negative opinions of the foreigners. However, if a well-known man like me, a target for the attacks, a rebel against the Goverment in Istanbul, the Caliphate and the Throne happens to be accepted as the only responsible person for this national movement -as the head of it- then my actions could be seen as something growing only out of my personal ambitions rather than my purely national considerations. Therefore, the Representative Committee must be formed from the delegates elected from the provinces and the autonomous sanjaks. Only in this way national power can be displayed."

I am not going to analyze whether these ideas were right or wrong. I will only mention the points that I based my ideas on. I certainly had to participate to the congress and be its leader. Because I believed that it was compulsory to put the national will into operation immediately and to urge the nation to take directly effective and armed measures. To evaluate and determine these essential points, I considered it necessary for me to work in the congress by informing and guidance and direct ruling. Indeed, this is what actually happened. I admit that I didn't believe that any representative committee could carry through the principles and decisions of the congress. Hence, time and events proved that I was right. Besides, I must openly state that I was not convinced that any representative committee could succeed in holding the congress in Sivas which I had already decided upon when I was in Amasya and brought to the knowledge of all the people by every possible means; or representing the nation and the country as a whole by a single representative body and finding ways to protect and save not only the Eastern Provinces but every part of the country with equal sensitivity, attention and care. Because, if I had had such a belief, I would have found a way not to resign but wait for the results of the efforts of those who had made some attempts until the day I started this work. I would not deem it necessary to rebel against the Government and the Sultan-Caliph. On the contrary, like certain double-dealers, I would continue to keep my positions as Army Inspector and Aide-de-Camp to Sultan, both of which seemed flamboyant and garish at that time. It was certainly risky for me to openly put myself forward and assume the leadership of the entire national and military movement. But could this risk mean something other than facing the severest penalties and suffering more than anybody else in the event of failure? But, could it be possible for a man who considers himself as a patriot to care about only his destiny while the existence of the country and the whole nation is at stake?

If I had allowed myself to be influenced by the imaginary fears and ideas expressed by some of my comrades, two great dangers might have emerged. First danger would be to admit that my ideas, decisions and character were insufficient and weak, which would be an unrepairable mistake made against the duty I adopted conscientiously.

The history has proved that to succeed in great causes a leader who has strong abilities and power is a must. When all of the statesmen are hopeless and ineffective, and the whole nation is plunged into darkness without any leader, in a turbulent time when everyone who calls themselves patriot thinks and acts in many different ways, is it possible for anybody to proceed safely and in a determined way and succeed in the end to achieve the very difficult aim by consulting and believing the necessity of trusting many respectable and effective persons? Is there a single community who succeeded this way in the history? Secondly, gentlemen, could the situation and the duty be placed in the hands of any representative body that consisted of random men who had no connection with or interest in issues regarding the nation, country, politics and the army and who had never showed any success and also failed in passing the test in issues such as a Nakşibendi sheikh from Erzincan or the Head of a clan from Mutki? And if we placed them to the hands of such men, wouldn't it be a great mistake, deceiving ourselves and the rest of the nation when we said that we would save the country and the nation? Even if it had been possible to help such a representative body in a secret way, could it be something regarded as safe?

There is no doubt that at the present moment what I have just said is seen as an undisputable truth by the whole word, although it did not appear to be so at that time. Nevertheless, with regard to the social and the political education of the next generations, I consider it to be my duty to support the things I mentioned with some memories and documents of the past.

The Manifesto of the congress was circulated throughout the country, as well as to the representatives of foreign countries in different ways. The Regulations were also telegraphed in code part by part to the commanding officers and to the other trustworthy authorities and printed out, copied and distributed within the areas. Naturally, this situation continued for several days. On this occasion, Selahattin Bey the commander of the 3rd Army corps in Sivas, informed me in a telegram, dated 22 August 1919, that "he found the publication of Articles 2 and 4 of the Regulations risky and they needed to be revised."

Article 2 is about the principle of united defence and resistance, and Article 4 is about the formation of a provisional Government.

While we were trying to make the decisions of the Congress be understood by everyone and applied as a whole in Erzurum, we received the news that certain published documents, called the "General Formation Regulations of the Karakol Society" and "General Duties Instructions of the Karakol Society," had been distributed among the army, the commanders and the officers.

Even the commanders who were close to me thought that I attempted to this and they got suspicious about me when they read those documents. They thought that while I was carrying out a national duty openly in congresses, I was also trying to form a mysterious and formidable committee. The leaders of that society and the attempts were in Istanbul and they were really acting by using my name.

According to the General Organization Regulations of this Karakol Society, the names of the members of the head office, their number, the place and the manner of their meetings as well as their election process and their duties are kept as an absolute secret.

Moreover, anyone who gives away even the smallest secret or created insecurity or danger or a suspicion that could lead to a danger will immediately be put to death.

A "National Army" is mentioned in the General Duties Instructions, and it is stated that the "Commander- in- Chief" of this Army and general Staff, the commanders of the troops, the Army Corps and the Divisions, with their Staff officers are selected and appointed. They are kept as a secret. Their duties are carried out secretly."

I warned the commanders immediately by instructing them that they should never carry the provisions of this regulations and the instructions into effect. 1 added that I was investigating the origin of this attempt.

After my arrival in Sivas I understood from Kara Vasif Bey that he and his companions were the ones behind this.

In any case, the way they acted was not right. It was very dangerous to try to make people obey the orders of an anonymous committee, with an unknown commander-in-chief and several unknown commanders, by threatening them with death penalty. Indeed, distrust and fear began, among the army members against each other. For instance, it was probable for the Army Corps commanders to worry about it and ask; "Who is this secret commander of the Army Corps I am serving to? When and how will this person seize the command? And how will I be treated?"

When I asked Kara Vasıf Bey in Sivas, who constituted this secret committee and who was the secret commander-in-chief and who were the high staff officers, he replied: "you and your comrades!" This answer really surprised me. It was, for sure, not reasonable or logical. Because no one had ever told me about such an organization and asked for my consent.

Later on it is understood that this Society kept working particularly in Istanbul under the same name, and it cannot be said that they were honest about both its formation and the information they gave us.

Beause it would accelerate and facilitate our success, it was important to persuade the Istanbul Government to stop preventing national attempts. I took the advantage of the fact that Ferit Pasha had returned to Istanbul without achieving anything, almost being humiliated, I decided to send him a telegram in code on 16 August 1919. The main points of this telegram were;

"When I read the detailed answer that Monsieur Clemenceau had given to your highness Grand Vizier, I can feel that you returned to Istanbul in such a pain and distress. I cannot think of a person who would not be shaken by the statement that shows the plan to split up and destroy our country in an openly humiliating way. Thank God, our nation, with the spirit of heroism, will never bow down before such a destiny or cruel decision like this by destroying its own long-standing presence and traditions."

Now I am sure that Your Highness don't see the general situation and the real interests of the State and the nation with the same eyes that you saw them three months ago.

"The Cabinets acceded during the last nine months had failed sharply and they became functionless at the end which is something very bad for the dignity of the nation. It is obvious that having a voice about the destiny of the nation and being heard inside and outside of the country is only possible if we trust in the national will."

"It is also pointless to see English guidance as a solution for salvation and it can only result in disappointment. Furthermore, even the English has finally accepted that the real power lies in the hands of the nation, and they believe that it is impossible to carry on a business and succeed in with a Government that has no supporters and can't give any guarantee in the name of the nation. Even if they attempted to do so, the nation would not obey them."

"The Government should stop opposing the national movement and they should rely on the national forces and take the national aims as its guide in every step it takes. And for this, it has to ensure that the Parliament representing the national entegrity and will should gather as quickly as possible. "

When we were in Amasya, we started to work and keep in touch to maintain the election of delegates to the congress to be held in Sivas, and we tried to enable them to arrive Sivas safely. All of the military commanders and a great number of patriots were making extraordinary efforts. But again the opponents' propagandas were going on and especially the impediments of the Istanbul Government also were making it difficult for us.

Some districts not only rejected to elect delegates but also replied to us in a manner that might weaken our morale and drive everyone to despair. For instance, the coded telegram dated 9 August 1919 from chief of staff Omer Halis Bey in the name of the commander of the 20th Army Corps contained the news from Istanbul which is worth noting:

"1. Istanbul is not sending any delegates. Although it approves the activities there, it does not want to make bold attempts.

"2. It is impossible to send delegates from Istanbul. The ones that we want to send will not go because they are in doubt that they will work there efficiently and fruitfully. Therefore, they do not want to make any expenditure or face the troubles of the journey. (as you know, we invited some of thoe by sending them a special letter.)"

While we were trying to overcome the obstacles related to the election of the delegates and their participation to the congress, there was a rush and an excitement in Sivas, the place where we had chosen to hold the congress because we believed that it was the safest place.

In August, we heard that several delegates had set out to Sivas from everywhere and some of them arrived in Sivas. The delegates who arrived there were asking when we would leave for Sivas.

After that moment it was time to leave Erzurum. As you can easily understand from what I have explained until now, in the Congress of Sivas our aim was to unite all the vilayets, the ones in the east and the west and those in Thrace, shortly the every part of the country. That's why there had to be the delegates from the eastern vilayets in the congress too. It was not practicle to try to choose delegates in these provinces for the Sivas Congress. It was also obvious that it was impossible to make those delegates, who had met at the Erzurum Congress, to come to Sivas. Besides, these delegates had been given only a limited authority by their districts in the name of the Association for Defence of the Rights of the Eastern Provinces and they did not have any authority relating to general purposes. It was also apparent that the Erzurum Congress had no authority to send a delegation to the Sivas Congress in the name of the Eastern Provinces.

Trying to make a new election for delegates was as useless as being lost in a labyrinth of theories.

The simplest and most practical way was to bring the Representative Committee of the "Defence of the National Rights of the Eastern Provinces Society" to Sivas and make them attend the Congress.

Altogether as the members of the Representative Committee we were five; three from Erzurum, one from Erzincan, and Bekir Sami Bey from Sivas and when we needed to examine the documents of the delegates, who had come to the Congress in Sivas, I wrote another document and sealed it in the name of the Representative Committee. It ran as follows:

"From the Representative Committee:

Mustafa Kemal Pasha,

Rauf Bey,

Raif Efendi, religious scholar,

Şeyh Fevzi Efendi,

Bekir Sami Bey.

"The persons whose names appear above have been elected by the Erzurum Congress to take part in the Congress in Sivas as the representatives of the Eastern Provinces."

We left Erzurum on 29 August 1919.

We arrived in Sivas on 2 September 1919. Starting from the far outside of the city, we were welcomed by the locals with huge cheers.

Selahattin Bey, the commander the 3rd Army Corps, was in Sivas. He and the Vali showed extraordinary hospitality in arranging accommodation for the delegates, who were coming to the congress. They prepared both the high school for the Representative Committee and the hall where the congress would be held.

The delegates, who had arrived before us, already held meetings among themselves and drawn up several projects while they were waiting for our arrival.

Several private meetings and discussions also took place after we came and it was said that some decisions were also taken this time.

The Sivas Congress was opened on 4th Thursday of the September 1919, at four o'clock in the afternoon.

Husrev Sami Bey, one of the delegates, whom I had known personally for a long time, gave me the following information; "Rauf Bey and several others held a private meeting at Bekir Sami Bey's house and decided not to elect you as the chairman." I could not believe it to be possible -that the friends, especially Rauf Bey— had taken up such an attitude and I must confess that I warned Husrev Sami Bey rather sharply not to tell me such meaningless words. I also added that what he said could not possibly be true; furthermore, it was not right to tell the things that could lead to misunderstandings among our friends.

Who would be the Chairman at the Congress was not something I cared for. I thought it would be proper to elect an older man as a chairman. I tried to learn what some of the others thought about this issue. By the way, before entering the congress hall I met Rauf Bey in the corridor. "Whom shall we elect as the chairman?" I asked him. Rauf Bey almost excitedly, in a way that it was obvious he had prepared to say that, told me in a decisive manner; "You shouldn't be the chairman!" Immediately, I believed that Husrev Sami Bey was right and, naturally, I was upset about it. In the Erzurum Congress there were also some people who had thought it was dangerous to elect me as the chairman but I have already told you what kind of people they were. But at this time, since my most intimate friends appeared to have the same kind of ideas, I felt concerned. "I understand," I said to Rauf Bey, "you are now acknowledging me about the decision you took at Bekir Sami Bey's house." And without waiting for him to reply, I left and walked into the congress room.

After the opening of the Congress, we listened to the following words of the person giving the first speech which was written in the minutes of the Congress word by word:

"It is natural that now we need to discuss who will be the chairman. I propose that the Chair shall be taken in turns daily or weekly in alphabetical order, either according to the names of the members or the vilayets or sancaks which they represent."

It was quite a surprising coincidence that the name of this man and the province he represented both began with the letter A. After I opened the congress with a speech as the host, I temporarily was on the Chair.

I asked "Why should that be necessary, sir?".

The man making the proposal said that "Because nothing will be turned into something personal which will leave a good impression in the outside world, showing our respect to the principle of equality."

While I was keeping in mind the fact that all the nation and the man proposing this were in such an abyss of misfortune, with all my heart and soul I kept trying to carry out every kind of attempt that I believed would be a way for rescue in spite of all the difficulties and the obstacles. Interestingly, my closest friends were talking about turning the issues into something personal just like this old man, for whom I had a great esteem, but he was a man who just arrived from Istanbul and therefore, didn't know anything about the underside of the real situation.

I put this suggestion to a vote. It was rejected by the majority and I held the chairman election by ballot. I was elected as the chairman with only three votes against me.

Finally, on the fourth day, we reached the principal object of our meeting and on the same day we discussed and quickly finalized the content of the Erzurum Congress's regulation. Because we had already prepared amendments to the regulation of the Erzurum Congress and informed the ones necessary.

Since the changes made caused oppositions, conflicts, correspondences and discussions, I will mention the most important ones;

1. The title of the society had been "Association for the Defence of the Rights of Eastern Anatolia". It later became "Association for the Defence of the Rights of Anatolia and Rumelia."
2. The phrase, "the Representative Committee represents the east of Anatolia" was amended to "The Representative Committee represents the whole country." And six new members were added to the members that existed.
3. Instead of saying "since every kind of occupation and interference will be considered as aiming to

form a Greek or an Armenian state, we will adopt the principle of united defence and resistance", we stated that "The principle of unified defence and united resistance will be adopted for the purpose of resisting any attempt of occupation or intervention, and particularly any movement designed to form any Greek or Armenian state."

Of course these two clauses very different meanings – naturally- when compared to each other. In the first one, there is no hostile attitude and no resistance against the Entente Powers. In the second one though it is the opposite, which is clear.

4. The subject of the Article 4 of the regulation led to many discussions. It was about:

"to decide and determine the administrative, the political and the military measures to be taken in case it is understood that due to the pressures from the Entente Powers, the Ottoman Government is forced to neglect and cede these territories (namely, the Eastern Provinces)." In short, it was about forming a provisional administration.

In the regulation of the Sivas Congress, the expression "these territories" was amended to a more comprehensive and a general phrase by saying "ceding or abandoning any part of the country."

After that, in our meeting on 8th September, the memorandum I mentioned was discussed. In this memorandum the main subject was the American mandate.

Many member took the floor. Before letting anyone to speak, I said following words as Chairman, which I quoted from the official minutes:

"I would like to draw your attention to certain points. For instance, Mr. Brown's name has been stated in this report and it is apparent that he talked about an army of 50,000 laborers that would be brought."

"Mr. Brown says that he has no official status, and whatever he says is totally personal. He says that America will not mandate; on the contrary, it is quite probable that they will not accept it anyhow. Therefore, his words are only his personal ideas and he does not speak on behalf of America. He has no idea what the mandate would be like! He says "you will name it in the way you like"! The chief subject of this report is the question of mandate.

Vasıf Bey made a long statement defining the mandate. Then he gave the word to others and later he began to speak again: "Let us accept the mandate in principle and leave the details to be discussed later on."

Macit Bey, another delegate: "The main question to be discussed in the general assembly is whether we will be able to live independently in the future or not. In what form shall we understand mandate and under which conditions shall we meet the Mandatory Power? Who will be the Mandatory Power? That is the main question." As the Chairman I said: "I guess two points arise from this report. First one is that the Government shall not give up its internal and external independence; and the other is whether the Government and the nation need a foreign support against destroying pressure coming from foreign countries. This is the point that causes the indecisiveness. If you let me, we shall refer the matter to the Commission of Motions to think and then submit to you. In any case, we don't want to lose our independence inside or outside of the counrty." Bekir Sami Bey said: "The issue that lies before us is very difficult and important, we shouldn't waste our time on empty discussions. Let us go on our discussion and make a quick decision without any further delay." From my chair, I said "Let me explain this question as the Chairman [I was also the Motions Commissioner]. The content of this memorandum was read in the Commission and discussed for a long time. However, at the end we could not make any definite decision. Before we read the commission in the general assebly, we sent it to the Commission of Motion. That's why; first we wanted to reach a final decision after reading it and deciding what the opinion of the general assembly would be like and then send it to the Commission of Motions." Ismail Fazil Pasha also said: "I agree with Bekir Sami Bey. We have no time to lose. After all, the question is very simple. Which one do we want? Full independence or mandate? It is the decision we should make. Let us lose no time by sending such an important question once more to the Committee and then to the general assembly again. This would make us dwell on the question unnecessarily and our time is precious. Today, tomorrow or the day after, we must definitely make decision on this question at the general assembly. We must not lose any time in the commission because this is quite an important question."

Hami Bey took the word. After he declared that he shared the opinion of His Excellency, Ismail Fazil Pasha and Bekir Sami Bey, he said: "Anyway, we need help. The basic evidence of this is the fact that the public revenues are barely sufficient to cover the interest of our debt."

The next speaker was Raif Efendi, who opposed the mandate. Ismail Fazil Pasha, made a long speech as an answer to him. After him, Bekir Sami Bey spoke again and said: "I would like to add a word to what his Excellency

Ismail Fazil Pasha has just been saying and I completely agree with him. If we compare the conditions that our allies imposed on us at the Paris Conference, which we attended after we won a victory in Crimean War, to the demands stated in this motion, then we will, I think, see which one is against to our independence more strongly."

After Bekir Sami Bey, Hami Bey and then Refet Bey (Refet Pasha) spoke. Refet Bey's speech was exactly as follows: "While it is certain that the mandate will not spoil our independence, some of the colleagues are asking questions like: "are we going to be independent or are we going to accept the mandate?" First of all, what mandate means should be understood. Moreover, before talking about the mandate, we need to explain in which context this word was used in the report that caused so much alarm. His excellency Fazil Pasha speaks of 'a mandate under the reservation of our independence.' The motion proposed by Hami Bey in regard to the mandate is divided into two parts; firstly there is a introduction, and then the next part gives a definition of mandate... To be able to evaluate the question of mandate according to the ideas herein, first I want to understand one thing: has the content of this motion been discussed in the general assembly or not?"

Ismail Fazil Pasha said: "since it has caused a lot of misunderstandings, three of us (that were Fazil Pasha, Bekir Sami Bey, Hami Bey) are withdrawing this motion. We disregard it."

I, as the Chairman, declared that the motion was withdrawn.

Although the motion had been withdrawn, Refet Bey made a very effective speech that filled five or six pages of the minutes. I think it will be quite enough if I quote a few passages from the minutes to show what the speaker was aiming at.

Refet Bey said: "Our object in preferring an American mandate is to avoid an English mandate, which leads communities into slavery and suffocates the minds and the consciousness of people; and to accept American mandate, which is moderate and respects the consciousness of other nations. The main issue has got nothing to do with money."

"Lexically, mandate and independence are not contradictory to each other; but if we are not strong in reality, then we will suffer while we are under mandate and it will destroy our independence. Furthermore, let's say we want complete independence inside and outside of the country! But are we going to realize this by ourselves or not? Moreover, will they let us to act as we like or not? Let's think about it! There is no doubt that today, England, France, Italy and Greece want to disintegrate us; but if we make peace under the guarantee of a foreign state today, we will be able to change the situation in our favour as soon as the conditions are avaliable. But if the situation grows worse, will it not be detrimental to us?

"We absolutely have to accept the guardianship of America. In the twentieth century, it is impossible for a nation, a ruined State, to continue its existence without a foreign aid, while it hasn't got any fruitful soil and only has got utmost a revenue of ten or fifteen million along with a debt of 500 million liras! If, in the future, we remain in this condition and cannot get developed with a foreign assistance, we might not defend ourselves against any attack, even from Greece."

"In case Greece might hold the control over İzmir— God forbid! —war may break out between the two countries.

The enemy could transport his troops by sea but we do not have any railway line to bring up our troops from Erzurum. Therefore, to have a guarantee and assistance American mandate is obligatory for us." He concluded his words by saying: "I will be really glad if I, with my words, managed to provide a base for you for the future discussions."

You can easily recognize the misleading effect of these dexterous and brilliant words on the minds of all who heard them. To prevent the minds of the deputies from being poisoned by the other speakers and to have a chance to inform and guide some of them privately, I immediately told them to have a ten-minute break.

The last parts of this speech were interesting. Refet Beyefendi thought that the Greeks were only in Izmir for a short period of time and he did not accept that we were already in the middle of war. He was convinced that if the Greeks remained in İzmir and we engaged into a war, we would not be able to handle it.

Afterwards Ahmet Nuri Bey, one of the delegates from Bursa, made a long speech against mandate. Then Hami Bey replied him by talking for a longer time than him:

"I shall now mention one part of the question which I am particularly well acquainted with. As I have been talking personally to competent persons on this matter, what I am about to say is not a prediction but a precise fact. Before I had left Istanbul, I visited his excellency Izzet Pasha, the former Grand Vizier. His Highness was also convinced that we definitely need mandate. He asked me what I thought about it and I explained my own point of view. Several days afterwards he sent for me and told me about the following problem: The members of the American Commission of Inquiry, who had arrived in Istanbul and were trying to learn the opinions of the political parties there, visited İzzet Pasha in his residence after they travelled through the districts of Syria and Adana. They expressed that the national organization in Anatolia represents the Turkish nation and that they recognize Pasha as the founder of this movement. They told him: 'If you can induce the Erzurum and Sivas Congresses to ask for an American mandate, America will also accept the mandate over Ottoman Empire!' After explaining it to me, the Pasha said that the nation had no strength to wage another war, and we definitely have to look for a solution of this kind. He advised me to explain this situation to people in Sivas when I went there. İzzet Pasha also thinks that mandate, demanded under these conditions, would be accepted for 90%; but we have to propose definite terms. The Pasha even added that as it is not possible for America to accept the mandate unless it corresponds to the desires of the nation. The will that is expressed through the Congress will be helpful for America to support this view before the European Powers. I communicated this to Rauf Bey in a coded telegram from Istanbul when he was in Erzurum." "The ones who are worried about mandate feel uneasy for only its form rather than its content. The word itself has no importance. The significant point is about its truthfulness and its content. If they wish, rather than saying we have been placed under mandate we could say 'we are imperishable as a state'."

Husrev Sami Bey began to speak; "But our aim here is to protect ourselves and prove that we will be 'imperishable as a nation'." Hami Bey answered this and he seemed as if he took a step back this time. Kara Vasıf took the word and spoke until the end of the meeting. As a summary of Vasıf Bey's long speech, I quote some paragraphs from his speech, just as they were recorded in the minutes: "Even if all the States agreed to grant us complete independence, we would still need help." (At the beginning of his speech Vasıf Bey had proposed to change the expression "mandate" with "help".) "We owe something between 400 and 500 million liras. No one would donate this amount to someone else. They will force us to pay our debt but our revenues are not enough to pay even the loan's interest. We will have to cope with quite a difficult situation. Our economic condition will not allow us to live independently. Besides this, we are surrounded by countries wishing to divide us into parts among themselves. Their desires would perish us all. What can we do without money and army? They are flying above us with their planes, while we are still dealin with ox-carts. They build warships, while we cannot even build sailing ships. Even if we preserve our independence today, they will sooner or later dismember our country." Vasıf Bey ended his speech with the words following:

"....the Americans in Istanbul say: 'Don't be afraid of mandate; it is mentioned in the regulations of the League of Nations.' This is why, I think of England as our eternal enemy but America seems a slightly better one when compared to the most evil. If you agree with me, we can write a letter to the representative in Istanbul and ask for a torpedo boat to be able to send a delegation in secret."

On Tuesday 9th September, Rauf Bey's speech about the mandate was the following: "There has been a great deal said and written in the Press and in other sources until now about the question of mandate. Although the assembly has agreed in principle in terms of mandate, it has not yet been clearly stated from whom we will get this help. It seems that America is implied here and I believe there is no harm in expressing it openly."

As it is obvious from these words, it was certain that there was a misunderstanding between Rauf Bey and the members of the Congresses, held in Erzurum and Sivas. It can be thought that the statements representing Rauf Bey's point of view arose from the wording of Article 7 in the manifesto issued by the Erzurum Congress and the Sivas Congress. Indeed, maybe the wording of this article was about to quieten those who were going too far on the question of mandate and to disturb the public opinion by their endless propaganda. Even it might only be about giving just an answer to their claims. But when we examine the wording of the article in a sensible way, it is obvious that neither the idea of mandate nor taking America as a focus on mandate issue was referred to. To explain this point, I would like to remind you of the article:

Article 7: "Our nation fully appreciates the greatness of modern ideals and is aware of our technical, industrial, economic condition and our needs. Consequently, so long as we preserve our internal and external independence and sovereignty, as well as the integrity of our country and our state; and within the borders of the article 6, we would appreciate technical, industrial and economic help from any state that is respectful to the essentials of nationalism and any state that doesn't wish to occupy our country. The immediate maintenance of peace with fair and humanly conditions is our wish for the sake of humanity and world peace."

Which part of the article is suggesting mandate or having America as the mandatory power? Only few people might say that the phrase, "we would appreciate technical, industrial and economic help from any state" suggests the idea of mandate. But it is certain that it is not what mandate stands for. We are always pleased to accept any help and we might even accept it today as long as it is as clear as a cristal. We have happily accepted the technical, the industrial and the financial help of a Swedish group for the construction of the railway lines running from Ankara to Ereğli and from Keller to Diyarbakır, and we have receieved the help of a Belgian group to construct the railway lines between Kayseri—Sivas—Turhal. We can also accept the help of a foreign investor who, for instance, could offer help to establish and improve Ankara, the other towns in Anatolia, and also offer any help to construct all the other railways, highways and harbors. Those who invest their capital in our country shoud have no secret intention to destroy the independence and the sovereignty of our nation and the integrity of our country. It is also groundless to think that The United States is the state implied in the phrase mentioned in the article, which I will now quote: "any state that is respectful to the essentials of nationalism and doesn't wish to occupy our country,". America is not the only nation that respects the essentials of nationalism. Haven't Sweden and Belgium got the same characteristics, for instance? Can any of these states be a mandatory power also? And then again, if we had had any intention to hint at the United States, it would have been necessary to say only "power" instead of saying "any power." Therefore, it is obvious that the favorable reception of scientific, industrial or financial help expressed in this article may well refer to all nations.

Is there anyone who could imagine that a comrade, who was close to me day and night for a long time, could not still get my viewpoint on the question of mandate? If that's the case then either Rauf Bey did not agree with me in principle or he changed his mind in Sivas after he had talked to some people coming from Istanbul. It is difficult to figure this out. Let us hear a little more of what Rauf Bey had to say.

"At the beginning as the ceasefire was declared, while it was thought that the Germans would not sign the treaty of peace, the English Press revealed some secrets. The first part of those were suggesting that Germany was going to sign the Treaty. It happened in the way that they told. The second part was about the dismemberment of Turkey. Thank God, it didn't happen. In that part, it was written that according to the decisions taken in the Conference, the districts situated in the east of Kızılırmak should be considered as the part of Armenia which would be under America's protection. It was also suggested that Georgia and Azerbaijan would probably be handed over to America. Turkey would own the districts situated at the west of Kızılırmak, except for Izmir and Istanbul, and would have access to sea through Antalya. The northern part of this territory would be administered by Italy and France which would be the protectorate, and the southern part of the country would be under the command of England. The occupation of Izmir proved that those secrets revealed were true. Since we are being threatened by such a danger, we are obliged to accept America's help which adopts the most objective attitude towards our country. This is what I think."

I do not know if it is necessary to listen to Rauf Bey any further in order to understand his opinion?

These long debates about mandate reached an end after finding sort of a mid-way which put the supporters of mandate to silence. By the way it was Rauf Bey who proposed the mid-way. He proposed "to invite a delegation from the United States Congress to study our country and see the real situation in order to fix the atmosphere created by the hostile propaganda carried against us for many years in America." We all agreed to it unanimously.

The Congress came to an end on 11th September. On 12th September, a public meeting was held and the inhabitants of Sivas were present. Many speeches were delivered. During the Congress, the most important questions were referred to such as to accelerate the process for the election of Chamber of Deputies and to decide where they should come together. But some issues that I will now explain made us put an end to the meetings. Some information that we obtained on 9 September 1919 were laid before the Congress in these words: "The English troops in Eskişehir and Afyon Karahisar have been doubled. General Milne has arrived in Konya. Cemal Bey, Vali of Konya, and Muhittin Pasha, Vali of Ankara, insist on showing resistance. It appears that Ali Rıza Bey, the new Vali of Kastamonu, is a man of similar character to that of Cemal Bey. Knowing that my honourable colleagues persist on having strict actions against this situation, I requested Fuat Pasha to take prompt and strict steps. Relying on the fact the Congress trusts in him, Fuat Pasha, acting in the name of the Congress, made the necessary communications and took the necessary steps. He requests your assembly to approve of these actions. Fuat Pasha severely warns the Valis. He appointed officers of high rank to take command of the national troops in the various districts and granted them with full power to act in the name of the nation." The Congress approved the request.

We pretended as if we had been convinced that the Sultan would punish the ones who deceived him as soon as he learned the facts and since it was natural for the Cabinet to be seen as distrustful after its obvious betreyal. We accepted that we could only fix the situation if we directly informed the Sultan about the truth and we made this our first objective. With this intention, we prepared a telegram on the eleventh day of September to send to the Sultan.

In this telegram, among many rigmaroles which were customary at that time, we wrote: "The Government has attempted to shed the blood of Muslims by planning to attack the Congress with armed men. It is also proved by certain documents that they received money to dismember our territory by raising Kurdistan into revolt. The men that Cabinet used for these works had to run away in a disgraceful manner. They will be handed over to the avenging arm of justice if they are caught. The nation has no confidence in a Government which organized such crimes and issued commands and had them executed via the Minister of the Interior and the Minister of Defense." And we added: "Since we, the undersigned officers commanding Army Corps in this district, had to lay before you that the nation demands a new Government composed of honorable men to be gathered and a fast and lawful investigation to be carried out to punish the criminals. The nation also decided to stop all communication and relations with the Government until a fair Government is formed, and the Army cannot do otherwise than declare itself in accord with the will of the people".

We thought that each of the Army Corps should send copies of this telegram to Istanbul

THE SPEECH FOR YOUNG READERS

On the 11th day of the September and especially the night of 12/13, all the Telegraph Offices were occupied by the Commanders of the Corps, who tried to communicate with Istanbul as agreed. However, the Grand Vizier seemed to have disappeared. He did not reply. We remained at the set and pressured Grand Vizier to receive telegrams and answer them.

On the twelfth day of the month, generally communications and relations with the Government were broken off.

Ferit Pasha's Government had given so called orders for the election of the legislative body. But up to that time, that is to say, 12 September, at date when Anatolia ended its communication with Istanbul, this order had not been carried out. You will also agree that after the turn of events that had taken place, the most important subject was to urgently held the legislative election. Therefore, we began to concern ourselves with this question on 13 September.

To defend our rights and protect the existence of our nation against the reactionary acts of the Government and the dangers we are facing currently, it is our most important duty to ensure the election and the meeting of the national assembly immediately.

The Government has postponed the elections from month to month by deceiving the nation and on different pretexts, it postpones the execution of the election order it has lately issued. The Note which Ferit Pasha has just laid before the Peace Conference shows that he gave up our vilayets beyond Toros, his attempts to determine the frontier line passing through the Vilayet of Aydın is evident that he accepted the occupation of this area as a fait accompli. The thoughtless and malicious policy he is pursuing in the other parts of the country that are not occupied, enables us to foresee that he will expose the country and the nation to dismemberment. Since we think that he is intended to sign the Peace Treaty before the National Assembly can meet and confront the people with a fait accompli, the General Assembly urges the Army and the people to be cautious, and declares that it is in the vital interest of the nation to proceed as rapidly as possible in the following manner:

First of all; Municipalities and the Associations for the Defense of the Rights must work efficiently to complete all the necessary preparations for the elections to take place in the shortest time possible in accordance with the laws.

Secondly: The number of deputies of each sancak must now be determined in proportion to the number of the inhabitants, and the Representative Committee must be duly informed in advance.

Thirdly: Any difficulties that may cause to postpone the elections or the preparations for the elections must be thought beforehand and they must be prevented, so that the elections can take place as quickly as possible.

You are requested to bring the order to the knowledge of the municipalities and the Associations for the Defense of the Rights in your district and help for the hastening of the arrangements.

The General Assembly of the Congress, which had to cut off all relations with Istanbul Government which, by interpreting the will of the nation in an treacherous way, declares the national actions and the national proceedings as unlawful, and which, although we are struggling to prove the endless loyalty of the Nation to the Sovereign and Caliph, interposes itself like a solid wall between the nation and its Sovereign, and which arms the citizens to fight against one another and incites them to do so, feels itself obliged to inform your highness about the facts below:

1. The official business of the State will be carried on strictly according to the laws in force and in the name of His Imperial Majesty. Without distinction of race or creed, the lives, the property, the honor and the rights of all citizens will be protected.
2. State officials should exercise their duties in accordance with the legitimate wishes of the nation. But those who are not willing to do their duties will therefore be considered to have resigned from their positions and they will be replaced with the suitable persons.
3. Those officials who work actively against the aims of the nation and the national movement will be punished severely in the name of people and their religion.
4. Whoever, whether he be a discharged official or a private individual, does or advises anything that is contrary to the national resolutions, inciting or disruptive, will likewise be punished severely.
5. The welfare and happiness of the country and nation can only be secured by justice, and by the maintenance of trust and security throughout the country. The Commanders of Corps, the Valis and the autonomous Mutasarrifs are expected to adopt measures to assure this.
6. Until the demands of the nation are laid before our Sultan and a proper Government which the nation fully trusts in is formed, the communication office

will be the Representative Committee of the General Congress in Sivas.
7. These resolutions will be communicated to all headquarters of the national unions and they will all be announced.

Mustafa Kemal.

In their telegram dated 14 September 1919, the Central Committee of the Defense of Rights Association in Erzincan wrote a harmless idea: "We have unanimously resolved that it would be appropriate to grant the Government a final extension of forty-eight hours before putting our decision into execution."

The Central Committee of the Association of Defense of Rights in Sivas, which we also attended, stated their long report: "it is understood from the all the decisions taken that the intention is to proclaim a provisional administration." They continued; "this did not seem to be supported by the regulations of the Association or by any clause belong to it." And at the end they advised us "to search for the means in a calm, sincere and a soft way to allow our Sultan to know our demands."

This Congress has adopted the resolutions of the Erzurum Congress and its organization, but of course widened them. Therefore, the "Association for Defense of the Rights of Eastern Anatolia" were consolidated and extended under the more comprehensive title of the "Association for the Defense of the Rights of Anatolia and Rumelia."

Article 3 of the regulations and the fundamental resolutions of the Congress has shown the realization of this highest aim as a certain object. The General Congress in Sivas has confirmed its full confidence in the Representative

Committee elected by the Erzurum Congress in the name of the Association for Defense of the Rights of Eastern Anatolia and has recognized it as the Representative Committee of the "Association for the Defense of the Rights of Anatolia and Rumelia."

After 12 September 1919 -the time when we suspended the communication with the Istanbul Government- till the day when the fall of Ferit Pasha's Cabinet happened, we repeatedly sent various messages to the Sultan, to the representatives of Foreign Powers, to Istanbul Municipalty and to the whole of the Press.

You will recall that on 20 September 1919, with a general a proclamation signed by the Grand Vizier Damat Ferit Pasha, a proclamation of Sultan was published.

I would like to remind you of its main points. I will state them one by one.

1. The tragic events in İzmir, which took place as a result of the policy followed by the Government, attracted the attention of the civilised States, the nations of Europe, it won their sympathy.
2. A special delegation has begun to lead an impartial inquiry on the spot. Our rights are being revealed to the modern world.
3. There have been no decision or proposal intended to destroy our national unity.
4. Some people tells about a so-called dissention between the people and the Government.
5. This situation leads to our postponing the elections, which we desire to carry through as soon as possible in accordance with the provisions of law, and our postponing the meeting of the Chamber of

Deputies, the existence of which is more necessary than ever, because of the approaching peace negotiations.

6. Today, what I expect from all my people is the complete obedience to the orders of the Government.
7. The justifying feelings of the Great Powers, the moderate manner shown by the European and American public opinion, strengthens my hope for soon reaching a peace which would save our dignity and position.

As you know, the publication of this Proclamation took place at the time when relations and communications between the country and the Government have been suspended and we insisted in maintaining this rupture.

If our orders and instructions had been obeyed strictly, this message would not have been received in anywhere and the nation would not have been aware of it. But, from the telegram I will read now, we understood that in spite of our orders and in opposition to our point of view, this message had been received in some localities:

The Proclamation which His Majesty has deigned to issue to his people must be immediately delivered to the officials and the inhabitants of the town. So that everybody sees that the present Government of traitors continue to deceive our Sultan with an impertinent courage — in case there are any who may still be ignorant of this.

What attracts the attention in this Proclamation, showing how His Majesty's heart is full of love and kindness for his nation and country, is the fact that the complaints of the treason of the Government presented by the people has not yet been laid before the Sultan. Because the sincere expression of this Proclamation proves beyond doubt that His Majesty would not permit these traitors to remain in their position if he knew about the weapon of treachery they hold against people. Since they are aware of this truth, these traitors prevent our Sultan from communicating directly with his nation.

Therefore, the duty of the people as decided yesterday, is to manifest their unshakeable devotion and loyalty to our glorious Sultan again and again and to directly declare to our Caliph that the Nation and the Army, united in striving for the same object, are working together to save the unquestionable rights of His Majesty, as well as the existence of the country and the nation; while this Government of traitors conceal this legitimate movement from him, and show it in quite a different way. The copy of the telegram that will be prepared by the inhabitants of Erzurum will be delivered.

To minimize the effect which the Imperial Proclamation would surely produce in certain minds as far as possible, the only solution we thought was to draw up a reply to the Sultan, rejecting the assertions made in this Proclamation, and to publish and circulate it so that the people could read it and we did so.

They informed me that they had sent telegrams to the Office of the Government in Istanbul, under the signature of the people, and that these messages had also been published in all the vilayets and sanjaks and they asked me several other questions. For example, "the people were saying: 1. Don't the people of other vilayets share the same opinion with us? 2. How long will it take to go on with these unusual affairs? 3. Which measures were taken in case the Government resists? Please enlighten us."

It was significnt to take into account these questions before answering them. Since these questions, which had been asked in the name of the people, were also troubling the minds of the deputy Vali and the Commandant.

Therefore, I sent them a long explanation that kept the telegraph line between Sivas and Kastamonu occupied for many hours. What I said may be summarized like this:

1. The national movement spreaded over to every part of the country in a vivid and a fervent way. The inhabitants, of even the smallest villages, and the Army, down to the smallest units, are applying our decisions in complete unity and sensitivity.

2. The position which you describe as being abnormal will change automatically on the day when the people of Kastamonu stops considering present state of affairs something abnormal and finding it something they have to worry about, and they will not hesitate to stand up until we realize the common ideal. It is natural that the Government will resist. Before thinking about other measurements against it, we must first carry through what we have decided to do in every direction and by all possible means. For instance, what has been done about Bolu? Are we sure that all the official communication between Istanbul and the towns around Bolu has been cut off? We still didn't receive the information that we are waiting for. I believe the government will lose its power of resistance if it extends this far till Istanbul. But if the Government continues to keep on their foolish obstinacy, there would surely be the different and still more effective methods for us to apply.

While we were trying hard to establish the national movement and organisation all over the country, we received threatening and intimidating telegrams from certain heads of the Civil Administration, who were the supporters of the Government. One of them, Mutasarrif of Urfa called Ali Rıza, telegraphed to us and stated that he had learned from the foreigners with whom he had been in touch that the national movement was seen by the Entente Powers as an organisation directed against them, and consequently, the Entente Powers intended to put an end to the Turkish Empire by militarily occupying the whole of Turkish territory. There is no doubt that this telegram was dictated to the Mutasarif by the foreigners. Of course, the reply he deserved was delivered to him.

At this time the American Government had sent a Commission, under the command of General Harbord, to study our country and the Caucasus. This Commission also came to Sivas. On 22 September 1919 I had a long conversation with General Harbord about the aims of the national movement, its structure and the main factors that would contribute to the establishment of the national unity, as well as about our attitude to the non-Muslims, and propaganda and the hostile acts performed by certain foreigners in our country.

The General also asked me some strange questions, such as: "What will you do if, in spite of the effort and sacrifice made by the nation, it all ends in failure?" If I remember right, I replied that; for a nation which made every imaginable effort and every possible sacrifice to secure its freedom and independence, there wass no other possibility than success. But if we had failed, we would have had to admit that our nation was dead. Therefore, the possibility of failure cannot be dreamed of if a nation is full of life and capable of making every kind of sacrifice. I did not even want to try to understand what could have been the General's genuine object for asking such a question to me. But I would like to say that he appreciated the reply I gave to him.

On the evening of 25 September, I received the following telegram from Mahmut Bey, the commander of the 20th Army Corps in Ankara:

"Last night Telegraph Office in Istanbul asked Fuat Pasha to go to the telegram set. They dictated a telegram via the code key which the Ministry of the Interior usually uses when they communicate with the vilayets. The summary of this telegram was something like this:

The salvation of the country will be achieved if the wise provisions of the Sultan's Proclamation are observed. The national struggle has been reflected to the civil world as something containing evil purposes. The split between the nation and the Government can lead us to foreign intervention. When the Conference makes a decision about us, the split will not be good for the success or the salvation.

It had been almost fifteen days since our rupture with the Government began. The districts that opposed the national resolution were forced to obey it. All the officers, faithful to the Government, either fled away or were arrested. Thousands of telegrams from all parts of the country demanding the overthrown of the Government were sent to Istanbul every day. The officers and the officials of the Entente Powers who were travelling around Anatolia started publicly to declare everywhere that they were impartial regarding the national movement and they would not interfere with the internal affairs of the country. I believe it won't be wrong to conclude that under these circumstances, the

Sultan and Ferit Pasha had finally realized that there was nothing left for them to do other than compromising with the leaders of the national movement, and that they had begun to seek for some means to compromise, provided that their own position would be safeguarded.

I announced the entire nation in a circular dated 3 October 1919, that Ferit Pasha's Cabinet had been overthrown and that Ali Rıza Pasha was entrusted with the formation of the new Cabinet. I sent a copy of this circular to the new Grand Vizier, marked: "For your information".

We tried to get into communication with the new head of the Cabinet on the same day. He promised that they would speak to the Representative Committee next day when the Cabinet Council would meet.

The main points I referred to in my circular were:

1. If the new Cabinet will be respectful to the aims of the nation and the national organizations formed by the Erzurum and the Sivas Congresses, the national forces will support it.
2. The new Cabinet will not enter into any agreements regarding the future of the nation until the National Assembly gathers and takes up the control.
3. The delegates that will be sent to the Peace Conference must be selected from the ones whom are wise, talented, fully trusted and recognizing the aims of the nation.

In my telegram to Ali Rıza Pasha, the Grand Vizier, dated 3 October 1919, I said:

"The nation has been in a deep sorrow due to the proceedings of the Governments that have succeeded until now which have been in contradiction to the Constitution and the demands of the nation.

For this reason, the nation has strictly resolved that its legitimate rights shall be recognized and that its future shall be entrusted to the capable and reliable people. The national forces, controlled by the regularly organized troops have the power to show and prove the will of the nation.

The nation has no desire to place Your Highness and your colleagues, who gained the confidence of the Sultan, into a difficult position. On the contrary, it is sincerely ready to assist you. However, the presence of the ones in the Cabinet of Ministry, collaborating with Ferit Pasha, obliges us to understand to what degree the policy of your Ministry agrees with the demands of the nation. Until the nation has a full confidence in you, it would be inappropriate to delay its demands for salvation and be satisfied with the half-way measures. Therefore, we would like to understand clearly and definitely whether you share the same views with us or not."

After this I repeated the three main points set out in the circular. Then I announced that "after we understand that we agree on the main principles, I will bring forward some certain considerations, holding the secondary importance, in order to alleviate the current state of dismay."

But, from certain events we had come to the conclusion that a considerable amount of uncertainty was reigning in Ali Rıza Pasha's Cabinet, and that the minds of some of those who were the members of the Cabinet were very confused. Therefore, we thought we had to take certain steps.

So, on the same day, we published another circular and declared that it was necessary to maintain the rupture of the official correspondence just like we had done until then unless an agreement was made between the Government and the nation on the issue of the demands stated beforehand.

We finally received, from the new Grand Vizier, the reply that we had been waiting for.

The Government has not been informed about the character of the organizations and the resolutions drawn up and passed by the Congresses of Erzurum and Sivas, which were referred to in Your Excellency's telegrams. Please send me urgently the resolutions passed by these congresses, so that we may be able to consider them and keep them for reference.

Isn't it surprising that the Grand Vizier and his colleagues pretended that they had known nothing up to the day of their taking office about the character of the national movement, when Cemal Pasha who, as we shall soon see, declared in his capacity as a delegate of the national forces was among them? And what is more remarkable is that they asked for the resolutions passed at the congresses so that they might be able to decide whether they would be respectful to the aims of the national movement. Could it be imagined that they were not well informed about the resolutions passed by the congresses, which had attracted so much attention throughout the country, resulting in the overthrow of the former Cabinet? I had no doubt that their object was to gain some time and, while not giving any promises to us, to devise some new devilish schemes to deceive the nation and shake its solidarity.

But if there would be break up, I decided to reveal all their real characteristics to the nation. So, I set conformed to the request of the Grand Vizier and his colleagues. In a telegram, dated 4 October 1919, I sent them, the Manifesto issued by the Congress word by word, and extracts from the essential points of its regulations regarding the organization.

General circulars were again distributed regarding the order to suspend all official correspondence.

On the same day we received the following telegram:

"The Cabinet is in complete agreement about working dedicatedly to save the country in accordance with the wishes of the nation. The maintenance of Ottoman unity, the protection of national independence, the throne and Caliphate can only be secured by leaning for support on the strength and the will of the nation, as provided by the Constitution. It is understood that the well-defined aim of the present Government must be to keep all the territories that belonged to the Empire at the time of the armistice, on the principles declared by Wilson, under the immediate sovereignty of the Ottoman State; to prevent the dismemberment of its territory within these frontiers inhabited by a Muslim majority, and to act in such a manner that a fair and equitable decision will be taken, which will safeguard the historical, national, religious, and geographical rights which we possess in these districts. It is natural that no formal obligation of a binding nature regarding the future of the nation can be undertaken until the National Assembly meets and that the delegates which will be chosen for the Peace Conference to be selected from among experts who are wise, strong, trustworthy and capable of understanding the demands of the nation. Since according to the Constitution of our country, the nation is the sovereign power, the present Government — recognizing that it cannot make decisions before appealing to the will of the nation — will take the necessary steps for holding the elections as early as possible, and therefore to hasten the opening of the Chamber of Deputies.

"The program of the present Government aims at bringing all its acts into agreement with the stipulations laid down by law as well as preventing and controlling any action that is contrary to this.

"If they continue for any length of time, any abnormal and unlawful case might result in a separation between the Sultan and Anatolia, which could produce very terrible consequences; it might — God forbid! — endanger the Capital and lead to the occupation of the different parts of the country.

"Therefore, the Government requests you to evacuate the State buildings which you now occupy as soon as possible, and stop preventing business from being carried on in the State offices, to respect the authority of the Government, which will not submit to any interference, stop entering into political relations with foreign countries, and, lastly, avoid restricting the freedom of the people in carrying out the Parliamentary elections."

The telegram had begun by pointing out that the Government would be guided by law and acknowledged that it would be their duty to prevent any illegal action, it referred to the abnormal and illegal character of our movement and added that such a state of affairs, if continued, would lead to a separation between the Capital and Anatolia, and suggested the dangers that would ensue.

In fact, the Cabinet showed its intention. It demanded that we should evacuate the State buildings we occupied, should not interfere with business being conducted in public offices, should respect the authority of the Government, should not to enter into political relations with the foreign countries, and should in no way restrict the freedom of the voters during the elections for the Chamber of Deputies. In brief, it implies that their intention is to get rid of our presence and, at the same time, ignore our movement.

The first action of the Cabinet was to expel the Representative Committee, so that it would be discredited in the eyes of the public. Following this telegram, which showed no sender or address, a correspondence began between the Telegraph Office in Sivas and that of Istanbul.

On the following day, which was 5 October 1919, we were told that the unsigned telegram was sent by the Grand Vizier as an answer to the Representative Committee. Even though there was no official and signed message, we considered it was unnecessary to lose any more time on such an unimportant point. We decided to send a reply to the Grand Vizier. I will summarize the main points in our long telegram dated 5th October:

After saying: "we understood that our suggestions were approved of and accepted fully." we continued to explain our opinion about the things we were asked to carry out and said: "Ferit Pasha's Government was the source of the abnormal and unlawful situations. This situation will disappear automatically if you take certain steps to put an end to the reasons and the consequences of the unlawful acts of that Government."

"Before our association promises its loyalty to the present Government and helps it, the Government must first declare, in concise and definite terms, that it has friendly feelings towards our national organization. Otherwise, it will be doubtful whether we were able to establish mutual trust and conciseness, and it will be possible to face an active opposition."

The telegram from Ali Rıza Pasha, which was not signed, contained the following phrase: "According to the Constitution of this country, the nation is the sovereign power." We answered it by saying: "Even though it is correct, while the Constitution stipulates openly that the Chamber of Deputies must be elected within four months after the dissolution of the previous one, until now even the registers of voters have not been compiled. This procedure is an open attack of Ferit Pasha's Government against the Constitution and a formal infringement of the constitutional charter.

Therefore, it is the first sacred duty of every Constitutional Government that recognizes the sovereignty of the nation and believes that the enforcement of the law is its duty, to look upon such actions as a crime, according to the related articles of the Penal Code, and to apply the provisions laid down by law as widely as possible in dealing with those who are found guilty." Then we started to put forward the following proposals:

1. Make a formal announcement declaring that peace and order prevail throughout the country and that the national movement is completely justified and legitimate; so that it will be seen that the Government supports the united nation.

2. There are some high ranked officials who were the agents of the former Government in their treachery. Bring them into the related courts. Make the necessary proceedings about certain former Valis, who have opposed the national movement, so that they will be debarred from any further state service. Certain officials who have been dismissed because they have served the national movement, shall be reinstated in their former positions.

3. Immediately dismiss the ones whose reinstatement have not been approved by the National Assembly, because such reinstatement was due to the false policy of the Government. Give important military positions to capable men.

4. Until the former Ministers, Ali Kemal Bey, Adil Bey, and Suleyman Shefik Pasha have been handed over to the Supreme Court when the National Assembly is opened, we demand, in the name of the inviolability of the law and the sacred character of national rights, that they should be not allowed to escape anywhere. We also demand that Refik Halit Bey, General Director of Posts and Telegraphs, shall be arrested immediately and brought before the related courts.

5. Put an end to all the proceedings or pressure on the ones who have participated in or have supported the national movement.

6. Set the Press free from foreign censorship.

We then reached the fifth day since Ali Rıza Pasha's Government had come to power. We still could not come to terms yet. The official connections and correspondence between the country and Istanbul were still suspended. His Highness the Grand Vizier did not reply to our proposals; you will see that he never replied. None of the members of the Cabinet wanted to meet with us.

Then we started to recieve message from Yunus Nadi Bey. He began with these words:

"I have thought that upon the change in the Government, which was solely due to the fact that the will of the nation has succeeded in realizing its sovereignty, there would be an agreement soon between the new Government and the national movement. As I result of my research, I understood that there are one or two points on which there is a conflict. Since getting late to reach an agreement would not be good in and outside of the country itself, I feel it my duty to submit some demands to you."

Then he declared their knowledge and thoughts about the points I will summarize now as the first subject.

1. It was groundless to think negatively about certain members of the Government only because they were also the members Ferit Pasha's Government and Abuk Pasha took part in overthrowing Ferit Pasha's Government.
2. Rıza Pasha's Government was only a temporary one and it could last until the result of the elections for the legislative body become known.
3. The present Government has done nothing that could cause any doubt that they were not favorable to the adoption of all the claims and aims of the nation and were not fully resolved in trying to realize them.
4. There was no reason to doubt about the people's, like Cemal Pasha's and Abuk Pasha's, being the delegates and guarantors of the national organization within the Cabinet.

As the second subject, Yunus Nadi Bey mentioned persons. Having entirely the same ideas with us in this regard, he said: "I will venture to advise you to act with moderation," and he explained his point of view that it would be very important to prevent the good effects, produced by the success of the national cause, from appearing to be a kind of a revenge in the eyes of certain persons.

Yunus Nadi Bey continued: "From my association with the members of the present Cabinet, I understand that they are determined to completely carry out the claims of the national organization." And he added:

"Cemal Pasha, the Minister of Defence, has declared that this idea has already been sufficiently expressed in the manifesto which will be published today, but, as the manifesto has been written in the official language, it was not advisable to lay too much emphasis on some formal expressions."

After Yunus Nadi Bey had informed us of the sincere desire of the new Grand Vizier and his Cabinet to meet directly a deputation appointed by the leaders of the national organization, so as to obviate any misunderstanding, he summarized his ideas in this sentence: "What I consider to be the most important thing at the present moment is that the crisis has not been solved yet and it should not continue in an uncertainty."

Since Yunus Nadi Bey said that he was waiting to hear my views, and I sent him this reply:

"Have you seen the essential and the minor, proposals which the Representative Committee has laid before the Grand Vizier, and the answer of him, especially the last paragraphs of it?

From your explanations and remarks, we understand that you have never seen those documents and they were told to you by the people who have not completely understood the content and the sincerity of our proposals.

For this reason, we find it difficult to discuss about this matter here. To throw a little light on some of your remarks, which seem to represent your own personal opinion, below we give some explanations in their proper order.

"We also believed that there would soon be a harmony between the new Government and our national movement. The cause of the delay should be searched not on our side, but to the hesitating and vacillating attitude that the new Government has taken up during the last four days. The new Government has not even told us that any difference of opinion exists between them and us. Without doubting on the honor of the former Ministers who kept their positions in the new Governement, it is still an important point and needs to be considered that, consciously or unconsciously, they have been taking part in the treacherous actions of the former Government. We do not know the role Abuk Pasha played in the overthrowing of the former Cabinet. But we know very well the power brought out this result. Our aim is not, as you think, to look upon this Government as a temporary one. On the contrary, we wish it will be an important Government that will decide upon the future of the nation and conclude the peace. The foreigners have no importance in our eyes when the main interests of the nation is the subject. We are among those who don't refuse to adopt their way according to the gossips of the foreigners. We know the internal and the external situation very clearly. Our steps have not been taken haphazardly, they are based on careful considerations, on a firm foundation, on the true force of the nation as a whole, consisting of a regular organization and the firm will of the nation. The nation is determined to make its full sovereignty recognized by the whole world. We have taken every necessary steps everywhere to ensure this. We demand that the present Government accept the national demands and claims and complete them. Because otherwise it can't keep the power. We do not know Abuk Pasha. But we can't expect Cemal Pasha to be anything other than being the representative of our national organization.

We hoped that as soon as Cemal Pasha became a Minister he would keep in touch with us before anyone else, so that he would understand the actual situation, and according to it he would try to bring the ideas of the Government and the national organization into an agreement. But now we see he is trying to avoid such a communication. The proposals and demands we addressed to the new Government were not personal or arbitrary. They were the summary of all the suggestions made to our Representative Committee by all the vilayets and autonomous sanjaks and the places under their administration, five commanders of Army Corps and all the heads of the Civil Administration who were faithful to the national organization. The Representative Committee made this summary of the proposals in such a way that it would not place the Government in a difficult position. The demands and the suggestions do not consist any of the inconveniencies that you describe. If the Government sincerely and seriously enters into communication with the Representative Committee, there is no reason to not to decide upon when and in which shape our proposals will be fulfilled by the Government. However, the concluding paragraphs of the Grand Vizier's telegraphic reply to Representative Committee on 4 October are remarkable. There is no doubt that there can be no agreement so long as the ides that our lawful national movement and its leaders are illegitimate and unlawful continues to exist.

If the manifesto, which as you said will be published today, for any reason or in any manner, uses a critical language about our national organization and our national movement, even if they would be some formal words, we will immediately come to the conclusion that there is no possibility for an agreement. Moreover, unless Istanbul Government comes to a definite understanding with the Representative Committee, their manifesto will not be received anywhere. It might remain within Istanbul.

Our Representative Committee is a national and legitimate committee that was elected by the Erzurum and Sivas Congresses, consisting of representatives chosen via a general election in all the vilayets and autonomous sanjaks. Its ability to represent and its strength can easily be seen in its works and actions. Until the day Chamber of Deputies assembles and takes the control, the Representative Commiitee must deal with the future of the country. Of course the Government will strengthen its position and its authority by keeping sincere relations and close contact with our Committee. It is natural that the interests of the country and the nation would be in risk if different courses of action are taken.

The Representative Committee assembled in Sivas is prepared and willing to enter into sincere and direct relations with the Government. It does not have the authority to give this duty to someone else. If we can reach a complete understanding with the Government, then we can consider taking further steps that will facilitate our relations and trust in each other.

In short, it will only be possible to put an end to the present complicated situation quickly, if first of all the Government publishes a manifesto in terms similar to those we have proposed and demanded, which will not consist merely of empty words, but will be expressed in sincere language and if the Grand Vizier gives us a straightforward answer, in which he will declare that he has favorably received our other proposals and that they will be carried out. Otherwise, when our telegrams and manifestos are being controlled, stolen, and kept by Refik Halit Bey, it seems very strange to speak about the sincerity of the Government.

If the Government continues its hesitant attitude even for a few days longer, they will completely lose the trust of nation, the thing which the nation has not experienced yet. In the telegrams we receive from all parts of the country, people are asking whether confidence can be established in the new Government or not."

Yunus Nadi Bey understood the real situation from the information and explanations I gave him. He did not consider it necessary to continue communicating with us. On the contrary, he tried to warn the new Government, and Cemal Pasha....

Finally the next day after our exchange of telegrams with Yunus Nadi Bey, we received the following telegram from Cemal Pasha — although no reply had yet arrived from the Grand Vizier.

The summary of correspondence made until now:

1. The Cabinet agrees with you and recognizes that the will of the nation is sovereign. It is only sad to be looked upon as a Government of revenge. The goverment also agrees that the ones who are guilty must be punished in accordance with law.
2. It undertakes to end the injustice that some Valis suffer from and indemnify them and to select and appoint the adequate ones, as well as to restore dignity and the order in the Army.

3. The State will rely on the national will and the Representative Committee to restore its dignity and its prestige in the eyes of the foreign countries.
4. In my position as the delegate of the Representative Committee, I declare to you in full sincerity and with respect that the Government wants to see the Representative Committee as a support, without being seen as a supreme authority inside and outside of the country and it appreciates its great power. Above all, the Government considers that it would be useful if telegrams are exchanged freely and mutually and it is contended that the Valis and Military Commanders who were newly appointed or re-installed in their former offices took up their posts immediately, and the Govermnment finds it useful that the recently accepted electoral law are circulated and published throughout the country.
5. When I promise that the actions against the will of the national will be avoided, the only point that will remain open for discussion would be to fix the time and the manner how the details would be carried out, which, I think, will be very easy. To be able to work together immediately to realize our aim, which is the salvation of our country, I request you not to insist on details and grant me your support. Yours respectfully.

We immediately gave a friendly and a sincere reply to this telegram:

Below is the reply to your telegram point by point and in their proper order.

1. We thank the Government in the name of the nation for accepting the sovereignty of the national will in

complete accord and unity with us. We, also think that it is something to be afraid of if the Government, the Representative Committee and the whole of the national organization were to be suspected of pursuing a revenge. On this point, we completely agree with the Cabinet; in regard to the necessity of punishing the ones who are guilty.

2. We thank you also specially for the consent of the section two. The reason why this point was required to be explained before was that: We were afraid that if certain Valis and commanding officers who were not accepted by the people because of their opposition to the national movement and to the national activities, would be — even temporarily — reinstated with the propose of complying formalities, they would not be accepted by the people again and this would be disrespectful to the Government.

3. We are grateful especially for the third section. With God's help, we will be able to secure the welfare and the freedom of our country and our nation.

4. We declare in all good faith that, in return for the sincerity and seriousness shown by the Cabinet, the Representative Committee will never assume the position of being a supreme authority, either in the country itself or in regard to foreign relations, on the contrary, it will consider that it is their duty, for the sake of the country and the nation, to support and uphold the authority and the power of the Government within the limits of the principles adopted. We request them not to have any doubts about this matter. That, in accordance with Article 8 of our regulations, Your Excellency's being a

member of the Cabinet as the delegate of our Reprentative Committee pleases us a lot because it ensures the harmony between the both parties in terms of actions and decisions.

Since now an agreement between the Government and our national organization has been made, it is natural to remove the limitations set on the communication. However, as the Representative Committee must keep its connection with the offices of organization throughout Anatolia and Rumelia, we especially request that we may be permitted to carry on our private telegraphic communication as we have been doing until now.

We earnestly request you to send us in confidence, before its publication, a copy of the manifesto that we asked the Government to issue because after that the instructions sent out by the Representative Committee might well be founded on it and thus the nation may confide in us. Even one inappropriate word of manifesto might cause the misunderstanding in the minds of the people to continue and might put the Representative Committee in a very difficult position in the eyes of the nation.

After we have circulate them, we will now send you a copy of a thanking note which will be presented to the Sultan, as well as a copy of the manifesto we will address to the nation and if the Government would have any remarks, it will be taken into consideration.

We kindly ask you to inform us what particular idea inspired you when you drafted the new electoral law, so that we will be able to make our comments on it.

5. After having arrived at a complete agreement on the main points, there can be no doubt as to the sincerity of your honorable colleagues, it is quite natural

that the details will be decided upon automatically. My colleagues and I ask you to be sure that we will work with all the strength, the sincerity and with all the possible energy to help the work carried on by Your Excellency and the Government of which you are a member, and our goal to save our country will be accomplished as soon as possible. I send you our greetings and the esteem of all my colleagues, who are with me here.

Since we understood that the Government did not want us to see their manifesto before it was published, we then published our own manifesto written for the nation without consulting them and we sent the telegram to the Sultan afterwards.

Our manifesto dated 7 October, 1919 showed people that our course was right and successful, and explained why it was necessary for us to continue to act in a perfect unity as we had been doing till then. In short, this manifesto was intended to inform, warn and strengthen the morale of people.

The telegram that was written to the Sultan expressed our thanks on behalf of the nation.

The principle accepted and observed in civilized States governed on the principle of the sovereignty of the nation provides that the administration of the State is confined to the hands of that political party which represents the general tendency of the nation most powerfully and which is able to serve its demands and interests with the greatest authority and power; and the responsibility of it is entrusted to the most prominent leaders of the nation.

A government which does not combine all of these cannot work anyhow. The idea to form a weak government composed of a second-rate elements chosen from a powerful party and try to carry on with such a government by the help of the advices and the instructions given by the first-rate leaders that belong to the same party is something unreasonable. The tragic results of such a system became quite evident especially in the last days of the Ottoman Empire.

As I have told you, since the Government did not tell the content of their manifesto to us before its publication, we made an announcement to the public without consulting them.

Thereupon, the Government informed us through Cemal Pasha on October 9 that they considered it necessary to publish the following four points by several means:

1. There was no connection between the national movement and the Committee of Union and Progress.
2. The Ottoman Empire's intervention to the World War I was wrong. It was essential to make publications that openly declares the names of the ones who were responsible for this mistake and to investigate this and punish them in accordance with law.
3. Anyone who committed crimes of any kind during the war could not escape from the punishment laid down by the law.
4. The elections must take place freely.

After telling these four points, Cemal Pasha mentioned that declaration and publication of them would end certain misunderstandings in the country itself, as well as in foreign countries, and he especially requested us, for the sake of the interests of the country, to receive these proposals with favor.

These requests can serve as a criterion to understand how Ali Riza Pasha's Cabinet thought superficially, and how weak was the foundation on which they based their decisions. These miserable persons who were incapable of seeing the depths of the terrible abyss into which the State was plunging, shut their eyes so that they would not see the real and serious way to salvation. The true and the serious way scared them more.

They were acting like this because their understanding was a narrowed and limited kind and they were weak and had an indecisive character.

Was it not actually a natural sign of The Sultan's impotence that he became practically a total servant to the others while he was supposed to serve his own country as the Sultan-Caliph?

What else could Ali Riza Pasha, who was Ferit Pasha's successor, and his colleagues who were transferred from the previous Government as well as new ones, do other than continuing to work from the point at which Ferit Pasha had left off and carry on the demands of the enemies?

We were perfectly well aware of this. However, due to various reasons and considerations, which were understandable things, there was no other way to reach success other than waiting and being patient.

In spite of the fact that the Government's manifesto was nonsensical and had misstatements in it, we resolved to support the new Government on 7 October in the name of the Representative Committee. We announced to the people the good news that the new Government and the national organizations had reached to a complete agreement and taken the necessary steps everywhere to prevent any interference with the affairs of the Government and to support its authority and its actions. We took up an attitude that could prove that real and complete unity existed internally and externally. In short, we tried to do every possible thing which anyone who supported the independence of their country in all sincerity and with pure intentions. We made suggestions and gave advice to hold the elections as quickly as possible. But there was one thing we did not do: We did not suppress the national organizations and did not dissolve the Representative Committee. This was our only fault.

There is no doubt that our agreement with the new Government, in which the nation trusts, will allow our domestic policy to influence our foreign policy very favorably and effectively. Under those unusual conditions, it was not possible to avoid some unpleasant incidents in certain places and it was an inevitable and a natural situation. If we consider for a moment the oppression and the malice that the innocent and downtrodden citizens of some districts -such as Kutahya, Bilecik and Eskisehir- face with, we can easily see how justified are the acts which we complain about. On the other hand, if we consider that the lethargic attitude of the former Government is the reason of the deplorable and heartrending state of affairs in these districts, I am convinced that it would be unjust to make the national movement a target for criticism and reproach. I ask you, also, to excuse the Vali of Kastamonu for his telegram that you mentioned. Because this kind of messages have been sent from not only Kastamonu, but also from the other places. If the former attitude of the Government, which appeared to be ambiguous at the beginning, had lasted for a few more days, millions of similar messages would have have been sent to you from all parts of the country. From now on, we will take all the necessary steps and exert the desired influence to prevent the recurrence of such an incident and in accordance with your advice, we will try in all good faith to secure the complete unity and have sincere relations with the Government within the limits of the law. Yours respectfully."

While I was reading Ahmet Izzet Pasha's advice letter and our answer to him, I remembered a thing. I will mention it so that it may be put on record and find a place for itself in history.

One day Ali Riza Pasha visited Ahmet Izzet Pasha. During their conversation he insulted me and exclaimed —just as though he had made a sudden discovery: "They will proclaim a republic— a republic!"

The things which proved the competency of our glorious nation were The Congress of Erzurum, The Congress of Sivas and the decisions taken in them. The application of these decisions which created the unity and solidarity and the downfall of The Government of Ferit Pasha, which attempted to eliminate those who gathered in The Congress of Sivas, and the attitude and the consciousness of the people were also the proofs of the nation's competency.

Cemal Pasha told a great and a clear lie when he said "the current government which gains the confidence of the nation". The nation had not yet had confidence in the government. This statement would be said only after the government actually voted to show its own confidence in the National Parliament itself. However, the members of the National Parliament had not been yet chosen when he said it.

When The Minister of Defence said that only one person trusted in them at the time. This person was the traitor Vahdettin, who exploited the chair of presidency.

He wanted to see that the Representation Committee found it necessary to make a compromise with him which would mean that he gained the confidence then on behalf of the nation. If what they aimed at was this, why did they need to eliminate the committee which was enabling them to get the confidence of the nation then?

The fall of the Government of Ferit Pasha had a positive impact on the morale and the emotions of some groups which were in doubts. Including senior civilian officer and military forces, all of them got organized rapidly.

Ali Fuat Pasha dealt with almost all the cities in the west. He went to Eskişehir, Bilecik, then Bursa and he got in contact with the people necessary.

The Colonel Mr. Kazım (Kazım Ozalp, the President of the Parliament), who was in Balıkesir, dealt with the national organization and the military order in that area.

Colonel Mr. Bekir Sami, who was in Bursa, sent a Vali who was working on behalf of Ferit Pasha to İstanbul on October 8. Thereby, Bekir Sami got the decisions of the Congress to be applied and he made a central commission to be formed. As well as taking care of the national organization, we were also dealing with the election of the parliament eagerly.

While dealing with choosing the parliamentarians, we were thinking of a place where the parliament should gather. As you remember, when I wrote a reply about this issue to Refet Pasha's telegram who was in Erzurum, I said that the Parliament should not gather in İstanbul; it should gather somewhere in Anatolia. I thought that it was totally unreasonable and pointless to gather the Parliament in İstanbul. However, without convincing the public and those who had the authority, our idea would not come true. The drawbacks of coming together in Istanbul had to be proved clearly. For this purpose, we attracted the attention of the Government in Istanbul. We did it through the help of Mr. Ali Kemal and Mr. Mehmet Ali's actions, we made the foreigners and the Greeks see the national aim something against Christianity and also we made it seem so thanks to the meetings in the Armenian Patriarchate and the attempts of the Party of Hurriyet and Itilaf.

On 13 October 1919, after opening the Parliament, we asked the government, through Cemal Pasha, how the Association for the Defense of the Rights would be treated. Also we asked them how they secured the safety if the Parliament might gather in Istanbul. On the same day, we asked Colonel Mr. Şevket, the participant in the central committee of our organization in İstanbul, what needed to be done to take the precautions for the security in case of a gathering in Istanbul.

It was important to point out that it was confirmed that the national organization and the Representation Committee were accepted as a political entity by the Government of Istanbul, our meetings were held officially; thereby, both sides accepted to follow the results.

Therefore, it was significant to make them regard the reports as protocols and make the Minister of Navy, who was a delegate of the Government of Istanbul, sign them.

The protocol dated October 21, 1919 comprised of the suggestions of Salih Pasha and some other issues which had no drawbacks in their contents to approve.

The second protocol, dated October 22, 1919, was the summary of the report of a long interview and the discussions.

The meeting started with a detailed discussion. Both sides had to give assurance about caliphate and sultanate. Then, the articles of Sivas Congress, which was held on September 11, 1919, were discussed.

1. In the first article of the proclamation, it was approved that the boundaries that were decided and fixed must be ensured in case even of a small demand. It was approved to prevent all the false actions practiced in the name of enabling Kurdish people the so-called freedom. It was discussed that Cilicia, the most fruitful and the richest land of Anatolia, occupied by the foreigners, cannot be divided from the country to establish a barrier between Arabic lands and Turkey under any conditions. It was also assured that Cilicia would never be seperated from the country, Aydın also cannot be seperated from the country.

   When it comes to Thrace; we discussed the issue about the separation of the area from the East of Thrace to the Midye-Enez line in the name of establishing a so-called free government but in reality it was going to be a colony. It was accepted that the border of Edirne and Maritza would never be abandoned even if it was intended to create a free Islamic government there. Following the ultimate decision of the Parliament was also approved.

2. The forth article of the proclamation was discussed carefully. It was totally unacceptable to give any political privilege to the non-Muslim communities which would harm our social stability. It was also emphasized that for the sake of gaining our total freedom, we were all obliged to oppose it and we would never

give up on this decision at any price; otherwise, it would be detrimental to our freedom. Not giving excessive amount of privileges to the Christian communities was fixed as a a purpose which could well be attained. Besides this; it was accepted that –like it was also emphasized at the end of the first article- the decisions of the National Parliament would be followed in this case and in the other cases to defend our rights.

3. According to the seventh article of the proclamation; we discussed how we would meet our needs in technical, industrial and financial issues without giving any compromise from our freedom. It was discussed that if there would be a state which could bring capitals to our country, since it would not be easy to foresee how much that state would be controlling our economy, we decided that this matter must first be pondered upon by experts and they should lay down the necessary limitations that would prevent it to harm our freedom and our national interests. Then, the plan they would come up with was also to be examined by the National Parliament.

4. The other articles of the decisions taken at the Sivas Congress held in September 11, 1919 were all approved on condition that they would also be presented to the National Parliament.

5. Then the decisions related to the organizational issues, taken in the Sivas Congress -held on September 4, 1919 -, were discussed and that part was the eleventh article and it was about the position of the

Association for the Defense of the Rights of Anatolia and Rumelia and how it would act in the future.

It was stated that after gathering the National Parliament when the utmost-level of security was provided the Representation Committee would be dismissed and the aim of the Committee would be determined in a specific meeting which would be the substitution of a congress.

It was stated that since the government ordered that the election should be made in a comfortable environment, when the election was made, the Representation Committee was not expected to intervene to it.

It was discussed that if there was any participant of Ittihat-Terakki who comitted crime in the army, they would not be selected as parliamentarians and to manage that The Representation Committee needed to get some certain advices about it. The Representation Comittee's position as a mediocre was added seperately as the third protocol.

The fourth protocol which was not signed due to secrecy was the following;

1. Dismissing some commanders from the army and reviewing certain decisions and the Sultan's command on putting some officers on trial.
2. Seeking a solution to bring those who were exiled to Malta for the purpose of making legal inquiry in the court.
3. Putting the villanous Armenians on trial (The Parliament was to take care of that.)
4. The government was to make a protest to release Izmir; if necessary, after informing the public secretly, we would also trigger them to make protests.

5. Change the general commander of the gendarmerie, the commander in chief, the police chief and the minister of internal affairs. (The Ministry of Defence and Interior would follow it.)
6. Preventing the Committee of Ingiliz Muhipleri [The supporters of Britain's mandate] to make people stamp pamphlets.
7. Stopping the publishing of the newspapers and the communities which were established with the money gained from a source outside the country. (Forbidding the officers to be a member of them.)
8. Helping Kuva-yı Milliye of Aydın; providing them food.
9. The officers who took part in the National Struggle would be stable until ensuring the absolute peace and security. Also, the officers who were dismissed because of their acts against the national struggle was to be discussed seperately before they were appointed with anew positions.
10. Trasporting the immigrants of The West of Thrace.
11. Providing Sadun Pasha and his officers whatever they needed.

In the fifth protocol, which did not have any signature on it, there were also the names of the people who were able to attend the Conference for Peace. The government would act free there on condition that it complied with the principles.

I guess you realize that the most significant point determined in these meetings was to make the National Parliament gather.

We made Salih Pasha accept our former thoughts and beliefs that it was inappropriate to gather the National Parliament in Istanbul. However, Pasha emphasized that he approved it himself. Therefore, he could not promise anything on behalf of the rest of the government. He promised that he would try all his best to convince the rest of the government and make them agree with him and he stated that if he would not succed in this, there would be left nothing for him other than resigning from the government.

Salih Pasha could not make it.

The order and information which are given to parliamentarians are:

First Matter: it is known that Istanbul is occupied by especially the naval forces and the land forces of English, and the forces which are attendant for providing order are under controlled by foreigners. Besides this, Greeks want to revolt with chosen 40 people called parliamentarians of Istanbul, Greek leaders who came from Athenian. It has to be said that the government cannot do anything in Istanbul. Because of all these reasons; the problem about the place where the National Parliament gathering appears. If the National Parliament will be gathered in Istanbul, parliamentarians would encounter danger. Really, it is possible that State of Alliances may cancel the decisions of cease-fire agreement, they may occupy significance point of our country, they may give opportunity minority of Christian to attack our rights, they may eliminate the Parliament which defends national unity and privacy of national independence, and they may arrest parliamentarians; just as English does to Islam National Shura in Kars. It came to mind that community of Nigehban and community of İngiliz Muhipleri will do every evil through realizing every request of enemies. Therefore, gathering National Parliament in Istanbul impedes the waited significant duty from Parliament. Since the National Parliament is a symbol of the independence of state and nation, eliminating its causes hurt our independence. The Minister of Navy Salih Pasha who meets behalf on the government in Amasya confirmed with his signature that National Parliament should be gathered in out of İstanbul. If National Parliament will be gathered in a place where is out of Istanbul, safe, far from the effect of enemies; all drawbacks will be prevented, also being caliphate and sovereignty in danger will be realized by all world, especially world of Islam; thereby National Parliament will realize their duties against taken possible decision against national entity and independence of it. Also it will be understood that the Parliament has the fate of the nation. The drawbacks of gathering Parliament in out of Istanbul are:

Enemies will get an opportunity saying to give up from Istanbul. The government would not communicate with Parliament, like Istanbul. The inauguration of Parliament would be through a person who is appointed as a substitute, because not creating travel trouble for Sultan. Based on these reasons, the current government thinks that the National Parliament will be started in Istanbul. Therefore, it was being added these drawbacks:

Gathering legally National Parliament depends on being the Parliament and Parliament of Ayan at the same time and the same place. Therefore; Parliament of Ayan and the government will not go to a meeting in out of İstanbul thereby they will impede opening Parliament in pursuance of Sultan.

According to this, there is no opportunity gathering National Parliament legally. Therefore, gathering in İstanbul is compulsory. If dear parliamentarians will not go to Istanbul and they will gather in out of Istanbul, such meeting does not represent the power of legislative of the National Parliament. Maybe it will be a meeting which represents the entity of the nation, aim of the nation, independence of the nation and which critics the decisions of future of the nation and does not accept them based on the nation. In this situation, the National Parliament does not have to gather in Istanbul. It may cause that government will take compelling precautions and all relations between the government of Istanbul and nation may end. Some of the parliamentarians going to Istanbul may increase in the possibility of the risk.

After Community of Anadolu ve Rumeli Müdafaa-i Hukuk discussing and examining all these problems, they inform all parliamentarians about all over these, and ask their ideas against gathering National Parliament in Istanbul. Besides this, it was seen as necessary that before dear parliamentarians going to National Parliament in Istanbul, they have to gather someplace, discuss these issues and report the results. The issues are:

a. All precautions which will be given in İstanbul and everywhere against the possibility of gathering in Istanbul.

b. Thinking to create a framework in the Parliament which defends and protects saving of independence of nation and state.

The places which are seen as appropriate for discussing these issues are Trabzon, Samsun, İnebolu, Eskişehir, Bursa, Bandırma, Edirne.

Second Matter: First matter has to been informed parliamentarians in your area, taking personal ideas, reporting these to the Representation Committee, and providing necessary works through giving this information to the central committee in your area.

The government does not regard the antagonists of the national organization as the enemy of the country and nation. In terms of the government; the national organization is the same thing with the organization of enemies; also we are same Ali Kemal and Mullah Sait. The events of Adapazarı, Karacabey, Steppe, Aznavour are not a crime for them.

After explaining these points in the given response to Cemal Pasha, we added this expression for clearly releasing tendency and emotions of the government: "According to our understanding from your reports, the government of Istanbul may see the entity of national organization as unnecessary. Really, if they have the power for saving the country without national organization, we kindly request that the situation will be informed clearly and all misunderstanding will be resolved."

I gave the letter who is sent to Sivas dated November 10, 1919 by Cemal Pasha and who is his own hand-writing after 18 days, so November 28, 1919. In this letter, Cemal Pasha summarized issues which are related to done correspondences, and he made an explanation for every matter.

By the way, when he mentioned gathering the Parliament in out of Istanbul, he said that "It is understood that Sultan will not give permission for it. Americans make clearly feel them that attacking to the Parliament may cause positive results for Ottoman Empire."

Cemal Pasha gave this information just as it is not known: "leader officers who do not have the spirit of Kuva-yı Milliye trust the armies of occupation. Also the former leader of government trusts them. For instance, it was understood clearly with changing police chief."

Cemal Pasha accused us with this expression: the government thought to commit many works, however they do not still believe the seriousness of the power which they trust. After this, he said that the header of those who regard this power (i.e. Kuva-yı Milliye) as necessary is the Minister of Interior.

Also there is such expression in a summary which is added later with his signature: "Antagonists and foreigners decided to prevent opening the Parliament. If the Representation Committee will contribute this prevention with a discussion of gathering place; our work will be left to God."

I will not mention the main reason, thought and vision of all letters. However, I will convey a part of the response dated November 28, 1919: "We do not see the matters are serious, saying the government of Istanbul no longer trusts in the seriousness of the power which they trust in deeply."

The first sentence dated November 24, 1919 code which belongs to the Minister of Defence Cemal Pasha: "Internal and political workings of the state do not accept partnership."

Our detailed response dated November 27, 1919, we said that: "It is obvious that the internal and political workings of the state do not accept partnership. However, it is clear that the nation will not give permission to any behaviour which disrupts national unify and causes impoverishment to the national organization against the incomparable current condition." The last sentence of this telegraph is that: "our committee is loyal for all expression under their signature... However, given promises should be mutual. Nonetheless, the government did not realize yet any promise under the signature of Salih Pasha; if there were prohibitive reasons, they were not reported."

I was absolutely certain that an attack would be made in Istanbul against the Chamber and that it would be dissolved. I had even decided what we would do if this should happen. We made preparations and gave instructions to the effect that the Chamber would meet in Ankara.

While doing all that I thought a precation against being misunderstood as a nation. This led me to wonder whether I ought to be elected President of the Chamber. My idea was, that as President of the Chamber I would have the necessary qualifications and authority to recall the representatives who had been dismissed. I admit that this step was only intended as a matter of form and that I could only make use of it temporarily. Nevertheless, in critical times it is necessary to take advantage of anything that might be of assistance, even if it should have only a temporary effect.

However, in any case I would not have gone to Istanbul. Without betraying my intention, however, I would have played for time; the business would have been carried on as though I were only absent for the time being and the Chamber would have continued under a Vice-President.

Of course, implementation of this precatuion would only be possible through the works and efforts of our colleagues who were able to grasp the true state of affairs and actually went to the Parliament in Istanbul.

I discussed this with the persons who were relevant. They agreed with me, and left for Istanbul promising and assuring me that they would carry out this plan.

But I heard afterwards that, with the exception of one or two of them, they did not even open their mouths to enunciate this opinion.

On this issue the reason and understanding was as follows. The question that should be asked was whether there was not one among so many representatives representing the nation who was worthy to be elected President of the Chamber, even if they had to vote for a representative who was not present? Would it not degrade the Chamber in the eyes of our enemies if the representatives who formed the Chamber were not people who recognised their own importance?

Another reason was that from the very beginning it will give the impression that the Chamber would be exposed to criticism if the leader of the national forces was to be elected President; therefore, this would not be expedient. Those who noticed that the people who came to such conclusions were not altogether strangers to me are reported to have preferred to keep silent.

In view of the possibility that foreigners might extend their aggressive intentions and might attempt to arrest certain Ministers and representatives in Istanbul, I resolved, in anticipation, to make reprisals by arresting some foreign officers who were in Anatolia. I informed Corps Commanders in Ankara, Konya, Sivas and Erzurum of my resolution in a private telegram in code on 22 January 1920, and ordered them to act accordingly on the same day.

The reply signed jointly by Vasıf Bey, Rauf Bey and Bekir Sami Bey came to the telegram I sent to the representatives. In this reply, it was told that as soon as the discussions in the Chamber officially began the Cabinet would resign as a result of the recent incident. In order to save the situation, it is necessary to keep the Cabinet in power till then. Abstain from any interference or actions. Give us your instructions. You may feel assured that your point of view will be unanimously defended by all the authorities".

I decided to issue no more communications, either to the Government or the Chamber, but to leave it to my honourable colleagues among the representatives to make the necessary arrangements.

I have already mentioned that I thought it would be advantageous and even necessary that I should be elected President of the Chamber, and that I had expressed my opinion about this to influential persons. In the first days when the representatives, as I have said, began to discuss thisquestion, Rauf Bey told me in his messages of 28 January 1920, and I February 1920, after having referred to other matters, that: "We did not continue to discuss the question, because it was surrounded by considerable difficulty" . And he continued . . . "the question has been discussed recently at a private and confidential meeting. Şerif Bey explained the advantages of you being elected... We feel that at the moment the votes will be divided and we declared that Your Excellency would rather continue to direct the affairs of the nation and remain the power behind the Chamber. Our statement was received with applause, and we could see the sincerity of the manifestations for the person of Your Excellency that was shown in all parts of the Chamber. At the full sitting Reşat Hikmet Bey was elected President, while Hüseyin Kazım Bey and Hodja Abdülaziz Mecdi Efendi were elected as the first and second Vice-presidents."

After all, Şeref Bey was the only member who advocated my election as President. At the meeting which they called "private and confidential," the other persons had not even suggested any reason for me being elected as the President. The question of my election ought to have been raised first of all, and then it could have been ascertained afterwards whether the proposal would have led to the votes being divided. Şeref Bey's arguments were so weak and in- conclusive that it was not easy to guess how the voting would have gone.

In my reply to Rauf Bey on the question of the election of the President, I said: "The doubts you express have been considered already and have been provided for. The reasons given in favour of my election are well known. They are that I would take care that the national forces are recognised by the nation; that I would carry on the duties of President very well in case the Chamber were to be dissolved; that I would endeavour, with the authority that would be vested in me as President, to consolidate the material and moral forces of the nation for its defence, in case a national upheaval should result from peace proposals that were irreconcilable with our future existence. What you say distinctly shows that these reasons relating to the defence of our country are regarded in certain circles in Istanbul as not being of any importance. If the defence of the nation was to be in jeopardy today or in the future on account of mistaken points of view, the responsibility would fall only on those who have committed this error. I need not assure you that I have no personal ambition concerning this question."

A telegram in code, dated 27 January 1920, in which Rauf Bey described the dilemma in which the Chamber was placed, contained some disturbing phrases. Here are some of them: "The Cabinet had first thought of resigning; but they did not. The present attitude of the Chamber does not help with the solution of this problem. The representatives who are present here are not inclined to allow telegrams to be read in a full sitting of the Chamber which the nation has addressed to the Chamber about the district of Maraş. We are advised to behave amicably on this subject towards the Allied Powers individually. There is not even a proper place for us to meet in".

In our telegram of 7 February 1920 we mentioned to Rauf Bey the following matters: The representatives, yielding to local and foreign influences which are increasingly felt in Istanbul, have lost sight of peace and are divided, some cringing before the foreigner and others trying to gain special favour for themselves or giving way to distrust. Our colleagues continually sacrifice their own conceptions and convictions with the object of winning as large a majority as possible of the representatives. In trying to be conciliatory, they have lost all their influence with the Government and recognised circles. If the present condition of things is allowed to go on, they will probably become the tools of anti-national movements and of ambitious people of various kinds, and decisions on national questions unfavourable to us will be the inevitable consequence. The only thing to obviate this is to be content with one party — even though it be a small one — consisting of friends who are absolutely loyal to our principles. This would be far better than giving in, as has been done hitherto. Without hesitation and unconditionally, the Government must be overthrown. We must take up a determined stand on this (Document 234).

Ali Rıza's Government had not resigned. To avoid creating a controversy, the Chamber did not have the courage to overthrow them, and had put their confidence in this newly-formed and inexperienced Cabinet.

I do not know whether you remember the terms of the declaration made by this Cabinet before the Chamber. In a kind of introduction to it, the Grand Vizier pointed out the most important task he had fulfilled, namely, to put an end to the discord existing between the Government and Anatolia, which had even reached a rupture between the relations of the two sides. He said that henceforward the national movement would find its expression in this High Assembly; that he did not see what there was to prevent them from acting together constitutionally in the future. He wanted it to be interpreted from these words that in the future the Representative Committee should no longer act in the name of the national will and would not maintain an opposition that was contradictory to the principles of the Constitution. The Grand Vizier did not think it necessary to speak about the injurious attack of which he himself had been objected to on the very day that the National Assembly had met — and with him the Chamber and the nation—and which was in contradiction to the national will and the principles recognised by the whole world. But he warmly resented the National Committee, and our honourable colleagues among the representatives stooped listening to him.

Declaring that the administration of the country needed improvement, and referring again to the old system in which the Ottoman Empire had always taken refuge when pressed by the Powers, the Grand Vizier promised new reforms. "We shall," he said, "introduce the system of decentralisation to a wide extent."

He enumerated the principles of the intended reforms and said that, for the purpose of safeguarding the rights of minorities, proportional representation would be introduced and necessary full powers would be given to foreign inspectors for the control of issues concerning Justice, Finance, Public Works, Police and even the Civil Administration.

Referring to foreign affairs, the Grand Vizier pointed out the obligation that: "The Imperial Government considered it their duty not to fail to carry out the stipulations of the Armistice," whilst on the other hand he was content to say that peace would put an end to the excitement and disorder caused by the occupation of İzmir, and he finished his speech by expressing his firm conviction that "foresight and determination" will turn the "misfortune" into "happiness".

A communication with Istanbul on 19 February 1920 brought us the news that: "The English diplomatic representative has verbally given definite information to the Government from the Foreign Office that the capital will be left to the Ottoman Empire, but, at the same time, he has demanded that the Armenian massacres shall cease forthwith and that our operations against the Allied troops — including those of Greece — shall also cease immediately. He added that if this was not done, our peace conditions would be altered. Certain advice was given to us at the same time to the effect that no incident, however insignificant, should be allowed to occur that could give rise to complaints being made concerning them."

What could be the meaning of this verbal threat? Could it mean that, in addition to the districts occupied by the Greeks, the French, and others, they resolved to occupy Istanbul as well or if conditions are accepted, will they abandon the idea of laying their hands on Istanbul?

Or, perhaps, it meant that the Greeks, French and Italians have only temporarily occupied certain districts. Perhaps the Allied Powers intended to seize Istanbul, but they would abandon the idea if we observe the conditions they imposed.

Or did the Allied Powers intend to indicate this: "The occupation by the Greeks, French and Italians is an accomplished fact; the occupation of Istanbul is contemplated; if you will allow the Greeks, French and Italians to remain in security and unmolested in their zones of occupation and if you actually give evidence that you consent to the occupation, we shall abandon the idea of occupying Istanbul?"

Finally, did the Allied Powers entertain some doubt about the Government not succeeding in disbanding troops at the front which the national forces had sent into the occupied districts to oppose the forces of the enemy and put an end to the fight they carried on and the movement they made against them, and did they consequently plan to occupy Istanbul on the pretext that the Government could neither prevent the attacks against the Allied Powers (including the Greeks) nor put an end to the Armenian massacres — which, by the way, did not exist?

I believe that later events showed that the last of these suggestions was the nearest of all to the truth. It was, however, noticeable that the Government, far from interpreting the proposal made by the English diplomatic representative in this light, had, on the contrary, founded their hopes on it.

In order to understand how ill-advised this proposal was, we shall recall certain phases of the situation as they presented themselves at that time. The assertions regarding the Armenian massacres were undoubtedly not in accordance with fact. For the Armenians in the south, armed by foreign troops and encouraged by the protection they enjoyed, attacked the Muslims in their district.

Animated with the spirit of revenge, they pursued a relentless policy of murder and extermination everywhere. This resulted in the tragic incident in Maraş. Making common cause with the foreign troops, the Armenians had completely destroyed an old Muslim town like Maraş by their artillery and machine-gun fire.

Threatened by the bayonets of the Armenians, who were armed to the teeth, the Muslims in the Province of Adana were at that time in danger of being annihilated. While this policy of oppression and annihilation carried on against the Muslims, who were only trying to save their lives and their independence, was liable to attract the attention of the civilised world and excite their commiseration, how could the denials or the proposal made to us to abandon the attitude attributed to us be taken seriously?

Was not the position in the districts of İzmir and Aydın similar or, perhaps, more tragic? The Greeks daily reinforced their troops and increased their munitions, and in this way completed their preparations for an offen- sive. On the other hand, they did not fail to deliver partial attacks all along the line. We had received news that during these days an infantry regiment, a fully equipped regiment of cavalry, twenty-four motor- lorries and a number of other wagons, six guns and a considerable quantity of ammunition had been disembarked onto İzmir, and that enormous quantities of ammunition were on the way to the various fronts.

The truth was that our nation had never taken up an aggressive attitude anywhere against any foreigners without good reason.

It was natural that the nation and the national forces refused to submit either to the demand of the foreigners or to the wishes and commands of the Government who tried to enforce them.

On 3 March 1920 I received a coded telegram which was of extreme importance. İsmet Pasha sent it from Istanbul. After I had arrived in Ankara, İsmet Pasha came to see me there. We were working together, but now His Excellency Fevzi Pasha had succeeded Cemal Pasha in the Ministry of War. In obedience to the explicit request of his Excellency and for an especially serious reason, I had sent İsmet Pasha back to İstanbul a few days before.

The matter which we regarded as of special importance was this. The Greeks had prepared an offensive. The reasonable thing to do in such a case was to mobilise our forces and begin a regular war. His Excellency Fevzi Pasha was perfectly convinced of the necessity of doing this.

The presence of İsmet Pasha in Istanbul would be expedient, so that he could take the necessary steps, and by appointing him chief of the General Staff we would have been able to rely on his official co-operation. That is why I thought it would be a good thing to send him to Istanbul.

As you already know, the British representative had proposed to the Government that the operations against the Allied troops, including those of Greece, to cease, and had informed them of the "gilded promise" made by the English, according to which Istanbul would still belong to the Ottoman Empire, on condition that this proposal was accepted. But we had been informed of the fact that at the precise moment when this proposal was made in Istanbul, the Greeks had landed fresh troops, new means of transport, and enormous quantities of ammunition in İzmir, on

18, 19 and 20 February, and were preparing for a new offensive. We lost no time in passing this information on to the Government and drawing their attention to it, ignoring the fuss they had made in trying to prevent our so-called interference in the affairs of the Government.

While the Greeks were preparing for this new offensive, Ali Rıza Pasha's Cabinet was confronted with a new proposal, namely, "to retire the national forces who had taken up a position against the Greeks for a distance of three kilometres!

The Greeks began their offensive on 3 March 1920. They seized the plateau of Gölcük and Bozdağ. Meanwhile, Ali Rıza Pasha resigned; the only thing he could do to extricate himself from his responsible position was to hand in his resignation and go. For, could it not be seen beforehand that Ali Rıza Pasha, who had done everything he possibly could to put an end to the activities of the national forces and had completely failed, would be held responsible by the Allied Powers if he had brought forward new proposals and had again failed?

To withdraw, therefore, was merely to follow the line of least resistance, and this he did. Ali Rıza Pasha had not consented to resign when we had asked him to do so during the first attack on the Cabinet. He had declared that he would be of greater service to the country if he did not resign. And the Chamber had supported him by accepting his opinion, which only showed their ignorance. Did it happen that the duty which he referred to consisted in letting the Greeks have as much freedom as they desired to complete their preparations for the offensive which was intended to tread another part of the sacred soil of our country underfoot and cause more of our beloved countrymen to groan under their yoke?

We spent 3 March and the whole of that night in telegraphic communication with İstanbul to keep them fully informed of all that was going on. Acting on the information we had received, partly from İsmet Pasha and partly from others, I sent a circular note to all the troops, the headquarters of the organisations and to the nation on 4 March.

The flood of telegrams which, in obedience to our instructions, inundated the entire country during the night of 4 March produced the desired effect in the Palace of the Sovereign and in the Chamber of representatives on the following day.

We shall now glance at what was going on in Edirne, and then return to Istanbul.

I think I have always mentioned in the course of my general remarks that we never lost sight of Thrace in our organisations and plans. Our connection and correspondence with Edirne were maintained and continued in just the same way as with every other district in the country.

Cafer Tayyar Bey, commanding the 1st Army Corps, described in an excellent way in a very detailed account, dated 31 August 1919, the activity of the Greeks in Thrace — especially in Western Thrace — and the enterprises they were engaged in there. He complained that he could not act efficiently in the face of their extraordinary activity there. In the instructions I had given to Cafer Tayyar Bey on 3 January 1920,1 repeatedly reminded him of the necessity of organising armed national troops, on the basis of the "Secret Instructions" with which we had furnished him.

"It is necessary," I said, "to gain, the advantage in this way, which cannot be attained by distributing the troops in any other"

On the same day, I also wrote to Cemal Pasha, Minister of War, telling him about the position of affairs and begging him to resist the preparations made by the Greeks, at least in Eastern Thrace.

From the reports coming from the union of "Trakya Pashaeli," it was clear that the formation of organisations had not been as successful as had been anticipated, and certain high officials were reproached for this.

From the very beginning, I sent certain observations to these officials.

General Milne did not allow Cafer Tayyar to dispose his troops as he wished to do. The Governor and Mutasarrıf remained neutral and abstained from leading and guiding the people who expect everything from the Government relating to the national organisations. And we cannot see how these organisations could possibly spread and be put on a solid foundation until these hindrances had been surmounted.

I have been told that some of our friends had arranged and prepared the way to reach Anatolia and come to Ankara. If that is so, the reason why they did not come to Ankara and preferred to give themselves up to the English and be taken to Malta deserves to be investigated. Indeed, starting with the idea that the position and the final destiny of Turkey is hanging by a thread, surrounded by gloom and danger, it is not improbable that, influenced by the fear of plunging into this dark peril and exposing themselves to such a horrible and terrifying fate, they preferred to surrender to the enemy and spend a certain time in prison.

At 10 a.m. on 16 March 1920, while we were at the telegraph set, we received the following message:

"The English have made a surprise attack this morning on a Government building at Şehzadebaşı and have had a skirmish with the soldiers. At the present moment they are beginning to occupy Istanbul. I send you this for your information."

Manastırlı Hamdi.

I made a pencil note on this telegram: "To be transmitted immediately to the Army Corps with my signature. Mustafa Kemal." Then I began to question the sender of the telegram. Manastırlı Hamdi Efendi continued without stopping to report as follows: "Not only one trustworthy man, but all who come here confirm what I have reported. We have just heard in this very moment that the Military School has been occupied. English soldiers are on guard outside the Telegraph Office in Beyoğlu, but it is not yet known whether they intend to occupy it or not."

Meanwhile an official of the Telegraph Office belonging to the Ministry of War told us that: "In the forenoon the English fought their way in; six have been killed and about fifteen wounded. At this moment the English are patrolling the town. They are now entering the Ministry. They have occupied it. They have reached the Nizamiye Gate. Interrupt the connection. The English are here."

When the Entente Powers occupied the Telegraph Offices in Istanbul their intention was to circulate an official communique throughout the country via telegraph. However, on account of the warning we had received, this communique was not accepted at almost any, except for a very few, of the Telegraph Offices. The most important of those who received it and replied to it were Suat Bey, Mutasarrıf of İzmit and Suphi Bey, the Governor of Konya.

Five-and-a-half years ago the leaders of the "Committee of Union and Progress," who had taken the destiny of the Ottoman Empire into their hands, aided by unknown circumstances but at the instigation of Germany, led the Ottoman Empire and people to enter the Great War.

The result of this iniquitous and fatal policy is known. After having passed through sufferings of every description, the Empire and the people had to submit to such a defeat that the leaders of the "Committee of Union and Progress" found that their only means of salvation was to ask for an armistice and flee.

After the armistice was concluded, the Entente Powers had one duty to fulfil. This consisted of preparing a ground for a peace that will secure the happiness, the future development, the social and economic life of the entire population of the former Ottoman Empire, without distinction of race or religion.

While the members of the Peace Conference were engaged with this question, certain individuals, partisans of the fugitive leaders of the "Committee of Union and Progress," formed an organisation, calling it a "National Organisation," and, disregarding the orders of the Sultan and the Central Government, dared to commit certain acts, such as calling the population, which was completely reduced through the fatal consequences of the War, under arms and creating discord between the individual elements, besides robbing the population on the pretence of levying national contributions. In this way they have not secured peace but have commenced a new period of war. In spite of these intrigues and provocations, the Peace Conference has continued to do its duty and has just decided that İstanbul shall remain under Turkish administration. This decision will have a soothing effect on Ottoman minds. While communicating this decision to the Sublime Porte, they have been informed of certain conditions which will affect the decision referred to.

These conditions consist in safeguarding the lives of the Christians living in Ottoman provinces and in putting an end to the continual attacks that are specially directed against the troops of the Entente Powers and their Allies. Although the Government has shown a certain amount of good-will in respect to this warning, the men who are working under the adopted name of "National Organisations" have unhappily not agreed to abandon their policy of provocation and intrigue.

On the contrary, they have tried to win the Government over to their side to co-operate with their enterprises. In view of this situation, which constitutes a grave danger to the Peace for which everybody is anxiously longing, the Entente Powers have seen themselves forced to consider certain steps that will secure the conduct of the Peace negotiations which will soon begin.

For this purpose, they have discovered only one way to do this, namely, to proceed to a temporary occupation of Istanbul.

The decision having been put into effect today, the following points are brought to public knowledge:

1. The occupation is temporary.
2. The aim of the Entente Powers is not to weaken, but rather to strengthen the authority of the Sultanate

in the territories that will remain under Ottoman administration.

3. The aim of the Entente Powers, also, is not to separate Istanbul from the Turks. But if — Allah forbid — extensive unrest or bloody persecution should occur, it is very likely that this decision will be altered.

The duty imposed on all Muslims and non-Muslims in this time of difficulty is to carry on their business, to assist in the maintenance of order, to close their ears to the lies of those who want by their acts of madness to destroy the last hope of building up a new Turkey on the ruins of the Ottoman Empire, and to obey the orders issued from Istanbul, which at the present moment is the seat of the Sultanate. Some of the persons who have been taking part in the intrigues referred to have been arrested in Istanbul. They will naturally be held responsible for their acts and for the events that have been produced thereby.

Simultaneously, I issued a proclamation to the entire Islamic world, in which the above-described infamous proceedings were referred to in detail. This proclamation was spread abroad by various means.

We learned that the representatives, who had scattered after they had been assured of the impossibility of performing their legislative functions, and several other persons in Istanbul had fled and were on their way to Ankara. I gave the necessary orders to the authorities along the line of their route to facilitate their journey.

You will have read in the first account of the Grand National Assembly some details of what was done about the disarming and removing of the foreign troops at Eskişehir, at Afyon Karahisar, the destruction of the railways in the districts of Geyve and Ulukışla, the arrest of foreign officers in Anatolia, and other matters.

The most important thing was our determination to fulfil our patriotic and national duty by securing the meeting of an assembly at Ankara furnished with extraordinary powers, and the way that this was to be carried out.

On 19 March 1920, that is to say three days after Istanbul had been occupied, I issued a communique regarding the question I have just described and the manner of its execution.

In the draft I had first made, I had used the expression "Constitutional Assembly." My intention was that the assembly which was to be convened would from the very first be endowed with full powers to alter the governmental system. But, because I did not or could not explain this expression with sufficient clearness, they pointed out to me from Sivas and Erzurum that the people were not familiar with it.

Thereupon, I contented myself by using the expression: "Assembly endowed with Extraordinary Powers."

To all Provinces;

To Autonomous Livas;

To the Officers commanding Army Corps.

The formal occupation of the capital by the Entente Powers has disorganised the national forces of the State, that is to say, the legislative, the executive and the judicial power. The Chamber of Representatives has been dissolved through the Government having been officially informed that under prevailing conditions there is no possibility for the representatives to perform their duties.

With the object of considering and carrying out the best way to secure the inviolability of the capital, the independence of the nation and the liberation of the country under these conditions, it has been deemed absolutely necessary to convene an assembly to be held at Ankara that will be furnished with extraordinary powers and will permit those members of the Chamber that has been dissolved to come to Ankara to take part in it. Therefore, we expect from your patriotism and your capabilities that you will proceed to carry out elections on the following lines:

1. An Assembly, furnished with extraordinary powers, will meet in Ankara for the purpose of conducting and controlling national affairs.
2. The persons elected as members of this Assembly are subject to the same legal conditions that apply to representatives.
3. The Livas will form the electoral constituencies.
4. Five representatives will be elected in each Liva.
5. The elections will take place in all the Livas on the same day and at one uninterrupted sitting of a committee consisting of electors of the second class, who will be chosen by the Kazas belonging to the Livas; of electors of the second class in the chief places in the Livas from among the administrative and local councils in the Livas; of the leading committees of the Defence of the Rights in the Livas. In the Provinces it shall consist of the central councils of the chief places in the Provinces; of the general councils of the Provinces; of the local councils of the chief places in the Provinces, of the electors of the second class in the chief provincial towns, in the chief towns in the Kazas, and of the electors of the second class in the Kazas belonging to the chief town.

6. In the same manner that each party, group and union may chose candidates, so every one individually has the right in his constituency to put forward his candidature and thus actually take part in the sacred struggle.
7. The elections will be conducted by the highest official of the town in which they take place, and he is held responsible for the regularity of the election.
8. The elections shall be conducted by secret ballot and there shall be a clear majority. The result of the polling shall be controlled by two persons nominated by the committee and in their presence.
9. A protocol shall be drawn up giving the result of the elections in triplicate, and attested by the signature or the personal seal of all the members. One copy shall be kept in the town, the second shall be handed to the successful candidate and the third sent to the Assembly.
10. The expenses incurred by the members shall be settled later on by the Assembly. Travelling expenses, however, are to be guaranteed by the local authorities and determined by the electoral committee, based on the unavoidable expenses that had been incurred.
11. The elections shall be finished so that within a fortnight, at latest, the majority of the members will be able to meet in Ankara. The members are to leave immediately, and the result of the elections, as well as the names of the members, shall be contacted forthwith.

12. You are requested to inform us of the hour when you receive this telegram.

Note: For the information of officers commanding Army Corps, the Provinces and the independent districts.

Mustafa Kemal, In the name of
the Representative Committee.

As for those who, in spite of the warnings we had been sending them in different ways for many a month, had not formed any organisation as we had instructed them to do and had worked for the "Karakol" Society, their leaders had been sent to Malta and their adherents in Istanbul had given no sign that they were still active or that they were still alive.

In the course of my general remarks I have spoken several times about the question of my election as President of the Chamber of Representatives in Istanbul and my intentions about this. I have already pointed out that in this attempt I met with certain difficulties and the plan did not succeed.

In fact, as the Chamber in Istanbul had become the object of a conspiracy and had broken up, I hesitated for a moment to call the representatives together and undertake to form an assembly, particularly of the nature I have described.

Let it be understood that I did not know whether Celalettin Arif Bey, President of the Chamber, would come to Ankara. I thought that in case he might come there, I would wait for him and let him call the Assembly himself. But at the same time, in order to secure the execution of the decision I had to make, I was obliged to put myself in telegraphic communication with all the commanders, and

I spent several days in obtaining their opinions and listening to what they had to say. Moreover, I did not think for a moment of calling a meeting of the Chamber of Representatives in its present form and comprising those representatives of the Chamber who had already been attacked and had been able to escape, with the addition of two members elected from each of the Provincial Councils and the Livas.

On the contrary, I had intended to organise an assembly of a totally different character and endowed with other powers, and with it to overcome the successive stages of the revolution that I had in my mind. For these reasons, I abandoned all hope of finding a possibility to bring our conceptions — between which I had no doubt there existed a very strong difference — into agreement by discussing them.

The elections began to take their normal course seriously and rapidly all over the country, according to the instructions issued on 19 March 1920. A certain amount of hesitation and reluctance was felt only in certain places, for a longer or shorter time according to the individual localities.

At last, the representatives from all the electoral districts, representing the whole country and nation, were present without exception at the Grand National Assembly. The places which originally intended to stay out were Dersim, Malatya, Elazığ, Konya, Diyarbakır and Trabzon.

I must call your attention to the fact that it was not the inhabitants of these districts who showed hesitation and reluctance, but the higher civil officials who were there at the time. As soon as they once understood the real position, the people no longer hesitated for a moment to identify themselves with the will of the nation.

Newspapers and travellers who came from Istanbul said that the buildings that had been commandeered were completely evacuated on the second day after the occupation had begun, that Salih Pasha's Cabinet was continuing its work and that the Senate was sitting; that during the last Selamlık the usual ceremonies were performed as usual in the presence of the Minister of War and the Minister of Marine, and so forth.

We finally decided to be satisfied with the delegates that had been able to come and to open the Assembly on Friday, 23 April 1920.

Soon after the Assembly was opened I described the position and circumstances in which we found ourselves. I also pointed out the course that I considered it would be necessary for us to follow. The most important thing being the political principles which Turkey and the Turkish Nation would have to adopt.

You know that life consists of struggles and conflicts. Success in life is only possible by overcoming difficulties. All depend upon strength, upon moral and material energy. Further than that, all the questions that engage the attention of mankind, all the dangers to which they are exposed and all the successes which they achieve arise from the turmoil of the general combat which is raging throughout human society. The conflicts between the Eastern and Western races mark some of the most important pages in history. It is a generally accepted fact that among the peoples of the East the Turks were the element who bore the brunt and who gave evidence of the greatest strength. In fact, both before and after the rise of Islam, the Turks penetrated into the heart of Europe and attacked and invaded in all directions. We must not omit to mention the Arabs also, for they attacked the West and carried their invasion as far as Spain and across the frontiers of France. But in every offensive we must always be prepared for a counter- attack. The end that awaits those who act without considering this possibility and without taking the necessary precautionary measures against it is defeat, annihilation, extinction.

What particularly interests foreign policy and upon which it is founded is the internal organisation of the state. Thus it is necessary that foreign policy should agree with the internal organisation. In a State which extends from the East to the West and which unites in its embrace contrary elements with opposite characters, goals and culture, it is natural that the internal organisation should be defective and weak in its foundations. Under these circumstances its foreign policy, having no solid foundation, cannot be strenuously carried out. In the same proportion as the internal organisation of such a state suffers especially from the defect of not being national, so also its foreign policy must lack this character. For this reason, the policy of the Ottoman State could not be national and was deficient in clarity and continuity.

To unite different nations under one common name, to give these different elements equal rights, subject them to the same conditions and thus to found a mighty State is a brilliant and attractive political ideal; but it is a misleading one. It is an unrealisable aim to attempt to unite in one tribe all the Turks existing on the earth, thereby abolishing all boundaries. Herein lies a truth which the centuries that have gone by and the men who have lived during these centuries have clearly shown in dark and sanguinary events.

There is nothing in history to show how the policy of Pan-Islamism and Pan-Turanism could have succeeded or how it could have found a basis for its realisation on this earth. As regards the result of the ambition to organise a

State which should be governed by the idea of world-supremacy and include the whole of humanity without distinction of race, history does not afford examples of this. For us, there can be no question of the lust of conquest. On the other hand, the theory which aims at founding a "humanitarian" State which shall embrace all mankind in perfect equality and brotherhood and at bringing it to the point of forgetting separatist sentiments and inclinations of every kind, is subject to conditions which are peculiar to itself.

The political system which we regard as clear and fully realisable is national policy. In view of the general conditions obtaining in the world at present, and the truths which in the course of centuries have rooted themselves in the minds of and have formed the characters of mankind, no greater mistake could be made than that of being a Utopian. This is borne out in history and is the expression of science, reason and common sense.

In order that our nation should be able live a happy, strenuous and permanent life, it is necessary that the State should pursue an exclusively national policy and that this policy should be in perfect agreement with our internal organisation and be based on it. When I speak of national policy, I mean it in this sense: To work within our national boundaries for the real happiness and welfare of the nation and the country by, above all, relying on our own strength in order to maintain our existence, but not to lead the people to follow fictitious aims, of whatever nature, which could only bring them misfortune, and expect from the civilised world civilised human treatment, friendship based on mutuality.

In reality, it was a question of acknowledging the collapse and the abolition of the Ottoman State and the Caliphate. It meant the creation of a new State standing on new foundations. But to speak openly of the position as it revealed itself might eventually jeopardise the goal we were aiming at, for the general opinion inclined to the opinion that the attitude of the Sultan-Caliph was excusable. Even in the Assembly during the first months there was a tendency to seek communion with the seat of the Caliphate, a union with the Central Government.

I tried to explain that the conditions under which Istanbul found itself equally prevented open or private, secret communication with the Caliph and Sultan. I asked what we considered we could attain by such communication and declared that it was quite unnecessary if it was a question of making known that the nation was struggling to preserve its independence and the integrity of its territory. For, was it possible that the person who held the office of Sultan and Caliph could have any other idea or desire? I stated that even were I to hear the contrary from his own lips I could not believe it but would incline to the assumption that every statement of that kind was only produced under pressure. While further insisting that the Fetva issued against us was an invention, that the orders and instructions of the Government must be made clear, I declared that there was no necessity for us to be cautious, as had been advocated by certain persons of weak character and superficial judgment.

So far as the formation of the Government was concerned, what I mean to say is that it was necessary to take account of opinions and sentiments before making a proposition. In bowing to this necessity, I brought forward my suggestion in the form of a motion, but a motion of which the intention remained concealed. After a short discussion it was carried, in spite of a few objections.

If we read this resolution, we shall see that fundamental principles were defined and formulated in it.

1. It is absolutely necessary to form a Government.
2. We cannot allow the chief of the Government to be defined as provisional, or a regency to be established.
3. It is a vital principle to recognise that the national will expressed by the Assembly is actually governing the destiny of the country. There is no power standing above the Grand National Assembly of Turkey.
4. The Grand National Assembly of Turkey combines in itself the Legislative and the Executive Power.

A Council elected and authorised by the Assembly conducts the affairs of the Government. The President of the Assembly is at the same time President of this Council.

(Note: As soon as the Sultan-Caliph is delivered from all pressure and coercion he will take his place within the frame of the legislative principles which will be determined by the Assembly.)

It is not difficult to appreciate the character of a Government standing upon such foundations. Such a Government is a People's Government, based on the principle of the sovereignty of the people. Such is the Republic. The fundamental principle in the organisation of such a Government is the theory of the unity of powers. As time advanced, we understood the force of these principles. Then followed discussions and incidents.

About a week had passed since 23 April when the Assembly was opened. Naturally, during this time the affairs of the country and the people could not stand still, especially as regards the measures which had to be taken against the activities and movements of our enemies. Several members elected by the Assembly as Commissioners had, however, when this Act was passed begun their work in co-operation with me. Among them was His Excellency İsmet Pasha, who had undertaken the duties of the General Staff.

While at that time the question of the duties that could appropriately have been assigned to the different members was being considered, I had made up my mind that İsmet Pasha should be Chief of the General Staff. Refet Pasha, who was in Ankara, had a private interview with me on which he asked me to make certain statements on this question. He wanted to know whether the Chief of the General Staff was the highest military authority. When I replied that this was actually the case and that only the Grand National Assembly was superior to it, he raised objections to my selection. He declared that he could not agree to it and that it would create a situation which would be tantamount to handing over the chief command to İsmet Pasha. I told him that these duties were very important and very delicate, and that I must be trusted to know all my comrades and to be impartial towards them. I added that it was not right on his part to hold such opinions.

Fuat Pasha, with whom I spoke later on the Western front, categorically opposed the appointment of İsmet Pasha as chief of the General Staff. I tried to persuade him also to my point of view, telling him it was the most feasible one at the moment. The argument Refet Pasha and Fuat Pasha advanced after they had made some personal remarks was that they had worked with me in Anatolia long before İsmet Pasha had done so, since he only joined us later. But in my previous statements I had already had an opportunity to emphasize the fact that İsmet Pasha had worked with me before I left İstanbul. In consequence of this he had come to Anatolia to work with me there; but when His Excellency Fevzi Pasha had been appointed War Minister he was again, for pressing reasons, sent on a special mission to İstanbul. There could be no question, therefore, of seniority as regards our unity of opinions and collaboration.

If the appointment of İsmet Pasha to the highest position on the General Staff had been unsatisfactory, it would have been the patriotic duty of Fevzi Pasha to direct my attention to it. However, on the contrary, his Excellency found the appointment perfectly satisfactory and, with feelings of sincere cordiality, He himself accepted the Ministry of National Defence which had been offered to him. The dignity and the great zeal which İsmet Pasha displayed as Chief of the General Staff, and later on as commander at the front, proved in practice how correct was the choice I had made, and in this I have a clear conscience before the nation, the Army and history.

When the Assembly passed the Act relating to crimes against the country on 29 April 1920 and in the course of the following months the Acts regulating the Independence Courts, it was following the natural consequence of the revolution.

We have mentioned certain hostile movements and events, especially the risings which began to take place after the occupation of Istanbul. They occurred and succeeded one another with great rapidity all over the country.

Damat Ferit Pasha was immediately put at the head of the Government in Istanbul. Damat Ferit Pasha's Cabinet, the party that all the hostile and traitorous organisations in İstanbul had formed, all the rebellious organisations of this party inside Anatolia and the Greek army, in short, all the enemies united against us in common action. The instructions of this unified policy of attack were contained in the Fetva, "Insurrection against the Sultan," which the Sultan-Caliph had circulated throughout the country, for which he utilised every possible means, even including enemy-aircraft.

Against this general, anti-patriotic attack, we took counter measures before the opening of the Assembly by driving the foreign troops that were in Afyon Karahisar, in Eskişehir and along the railway out of Anatolia; by destroying the bridges at Geyve, Lefke, at Carablus, and by causing the honourable ulema of Anatolia to draw up a Fetva after the Assembly had met.

The internal upheavals, which began during the year 1920 against our national organisation, spread rapidly throughout the country.

It is remarkable that a general insurrection of this kind did not take place eight months before, when the nation had gathered round the Representative Committee and had cut off all communication with Damat Ferit's Government, and when only a few incidents, such as Ali Galip's enterprise, were to be recorded. The universal insurrections which now took place showed that they had been consistently prepared in the country during the previous eight months. With the Governments that followed that of Damat Ferit it was felt very bitterly once more how correct the reasons were on which our struggle for the preservation and strengthening of the national consciousness were based. On the other hand, the sad results of an omission of another description on the part of the Government in İstanbul would be seen when it became a question of occupying ourselves with the front and the Army in order to give more force to the national struggle.

I would like to tell you here something that comes to my recol- lection about Suphi Pasha. I had known him since we were at Salonika together. I held the rank of Major and Adjutant then, while he was already a Brigadier General commanding the cavalry. In spite of the difference in our rank and seniority, there was a sincere feeling of comradeship between us. When the Constitution was proclaimed he carried out for the first time some cavalry manoeuvres in Cumali in the district of İştip. He had invited me and several other officers to be present for these manoeuvres and exercises. He had studied in Germany and was a very skilful rider but by no means an officer who understood his work as a leader. Although I was not entitled by my rank or authority to do so, at the end of the manoeuvres I sharply criticised the Pasha in the presence of all the officers, and sub- sequently published a little work called "The Camp of Cumali". On account of my public criticism as well as my little book, Suphi Pasha felt that he was very much offended; as he confessed himself, his spirit was broken. But he was not really angry with me personally; our comradeship continued as before. It was this same Suphi Pasha whom they had sought out and put in command of the Army of the Caliphate. Later on, the Pasha came to Ankara when I was just leaving. We met in the middle of a great crowd. The first thing I said to him was: "Pasha, why have you accepted the command of the Army of the Caliphate?" Without a moment's hesitation, Suphi Pasha replied: "In order to be beaten by you." By this he meant to say that he had taken over that position for this purpose. But in reality his troops were already beaten before he accepted the command.

Now let us recall the situation on the different fronts immediately after the Assembly was opened.

1. The Greek Front at İzmir.

When the Greek Army extended their territory of occupation, they landed troops in Ayvalık. On 28 May, 1919 Ali Bey was fighting against these Greek troops. Up till then no resistance had been offered to the Greek Army. On the contrary, under the influence of fear and in obedience to the orders of the Central Government, the inhabitants of some towns and smaller places had sent special representatives with high officials to their leader to meet them. After Ali Bey had established a fighting front in Ayvalık, national forces gradually began to organise fronts in Soma, Akhisar, and Salihli.

On 5 June 1919 Colonel Kazım Bey (His Excellency Kazım Pasha, President of the Assembly) took over the temporary command of the 61st Division at Balıkesir. Later on, he commanded the Northern front, comprising the districts of Ayvalık, Soma and Akhisar. After the appointment of Fuat Pasha to the command of the West front, Kazım Bey was promoted to the rank of a Corps Commander in the Northern Army.

After İzmir was occupied, some patriots were active amongst the military force and the population in the district of Aydın organising the defences against the Greeks, rousing the enthusiasm of the population and forming a proper armed national force. The courage of sacrifice and the ardour of Celal Bey (Representative for İzmir) deserve to be mentioned here. He had left İzmir under an assumed name and in disguise, and had succeeded in reaching that district. During the night of 15 June 1919 the troops sent by Ali Bey from Ayvalık had attempted a sudden attack on the Greek occupation troops at Bergama and had annihilated them. Troops sent from Balıkesir and Bandırma had participated in this attack. Following this event the Greeks considered it necessary to retire and rally their scattered, weak forces. They abandoned Nazilli. The troops recruited from among the population in the vicinity began to press upon the Greeks, while preparations were being carried on at Aydın. A violent encounter took place between the Greeks and the people, which resulted in the Greeks abandoning Aydın and retiring their troops.

Thus in the middle of June 1919 the Aydın front was established. In this district were Colonel Mehmet Şefik Bey, commanding the 57th Division, Major Hakkı Bey, commanding the artillery, Major Hacı Şükrü Bey, commanding an infantry regiment, and Yörük Ali Efe and Demirci Mehmet Efe at the head of the National Forces. Being master of the situation, the latter assumed command of the Aydın front. I have already had an opportunity of telling you that Colonel Refet Bey (Refet Pasha), whom I had sent later on to the front, was also under Demirci Mehmet Efe.

Provisioning the National Forces on the different İzmir fronts, and the gradual reinforcement of which by officers and men had made the object of our efforts, was safely secured by the population of these districts. National organisations had been formed for this purpose in the districts behind the Army. It was only after the formation of the

Government by the Grand National Assembly that this task could be transferred to the Government.

2. *The French Southern Front.*
a) In the district of Adana national forces had been drawn up immediately in front of the French troops in the country around Mersin, Tarsus, İslahiye and in the district of Silifke, and with great courage had begun active operations against them. The heroic deeds of Major Osman Bey, who concealed his identity under the name of Tufan Bey, in the district east of Adana especially deserve to be mentioned. The national troops made themselves masters of the district right up to the gates of the towns of Mersin, Tarsus and Adana. They besieged the French in Pozantı and forced them to retreat.
b) Skirmishes and serious fighting took place in Maraş, Antep and Urfa. Eventually the occupying troops found themselves compelled to abandon these places. It is my duty to mention here the names of Kılıç Ali Bey and Ali Saip Bey, who were chiefly responsible for these successes.

The National Forces gained solidarity day by day in the French occupied districts and on the French front. The occupying troops were strongly pressed everywhere.

As a result of this, the French tried to get in touch and enter into negotiations with us after the beginning of May 1920. A major and a civilian coming from Istanbul arrived first in Ankara. These gentlemen intended to go to Beirut straight from Istanbul. Haydar Bey, former representative for Van, acted as their dragoman. Our conversations did not lead to any important practical result. However, towards the end of May, a French deputation led by M. Duquest, who acted in the name of the High Commissioner of Syria, came to Ankara. We agreed with this deputation to an armistice of twenty days. During the temporary armistice we prepared for the evacuation of the Adana district.

During the secret sitting of the Assembly on 9 May 1920, when I had given certain explanations and had mentioned that French officials and the French deputation had put out a feeler and had tried to get into contact with us, one of the representatives (if my memory does not deceive me, it was the late Fuat Bey, Representative for Çorum) told me that "apparently Istanbul had been trying for several days to come to an agreement with us," and he asked me whether I was willing to give him some information about this.

As at this time certain enemy preparations on the Greek front became noticeable, a certain amount of uneasiness was felt. On this occasion I had to start for the Western front in great haste without having been able to complete the arrangements for Nurettin Pasha's appointment and his departure for his new post. I left this to İsmet Pasha, Chief of the General Staff, to attend to and ordered him to carry out all the necessary formalities. The enemy had actually begun his attack along the whole line. Our troops retired. When Nurettin Pasha saw how unfavourable our position at the front was, he told İsmet Pasha that before he could accept his post the Government must consent to certain conditions. For instance, the Government ought to ask for the opinion and agreement of Nurettin Pasha before coming to a definite decision on important questions relating to the administration of the country. For among those who formed the Government of the Grand National

Assembly were apparently some young men and not experienced persons like Tevfik Pasha and certain others who had reached the age of wisdom. İsmet Pasha, finding these ideas somewhat strange, immediately sent me a telegram about the matter. As for myself, I found it significant that Nurettin Pasha had put forward these requests at the very moment when the general position had become critical, while he had abstained from doing so at the time I offered him the appointment. In the reply I sent to İsmet Pasha, I ordered that no office was to be entrusted to him. I also looked upon the contents of a letter that Nurettin Pasha had sent me two days after the Greek offensive had begun as being rather strange.

The first decision arrived at by the recently formed Government of the Grand National Assembly of Turkey was to send an Embassy to Moscow. It was under the leadership of Bekir Sami Bey, Minister for Foreign Affairs. Yusuf Kemal Bey, Minister of Economy, was one of its members. The chief object of this Embassy, which left Ankara on 11 May 1920, was to establish relations between Russia and ourselves. Although certain essential points in the Treaty that Russia wanted to make with our Government had been agreed to on 24 August 1920, the actual signature to the Treaty was postponed on account of certain details about which no agreement had been arrived at, concerning some matters that affected the situation. The signing of the document, known as the Moscow Treaty, was not possible before 16 March 1921.

The Greeks began their general attack on 22 June 1920 along the Milne line. A Greek column was marching from Aydın, advanced as far as Nazilli.

You are probably aware that at the time of these operations our troops were mere skeletons without ammunition and incapable of being reinforced.

I went personally to Eskişehir and from there to the front line. I ordered our forces which were in this district and elsewhere to be reorganised. I took every care that new fronts under a regular command were established against the enemy.

The Greek offensive and the break up of our defences caused by it produced a great crisis in the Assembly, which found its expression in violent attacks and severe criticism.

It was necessary for me to intervene in these protracted and heated debates. Appreciating the feelings of the Assembly in the difficult position that had been created and the interest they took in it, I gave information and explanations with the object of calming down the minds of the representatives and allaying these unhappy sentiments. After replying to some minor attacks against my statements, I declared that those I had already given were quite sufficient.

Before these lively discussions had taken place, the particulars of which you will have read in the proceedings of the Assembly, similar debates had taken place on 26 July 1920 during the secret sitting. I had then also been compelled to give long explanations. In face of the criticisms and the motions that had been made and which were based on the general misfortune, everybody seemed to have forgotten the real causes and factors of the defeat. Attempts were made to put the responsibility for every reverse on the Council of Ministers that had been formed scarcely two months previously and that had taken over the responsibility of the Government. Nobody thought of the fact that the Greek Army had established itself and had continued to make preparations in the İzmir district for more than a year past and that, in opposition to this fact, the Istanbul Governments had done everything possible to render our army defenceless and had done nothing else but tried to break up and destroy the forces which the nation had been able to collect. They were not possessed of a sufficient sense of justice to recognise that it was only due to the energy and efforts of about five or ten determined and devoted men that in the course of a year we had, more or less, succeeded in creating a situation which the enemy had to reckon with. Nobody seemed to have judged or discussed the operations from the point of view of the military exigencies or with any knowledge of the actual state of affairs. The speeches that were delivered developed into shouts and complaints, either from overstrained patriotism or from moral weakness. Among those who spoke were men — although they were few — whose faith in the nation and whose patriotism were doubtful.

To avoid any possible misfortune we must first think of preventive means to meet it. When the misfortune has happened it is no good to complain. Before it began the Greek offensive was regarded as very probable. If the necessary precautions and measures had not been taken to meet it, the responsibility must not be put on the Grand National Assembly of Turkey and their Government. The Governments of Istanbul, together with the whole of the nation, ought to have begun seriously at least a year before to take the steps which the Grand National Assembly had on their part undertaken as soon as they had assumed the responsibility of the Government. Calling up troops at the front to suppress the internal unrest was considered to be of greater importance and urgency than arraying them against the Greeks, advisable as that might have been. Even today this is still the case. Possibly the enemy's attack could not have been pushed forward so far if the following troops had been at our disposition at the front: Those detachments that we had to take from Bursa; the two columns which had been sent into the disturbed district of Adapazarı; the column that had been scattered at Hendek—these four bodies of troops and the other that was fighting against the insurgents in the districts of Zile and Yenihan and those national troops which were supporting all these regular forces. Not until peace is secured in the country and the unity and firmness of the nation and their desire for liberation is established will it be possible to work with the object of opposing a foreign enemy, and even from such an effort no essential advantage can be expected. But if the nation and the country observed the attitude I recommend, a success which the enemy might gain at any time and which might lead to the occupation of a large territory, could only be of a temporary character. A nation that asserts and maintains its unity and its will, sooner or later will be able to make any proud enemy who attacks it to suffer for his presumption. For this reason, it is surely more important to suppress the upheavals in the country than to fight the Greek offensive. Besides, it was scarcely to be expected that the Greek offensive could have been otherwise, even if those troops which were appointed to oppose it would not have been withdrawn from the front on account of the trouble in the country. For instance, on the Northern front the enemy attacked with three divisions; we had no troops there of proportionate strength. It is not reasonable to make a great fuss and to say that the catastrophe would not have happened if our troops had taken up a position on this or that river or in this or that village, or if the officers commanding them would have stopped the enemy in his advance. There is no instance in history to show that a front has not been or could not be broken through. And this is specially the case if the front in question is not limited in proportion to the troops defending it but extending over hundreds of kilometres, for it would be a false conclusion to expect that weak troops at one or other point in the line could defend it indefinitely. Fronts can be broken through, but it is necessary to fill up the gaps in the line as soon as possible. This is only possible if reserves drawn up in echelon can be held in rear of the forces in the front line. But were our national forces facing the Greek Army in such a position and had they such reserves behind them? Was even the smallest unit worthy of the name of a fighting force still left in our West-Anatolian provinces, including the town and district of Ankara or, more precisely, in the whole of our country?

Apparently there was a great amount of neglect and terrible abuses going on in our Eastern Army. This neglect seemed to have assumed such proportions that it interfered with the patriotism of the people, and this had caused a great deal of excitement. Nevertheless, it is evident that neither the acting governor nor the officer commanding the Army Corps had a very clear idea about this growing excitement which was impossible to allay.

Not one of all the persons interested and those in the town who had official duties to attend to had noticed it; no one had come forward to warn the Government, but when the population learned that Celalettin Arif Bey and Hüseyin Avni Bey had left for Erzurum —the former on leave on account of over-exertion of the brain and the other sent on a special mission by me— their excitement and all the unrest had suddenly stopped. When, however, the two representatives arrived the excitement broke out again!

On 16 September 1920 I wired the Vice-president of the Grand National Assembly in Erzurum to the following effect: "Your telegram has been read before the Council of Ministers; we are in correspondence on this question with the officer commanding at the front." I asked the Commandant at the Eastern front for information and his opinion in respect to the communications from Celalettin Arif Bey, which I transmitted to him in a summarised form.

Celalettin Arif Bey, speaking about the abuses in the Army and of the appointment of the Governor of Erzurum with the approval of the people, and declaring that distrust would arise unless an immediate answer were given, actually has an interview with the officer commanding the forces and induces him to propose that he should be appointed Governor of the Eastern Provinces with very wide powers. And apparently this Army commander knows nothing about Celalettin Arif Bey's complaints, which, as a matter of fact, are aimed at himself! It is difficult to gather any other impression than that there was a conspiracy, or a network of intrigue going on with a certain aim in view.

In Kazım Karabekir Pasha's reply on 18 September to my telegram of the 16th, he said: "The messages from Celalettin Arif Bey are based on malicious gossip which has been disseminated by some persons for the sole purpose of getting rid of Colonel Kazım Bey, the Acting Governor of Erzurum. Unfortunately I believe that the excitement of the people and the appointment of a governor who shall be chosen by the people only means that Celalettin Arif Bey has chosen a wrong path. The fact that the complaint in question has not been directed personally to me, who possesses universal confidence and is greatly honoured by high and low I may say, in the whole of the East, affords a reason for believing that those who are intriguing well know that they have little chance of success.

"Celalettin Arif Bey has proposed to me that I remove Colonel Kazım Bey from Erzurum by depriving him of his position as Acting Governor and temporary commander of the Army Corps. I replied that if he would personally accept these appointments temporarily, Kazım Bey would be relieved of them by the order of the Ministry of the Interior.

"I believe that the position of Celalettin Arif Bey in Erzurum, he being here in no official capacity, may damage his authority. It is absolutely necessary for him to be appointed Acting Governor of Erzurum as soon as possible, so that he can bring this matter which he has undertaken to a happy issue without any interference.

"If you think proper, you could later on appoint him to be the Inspector and Governor of the Eastern Provinces. In any case I do not share his view that the excitement he mentions was only held back until his arrival. I believe that these statements are the exaggeration of an individual who met with a good reception."

In the reply that I sent on 20 September to Kazım Karabekir Pasha to his two telegrams of 14 and 18 September I quoted a clause of the Act of 5 September 1920 which provides that "the same person cannot hold the position of a member of the Grand National Assembly and be an official of the State at the same time." I added: "The appointment of Celalettin as the Governor of Erzurum is out of the question unless he resigns his position as a representative.

His appointment to the governorship of this Province could only be proposed to the Council of Ministers."

However, on 18 September, the date of Kazım Karabekir Pasha's last telegram, the anticipated attitude had already been adopted in Erzurum in contradiction to the stipulations of the Act to which we referred in our communication of 20 September. I was informed of this illegal procedure in a telegram from Celalettin Arif Bey, who was at that time Minister of Justice in New Turkey. He had drafted it on 18 September and I received it on the 21st. This telegram from the Minister of Justice, who had meanwhile appointed himself Acting Governor of Erzurum, read as follows:

The situation was indeed serious and grave, because at this moment we had decided to attack Armenia on our Eastern front. We were engaged in making preparations and taking dispositions for this purpose. The officer commanding the Eastern front had already received the necessary orders. The Minister of Justice in the National Government who was immediately behind the army which was destined to proceed to the east and who apparently was engaged in discovering thefts committed in this army and proving that its members were rogues, found that the only thing to be done was to unlawfully appoint himself the Acting Governor of this Province.

The officer commanding at the front, who had left Erzurum and gone to his headquarters, wrote on 22 September: "The proposal I formerly made about Celalettin Arif Bey's appointment as Governor of the Eastern Provinces had been suggested to me, and I believed it was a sincere idea. As I have since learned the actual facts of the case through

Celalettin Arif Bey's actions, I would like to inform Your Excellency that naturally I withdraw my proposal."

On the same day, that is to say, 22 September 1920, I received a telegram from the Vice-president of the Grand National Assembly, who had assumed the office of Acting Governor of Erzurum. In this telegram he said: "The abuses regarding arms and ammunition, as well as food supplies and the abandoned goods, the unlimited illegal requisitions, the acts of violence and violation of personal rights contrary to law, have deeply offended the people. We arrived here at the moment when Erzurum, under the influence of despair and distrust, had gone so far as to contemplate the necessity of governing itself as the only means of protection.

"Kazım Karabekir Pasha's attitude was still less in accord with the interests of the country. For this reason the population insisted on putting a speedy end to the abuses which were being perpetrated openly and bringing the guilty ones to justice. In agreement with Kazım Pasha, the people have demanded that immediate steps should be taken to inspire confidence, and have appealed to me personally to take over the office of governor temporarily.

"I have wanted you to entrust Hüseyin Avni Bey with this office. I would like you to inform the representative Hüseyin Avni Bey, who possesses the confidence of the country because he is regarded as one of them, of his appointment within the next twenty-four hours".

We had ourselves advocated the principle of the government of the people by the people; but we had never anticipated that every province or every district should individually constitute a separate administration. In the early days of the Grand National Assembly, we had clearly defined our aims.

These had been approved of and formulated in such a manner by the Grand National Assembly that this forum was the only place in which the national will to be master of the destiny of our country found its expression. Could the methods which such a personality, who was one of the leaders of this Assembly and at the same time their Minister of Justice, was allowed to adopt for the purpose of discovering illegal acts committed in the Army and elsewhere and of delivering their perpetrators to justice, consist in the fact that he allowed himself to be taken in tow by some stupid persons and assume a rebellious attitude to which my fellow-citizens at Erzurum — true patriots as I know them to be — would never have given their consent?

Celalettin Arif Bey made the same proposal to Kazım Karabekir Pasha, and it is reported that the latter replied: "Hüseyin Avni Bey is a man of moderate ability and has never held any public office; he entertained his fellow officers as a comedian on the stage when he was a lieutenant in the reserve. To make this man into a temporary governor would mean to make a mockery of the office."

Kazım Karabekir Pasha sent this telegram in code on 22 September 1920: "I am now perfectly certain that Celalettin Arif Bey and some ambitious men had worked out a neat little programme with the idea of snatching up appointments and honours while he was still at Ankara.

We quite understood how the game was intended to be played through a telegram that was sent in the name of the entire population of Erzurum, signed by forty or fifty people, when another telegram arrived which also came from the population of Erzurum and which clearly showed how loyal this population was to the Government and the

Grand National Assembly and how willing they were to submit to sacrifices.

Celalettin Arif Bey, having at last seen with his own eyes that the armies of the Grand National Assembly were victorious in the Armenian expedition forty-seven days after he had been ordered to return, was eventually convinced that he would have to leave Erzurum. He had, however, informed the Assembly of his departure via a telegram.

We appointed Kazım Karabekir Pasha, commanding the XVth Army Corps, to command the troops on the Eastern front. The Armenians were successful in a general surprise attack which they made before Bardiz on the morning of 24 September 1920.

The Armenians were driven back, and on the morning of 28 September our troops began to advance. On the same day the fifty signatories to the Erzurum telegram opened their offensive against Ankara.

The Army entered Sarıkamış on 29 September. Göle was occupied on 30 September. Now for certain reasons our Army remained stationary for a month —until 28 October— on the Sarıkamış—Laloğlu line.

Our Eastern Army, which was waiting on the battlefield, began its advance on Kars on 28 October 1920. The enemy abandoned this town without offering any resistance; it was occupied on 30 October. On 7 November, our troops occupied the country as far as Arpaçay and Gümrü. On the 6th November the Armenians requested for a cessation of hostilities and asked for peace. On the 8th of the same month we informed the Armenian Army through the Ministry of Foreign Affairs of the terms of the armistice. Peace negotiations began on 26 November and ended on 2 December, and during that night the treaty was signed at Gümrü.

The Treaty of Gümrü is the first that was made by the National Government. By this treaty Armenia, which in the imagination of our enemies had already been given the Turkish districts as far as the valley of Harşit, was blotted out through the fact that it had to cede to us - the National Government - the districts which the "Ottoman Government" had lost in the campaign of 1876—77.

The Central Committee of the "Trakya Pashaeli" Society for the Defence of the Rights of Anatolia and Rumelia held a congress in Eastern Thrace, which entrusted the administration of Thrace to the General Committee of "Thrace and Pashaeli." Cafer Tayyar Bey (Cafer Tayyar Pasha), a member of this committee, commanded the Army Corps in Thrace and had been elected Representative for Edirne in our Assembly.

The instructions which we had given to the Central Committee of Thrace and the officer commanding the Army Corps were based on the principle that the fate of Thrace would be settled at the same time as the destiny of the whole country.

These were the instructions we had given concerning military operations:

"In case of an attack by superior forces, resistance should be maintained to the end; even if the whole of Thrace were to be occupied, every single after for negotiation .— whatever solution might be proposed—was to be declined."

We declared that such was also the resolution of the commander in Thrace. But after a time, Cafer Tayyar Bey, relying on the promises made to him by foreigners, had accepted an invitation and had gone to Istanbul, and had only informed us of this after he had returned.

Apparently certain rumours had been spread, for instance, that Eastern Thrace could not exist by itself but could only do so under a foreign administration in combination with Western Thrace. In any case, a certain amount of propaganda was spread which was calculated to injure the morale of the country.

The destiny of Thrace was consequently left to those decisions which were made under the influence of political circles in Istanbul.

After their success in the general offensive which was undertaken on the Western front of Anatolia, the Greek Army landed a division at Tekirdağ on 20 July 1920.

Before the 55th Division, which was very much scattered about in the district of Tekirdağ, had time to rally, the Greek Division began to advance in the direction of Edirne.

The Greek troops, who intended to begin their attack from Western Thrace by crossing the Maritza River, were stopped and prevented from advancing any further thanks to the vigilance of Cemil Bey (at present Minister of the Interior), who was in command of the 60th Division, and of Şükrü Naili Bey (Şükrü Naili Pasha), who had arrived in Edirne with his troops on 15 June 1920, and who had already been seriously engaged in Edirne and the railway station of Karaağaç.

According to the news that reached me, Cafer Tayyar Bey was taken prisoner by the enemy whilst he was wandering about on horseback in the district of Havza, without having been able to get in touch with any of our troops. This is the reason that our first Corps was completely scattered and deprived of its commanding officer and leadership. Some of the troops were taken prisoner and the remainder fled to Bulgaria. Eventually the whole of Thrace fell into the hands of the Greeks.

When I spoke to you about the organisations of the "Green Army," I told you that there were two opposite views about the question of organisation. Efforts were made to compromise the movement by fostering the idea of a kind of organisation which we might call "Militia" in contrast to the idea of the formation of a regular Army which we favoured.

In the Kütahya district, the brothers Reşit, Ethem and Tevfik carried on this movement with great zeal making use of the forces known as "Flying Columns" which were at their disposal. On the Western front propaganda made for this movement became so powerful and effective in the Army, among the population and even in the Assembly, that it was everywhere proclaimed: "The Army is good for nothing; it must be disbanded. We all want to become National soldiers." Ethem Bey's troops which, being national, occupied a zone to itself and formed a special front among the Western lines of defence, began to be regarded as possessing special privileges and as being employed in preference to the regular forces, that is to say, as troops of which the others were jealous. Ethem Bey and his brothers began to exert a certain amount of influence and predominance everywhere.

Meanwhile, the officer commanding the Western front made a suggestion to the General Staff which was attached to the brothers Ethem and Tevfik and which consisted in "beginning an offensive against an isolated Greek detachment in the district of Gediz."

After some confused operations, which were carried on without any discipline, without any clear aim or order, we were, as you know, defeated in Gediz.

To counter this offensive, the Greek Army opened an attack on 25 October 1920 at Bursa. They occupied Yenişehir and İnegöl. They attacked our troops from Uşak in front of the heights of Dumlupınar, and our troops retired. Thus again we suffered a general defeat along the entire front.

The Army maintained and proved that the "Flying Columns" had done nothing at all and that they were incapable of doing anything; that during the battle they had not obeyed orders and that they always kept as far as possible away from danger.

You are well aware that the greatest danger to our country and nation in those territories which were or still are governed by Sultans and Caliphs consists of the fact that the latter are bought by the enemy. Generally speaking, this is easily achieved. On the other hand, for those territories governed by National Assemblies, the most dangerous thing is that certain representatives can be bought and enlisted for the service and in the name of foreign countries. If we look at examples in history, we must indeed admit that it is not impossible to find men devoid of patriotism who have succeeded in getting into National Assemblies. For this reason a nation must be very careful whom they elect as their representatives.

The safest way to protect the nation from error is to guide it during the elections by a political party which has gained the confidence of the people through its ideas and actions. Even if we accept in theory that the majority of citizens is equipped with authentic information enabling them to express themselves about each of the candidates and to form a correct judgment of him — experience bears this out— this is apparently not an infallible truth.

I shall now return to the point where I had left off, namely, concerning the Western front. After the battle of Gediz and its painful moral and material consequences, Ali Fuat Pasha's authority and influence as the commander of the forces appeared to have been shaken. Just at this moment Ali Fuat Pasha asked in a telegram in code on 5 November 1920 for permission to come to Ankara for the purpose of consulting with us. I had begun to feel that I would have to recall him from his command. The unfavourable criticisms levelled against Ali Fuat Pasha and the fatal effect which the existence of the "Flying Columns" had had on the discipline of the Army, had actually begun to be so noticeable that I considered it necessary on 7 November to order Ali Fuat Pasha to return to Ankara as quickly as possible.

As regards to the Western front, which required very serious and careful handling, it appeared to me that the quickest and best thing to do would be to send İsmet Pasha, Chief of the General Staff, who was already engaged in studying the general military operations, to take over the command.

I considered it expedient to send Refet Bey (now Refet Pasha), Minister of the Interior, to Konya and the surrounding districts for the sole purpose of recruiting such units, and I added this appointment to his other duties. Refet Bey had often for different purposes been to Konya and Denizli, where he had taken an interest in the southern part of the Western front, and was therefore well acquainted with this part of the country. Thus I was able to solve the problem in this way: The entire front was divided into two parts, of which İsmet Pasha was given the command of the most important one, called the Western front, while the southern portion of it could be given to Refet Bey, whom I had to send to the Konya district, and both fronts were directly under the General Staff.

Fevzi Pasha, Minister of National Defence, could undertake the administration of the General Staff.

In Fuat Pasha's time there was another zone behind the front line extending from the front to Sivas. To control this zone Fuat Pasha had been obliged to create the post of an acting commander. It was clear that this was scarcely practicable. Consequently, it was natural that part of this zone which was included as the base in the territory of the front came under the administration of the Ministry of National Defence in the new scheme.

To secure the quick preparation and reorganisation of the Army, it seemed advisable that for a certain time İsmet Pasha should still remain at the head of the General Staff, in the same manner as it was necessary that Refet Bey should temporarily retain his office as Minister of the Interior. In this we had the special object in view of securing the organisation of the cavalry with which he was entrusted as quickly as possible by preserving order in his district and requisitioning animals and material from the populace.

Fuat Pasha arrived at Ankara on 8 November 1920. I went to the station personally to meet him. I noticed that he was dressed in the uniform worn by the men of the national units and carried a carbine on his shoulder. There could no longer be any doubt about the great influence which such ideas and ways of thinking had gained on the whole of the Western front, considering that they had even induced the officer in command to wear this uniform himself.

Therefore, after I had explained my ideas in short to Fuat Pasha, I mentioned the new duties which he could undertake. He accepted them willingly. On the following night I asked İsmet Pasha and Refet Pasha to come to me and we arranged what their new appointments and powers would be.

The emphatic instructions I gave them were "to create a regular army and a strong cavalry force as quickly as possible."

This was the beginning of the execution of our determination "to destroy the spirit and system of the irregular organisations" which we had resolved upon on 8 November 1920.

The plan followed by Damat Ferit's Government in collusion with our enemies of all descriptions "to put an end by force of arms" had not been successful.

We had resisted the internal upheavals and had suppressed them. The Greek offensive had at last been brought to a standstill on a certain line. The operations undertaken by the Greeks were confined to limited areas.

It became evident that we had undertaken as serious steps against the internal unrest as against the Greek forces. It was also apparent that armed attacks whether from the interior or the exterior of the country would not succeed, and particularly that the position of the National Government at Ankara could not be shaken.

Consequently, the policy of armed attack pursued by Istanbul had been wrecked. The conviction that the policy would have to be altered naturally followed. In that case it would be better to adopt a policy of internal disintegration under cover of a policy of under- standing exactly as happened in September 1919, after the first resignation of Damat Ferit Pasha and the Cabinet of Ali Rıza Pasha came into power, when the question arose of pursuing a policy which was apparently one reconcilable towards us with the intention thereby of producing our inner disintegration.

We shall see that in the struggles that followed we had to combat ideas which were aimed at tempting us into internal and external enterprises and internal intrigues through the mediation of Istanbul in the same way as against the Greek Army, but under conditions which were far more difficult to understand and to explain.

Tevfik Pasha was at the head of the Government in İstanbul.

Ahmet İzzet Pasha and Salih Pasha, respectively, occupied the offices of Minister of the Interior and Minister of Marine in this Cabinet, which soon tried to come into contact with us. It was Ahmet İzzet Pasha chiefly who made this effort.

An officer among the military leaders of the Palace was furnished with certain documents and sent to Ankara by Ahmet İzzet Pasha. In them we were informed that they hoped to arrive at a peace under more favourable conditions than hitherto. İzmir, for example, with the consent of the Greeks, would come under a special regime under Ottoman sovereignty. Above all, it was important to come to an agreement with the Istanbul Government.

It was remarked that Ahmet İzzet Pasha and the Cabinet to which he belonged were not clear about the character and authority of the Grand National Assembly and their Government, and that they had conceived the idea of forming a Government in Istanbul as a means to solve the problems concerning the destiny of the country and the nation.

To fully enlighten İzzet Pasha and Tevfik Pasha's Cabinet and to inform them about the situation, we drew up a document containing in full detail all the communications and obervations we considered necessary and sent it to them by the special agent who had come to Ankara and who left in the direction of İnebolu on 8 November 1920.

In a telegram written in İstanbul on 23 November, which was signed by the special messenger who had arrived in Istanbul and which had been sent to Inebolu and transmitted from there to Ankara on 27 November, the following was said:

"When I was with İzzet Pasha today, 23 November 1920, the Minister of Foreign Affairs made the following statements regarding the latest political situation:

"It is reported that the English Ambassador, who arrived here a few days ago, has declared that a favourable solution would be found for the Ottoman Government on the important questions of Armenia and Georgia, and afterwards on the question of İzmir. It seems advisable to profit by this favourable situation and not miss the opportunity of doing everything that is possible to safeguard the future of the country. If Ankara wants to gain time, feelers must be put out immediately and the following resolutions adopted unanimously."

"After making these statements İzzet Pasha said that it is our duty to make use of the advantages which our continued struggles have gained for us. If Anatolia would not receive the deputation which it is intended to send there, we must get in touch with him personally and explain our aims privately to him. If we were not to consent to this, the conclusion would be drawn that we had abandoned the idea expressed in the above-mentioned statement. In that case he would no longer remain in the Cabinet but would resign and, if it was desired, he would go to Ankara without taking any notice of Istanbul."

In the same telegram we were told that the following statements appearing in the Istanbul Press were attributed to İzzet Pasha: "In sending a special agent to Anatolia the Government wanted to find out whether any connection could be arranged with the people in Ankara or not. The agent who had just returned has stated that such connection could be established. Correspondence with this object has been opened. We shall naturally do what is necessary."

In answer to the observation that statements of this kind were not in accordance with the point of view of Anatolia and that they should be altered, the Cabinet told us that they did not agree with us. İzzet Pasha, however, gave the following explanations to the journal called "Tercümanı Hakikat": "The higher interests of the country emphatically demand that the Press should be silent for the moment on this question. Consequently, I wish to be excused for the present from giving any information."

You will remember that on the day on which İzzet Pasha's messenger had started via İnebolu for İstanbul, that is to say, on 8 November 1920, we decided to appoint Fuat Pasha our Ambassador in Moscow and İsmet Pasha and Refet Pasha to commands on the Western front. İsmet Pasha left for the front on the following day and took over his command on 10 November. Shortly afterwards, I received a telegram in code, dated 13 November 1920, from a close friend of Ethem Bey's, which was sent from Eskişehir. It ran: "The rumour that Ethem Bey, accompanied by Fuat Pasha, will go to Moscow is regarded by the men at the front and the population to have a sinister purpose.

The fact that such men are being removed from your environment has given support to the opinion that your Excellency intends to establish a dictatorship."

In fact, the removal of these persons from Turkey was desirable both in the interests of Ethem and his brothers and for the salvation of Turkey. For this reason, I had told Fuat Pasha that if they wished he might take them with him and appoint them to carry out any duties he might think desirable. It was not to be expected that the contents of this telegram sent by one of Ethem Bey's friends expressed merely the ideas of the sender, or that it represented the truth, because neither the men at the front nor the people were interested in the question of Ethem Bey being sent to Russia or not. What particularly attracted my attention was the fact that there were people who could imagine that I was aiming at a dictatorship and that this had led me to get rid of Ethem and men of his type, who were in my way.

Soon after İsmet Pasha had begun to take up his duties at the front, Ethem Bey, on the pretext that he was ill, came to Ankara and stayed there for a long time. While he was away, his brother Tevfik Bey took over the acting command of the "Flying Columns."

On 24 November 1920 Tevfik Bey sent a telegram to the officer commanding at the front in which, after using some provocative expressions, he said: "It would seem that the Northern and Southern fronts are under the same Government; but as this is not so in reality, I shall not allow the sons of our country to be thrown away for no object, simply because the administration is lacking in competence. If our left flank is not protected within twenty-four hours I shall retire my mobile columns to the district of the Efendi Bridge. I leave it to the Government to decide who will be responsible for this."

İsmet Pasha replied to the commander of the mobile troops in these terms: "The XIIth Army Corps is forty kilometres away from your left wing. Our troops have not been ordered to go into a decisive battle or to drive the enemy back after they have retreated.

Consequently, the flying columns practically constitute an independent cavalry force pursuing the enemy. Its function is to take the necessary dispositions to deal with the superior forces of the enemy, yet whenever the enemy undertakes a local and serious movement of any importance you must avoid decisive battle. This is always the duty of cavalry troops in such circumstances. As there is not a strong cavalry force on the Western front, it is impossible that they can reinforce your line of defence; but it is possible and even essential that the flying columns shall keep touch and maintain communication with the Southern front by the means at present at their disposal.

It was natural that the commanding officer of the Western front intended to put forward a regular budget for his armies. For this purpose he demanded on 22 November 1920 that there be an inspection of the actual strength of all the troops under his command. This was carried out in all its details, with the exception of the flying columns. In his reply, Tevfik Bey said: "The flying columns can neither be altered nor converted into regular troops ... It is impossible to put officers or paymasters in charge of these vagabonds or induce them to agree to such a thing. At the sight of officers they will go mad as though they had seen the Angel of Death. Our troops are led by men like Pehlivan Ağa, Ahmet Onbaşı, San Mehmet, Halil Efe, Topal İsmail;

their non-commissioned quartermasters are men who can scarcely read or write. They cannot be moved about by telling them that they are not at the proper place. The flying columns must be commanded in an irregular way as they have been hitherto ...

I would like to tell you how the correspondence between the command of the Western front and the command of the flying columns, as well as the news about the situation, came to my knowledge.

The telegram sent by Tevfik Bey, acting commander of the flying columns, to İsmet Pasha in which he hesitated to hand over spies and deserters to the Independence Court and declared his intention of retiring his troops in the direction of the Efendi Bridge if the XIIth Army Corps would not protect the left flank of the flying columns within twenty-four hours, had been handed over to me by Ethem Bey, who was in Ankara.

I naturally found these telegrams very significant. In the attitude taken up by the flying columns I saw a peculiar state of affairs which required that certain steps should be taken. For this reason I had said in my telegram of 25 November in which I told İsmet Pasha that Ethem Bey had informed me of the contents of the telegrams in question: "I would like you to inform me tonight what has been done in reply to this step taken by Tevfik Bey, which I regard as a very important one, and what is going to be done about it."

İsmet Pasha sent me a detailed report on the correspondence.

The reports on military events from the flying columns were addressed to Ethem Bey in Ankara and transmitted by him to the Western front.

It was easily understood that the brothers Ethem and Tevfik, together with some of their friends who shared their opinions, had decided to revolt against the National Government. Whilst Tevfik Bey was looking out at the front for an opportunity to carry out his resolution to assemble his forces and leave the front, Ethem Bey and Reşit Bey his brother, who was a representative, and some of the others, occupied themselves with the political side of their enterprise. To secure the success of this plan of revolt they had first to make sure of getting the command over the army by discrediting and overthrowing the leaders at the head of the Army at the Western front, whom they considered were standing in their way.

Another question was to win the opinion of the whole of the Assembly to their side, in order to facilitate to overthrow the Army commanders, the Ministers and the Government.

There could no longer be any doubt about this being their intention. It was scarcely possible to avoid assuming that some reconciliatory and amiable words which Ethem Bey employed in his telegram to İsmet Pasha and his brother Tevfik Bey were based on the intention of gaining time, and that they were meant to show modesty and complete subjection for a certain time by interpreting the question as being due to a certain feeling of bitterness resulting from a misunder- standing between İsmet Pasha and Tevfik Bey. This implied that Tevfik Bey, after having permitted himself to be overcome by nervous excitement, had gone too far.

I wish to assure you that I had done everything that was necessary from every point of view, both at the front and in Ankara. I had no fear at all of the revolt by Ethem Bey and his brothers. I was convinced that if they did break out into open revolt, they would be suppressed and punished, and I proceeded, therefore, with great forbearance and equanimity. I preferred as far as possible to try to reduce them to obedience and a better disposition by giving them some good advice. If I could not succeed in this I decided to act in a manner such as their acts and provocative behaviour necessitated, and which would then be exposed to the public in their true light. With this in view, I resolved to go on 2 December 1920 personally with Ethem Bey and Reşit Bey, who were in Ankara, and some others to Eskişehir to meet İsmet Pasha there and come to an understanding with them.

I expected that Ethem Bey would avoid accompanying me on this journey, but it was absolutely necessary to take him with me. I arranged, whether he wished it or not, that he should come, and in case he would not do so I decided to act accordingly.

The next day Ethem Bey made the excuse that he could not go, because he was ill, and Dr. Adnan Bey stated that the condition of Ethem Bey's health would not allow him to make this journey. But I insisted on his coming with me.

At last, we left in a special train for Eskişehir on the evening of 3 December 1920. In addition to Ethem Bey and Reşit Bey, these very important persons accompanied me: Kazım Pasha, Celal Bey, Kılıç Ali Bey, Eyüp Sabri Bey, Hakkı Behiç Bey and Hacı Şükrü Bey.

While I was still asleep, early on the morning of 4 December 1920 the train arrived at Eskişehir.

As I had heard that İsmet Pasha was still in Bilecik, we decided to go on to the railway station there without stopping at Eskişehir. When I awoke at Eskişehir I inquired why the train was not going on. My orderly officer replied that our comrades had gone to the restaurant opposite the station to get some breakfast and that they would be back immediately. A few minutes later I was told that everything was ready. I asked whether our comrades were all there. A rapid count was made, and it was found that the number was complete, with the exception of Ethem Bey and one of his companions. I felt certain at once that Ethem Bey's flight had been pre-arranged; but I did not mention my suspicion to anybody. I was content to assure myself that in that case it was of no use to go on to Bilecik without Ethem Bey, and I decided to order İsmet Pasha to come to me.

After I had had a private conversation with him by telegraph, İsmet Pasha came to Eskişehir. As I wished to have a private conversation with him first, I went to meet him at a station some way off, and on the evening of 4 December 1920, we arrived at Eskişehir together. We dined at a restaurant with our comrades who were waiting there for us. Ethem Bey was not present. I asked his brother where he was, and he replied: "He is ill in bed." A meeting had been arranged for that night at İsmet Pasha's headquarters between Reşit Bey, Ethem Bey and ourselves, in the presence of Kazım Pasha, Celal Bey and Hakkı Behiç Bey. When Reşit Bey told me that Ethem Bey was ill he had added that he would be able to come to the meeting at the headquarters. After dinner we went there; but Ethem Bey had not arrived. I asked Reşit Bey when his brother was coming. He replied: "At the present moment Ethem Bey is at the head of his troops."

Reşit Bey spoke in the name of his brothers and himself. He was bold enough to say that his brothers were heroes and that they would not take orders from anybody, whoever he might be, and that everyone had to take matters as they were. He would not even listen to any remarks about principles of discipline made in the name of the Government or of the issuing of commands or about claims based on such principles. Then I declared:

"Hitherto I have been speaking in my capacity as an old friend of yours and animated by the sincere desire to arrive at a result that would be favourable to you. From this moment, however, our comradeship and private relations with one another must be set aside. You have before you now the President of the Grand National Assembly of Turkey and of her Government. In my position as the head of the State, I order the command at the Western front to make use of their powers and to act as the situation shall demand."

İsmet Pasha replied to this: "Some of those in command under me may have refused to obey me. I can punish them and teach them a lesson. Hitherto I have shown myself weak in this direction towards anybody, nor have I asked any one to help me in the duty which I have to perform. In future I shall do what is required."

Following the decisive attitude shown by myself and İsmet Pasha, Reşit Bey, who spoke in a very high voice, immediately assumed a humble attitude and declared that we must not be in a hurry to push things as far as that, and that he would find a way out if he were to go to his brothers. It was quite clear that this would have no result and that he only wanted to inform his brothers and gain time.

Nevertheless, we agreed to Reşit Bey's proposal. We consented that he should leave for Kütahya to see his brothers by a special train which İsmet Pasha would arrange for him on the following day. We thought it advisable that Kazım Pasha should accompany Reşit Bey, and so they left together.

You remember that following İzzet Pasha's action and proposal, a meeting had been decided upon to take place in Bilecik. The deputation had been waiting for me at the railway station in Bilecik since the previous day. It consisted of İzzet Pasha, Salih Pasha, Cevat Bey the Minister Plenipotentiary, Hüseyin Kazım Bey, Minister of Agriculture, Münir Bey, the legal advisor, and Hodja Fatin Efendi.

We met in a room at the railway station. İsmet Pasha was also present. I was the first to speak. After I had introduced myself as "President of the Grand National Assembly of Turkey and her Government," I asked: "With whom have I the honour of speaking?"

Not having understood my intention, Salih Pasha began to explain that he was the Minister of Marine and İzzet Pasha the Minister of the Interior. I said immediately that I recognised neither the Government of İstanbul nor themselves as members of such a government. I said that I did not feel inclined to carry on a conversation with them if they wished to appear at this interview in their capacities as Ministers of a Government in İstanbul.

Thereupon we agreed to proceed to an exchange of opinion without touching the question of our respective positions and authority.

I allowed some of the representatives who had accompanied me from Ankara to take part during certain stages of the conversation. During the course of the interview, which lasted for several hours, it became evident that the deputation had no fixed information or convictions.

In the end, I told them that I would not allow them to return to İstanbul and that they would have to come with me to Ankara.

On 5 December —the day we were with İzzet Pasha's deputation on the way from Bilecik to Ankara— I received a telegram from Reşit Bey, in which he told me of his arrival in Kütahya, of the meeting he expected to have on the following day with Tevfik Bey, and the arrival of Ethem Bey; but this telegram did not contain anything of a positive character. Four days later Reşit Bey said in a telegram, dated 9 December and sent on his departure from Eskişehir: "The incident with Tevfik Bey has come to a satisfactory conclusion." Another sentence in this telegram ran as follows:

"But we have noticed, over and over again, that the persons whose acquaintance we wanted to make and to whom we wanted to show who we are, cannot or do not wish to think in a reasonable manner adapted to the situation."

Reşit Bey had also informed İsmet Pasha, commanding the Western front, in Eskişehir that the question was settled, that telegraphic communication was restored, and that the Simav command could be re-established. Ethem Bey endeavoured to show us in a telegram in code, which I received on 9 December 1920, that the question had been put forward intentionally and inappropriately by İsmet Pasha. Ethem Bey further remarked that they had been informed of all the steps presumably taken by Salih Pasha, who was at that time my principal A.D.C. He added that he was in possession of certain proof, based on irrefutable evidence, of the fact that an erroneous suspicion had taken hold of me. Then he tried by insidious effort to secure that a detachment of the flying columns that had been sent to the Southern front by order of the General Staff and which returned from Maden on its way back from the front, be placed under his command. Referring to the fact that the flying columns had been provided for in the budget under the head of gendarmerie at the time of Fuat Pasha, he wanted to get some more money.

In the favourable reply I sent to him three days later, I said: "I must admit that appearances during these last days, although they did not cause me any fear, gave rise to some doubts in my mind," and I urgently asked him to act very strictly towards anybody who would try to disturb the order and concord prevailing in our general situation.

In reality, the difficulty had not been solved. From what I will now tell you, you will see that Ethem Bey and his brothers were trying to mislead us with the object of gaining time. Their intention was to recruit and collect as many men as possible, to act in such a way that Sarı Efe's fighting troops from Düzce and the Gökbayrak battalion in Lefke would rejoin them. They wanted to incite Demirci Mehmet Efe to revolt with them and then compel the officers commanding at the front to desert. This would offer them an opportunity of spreading propaganda among the troops and to get the officers and men to refuse to fight against them.

Ethem Bey sent agents whom he called liaison officers in every direction, including Konya, Ankara and Haymana. They were provided with special code-keys, and he began to collect ammunition and animals.

When the officer commanding the Western front had asked the commander of the flying columns how much rifle and artillery ammunition had been expended in the battle of Gediz, he received from "Tevfik, acting commander of the flying columns," the following reply: "Your question convinces me that you have no confidence in us. Ammunition is neither eaten nor drunk, it is only used against the enemy. If you have no confidence in us, you need not take the trouble to send us any ammunition at all."

You can see that Tevfik Bey was still acting commander and that in that capacity, although Ethem Bey was at the head of his forces at the front, he carried on correspondence which meant that there were two chiefs at the head, of the same forces exercising the same full authority.

The officer commanding at the front had sent me a copy of the document containing the question that was put on the 13th and the reply to it, for my information.

The employment of a code, the key of which was not in the possession of the Government, as well as private codes, had been universally prohibited; but in spite of this prohibition Ethem Bey's agents, and some representatives who were his companions, continued to communicate in code. This practice was obviously forbidden. Thereupon Ethem Bey addressed himself to İsmet Pasha on 13 December 1920, and told him that it had been reported that telegrams sent to the liaison officers belonging to the flying columns in Ankara and Eskişehir, referring to certain requisitions and sundry other matters, had been intercepted, and he wanted him to have these orders cancelled because they interfered with their communication and led to difficulties.

After Kazım Pasha, accompanied by Recep Bey, had had their interview with Ethem Bey and Tevfik Bey in Kütahya, he gave me the important points contained in the statements made by Ethem Bey in this condensed form:

I. The Government of Ankara is neither fit nor able to realise the national aims. We cannot tamely submit to this Government.

2. The character of our enterprise will be unfavourably construed. If, however, I do succeed in the end, everybody will say that I am right.
3. The question between Refet Bey and ourselves is one of personal dignity. Mustafa Kemal Pasha prefers to respect Refet Bey's pride and hurt ours. In any case, I feel inclined to oppose Refet Bey and to pursue him as far as Ankara; if I have to die I would prefer to do so in pursuit of him.
4. We would have finished this affair long ago if it had not been for Reşit's position in the Assembly in Ankara, which has misled us. What is the Assembly and what importance is to be attached to it?

After having listened to these expressions, Kazım Pasha had been trying to preach calmness and moderation to these people by telling them that, in addition to the Western front, Turkey had armies also in the east, south and centre of the country, that these armies had capable leaders and officers of high merit at their head and in their midst, and that, finally, the nation were on the side of all of them.

The committee was instructed to inform the flying columns of the following points which contained the final emphatic demands of the Government:

1. The flying columns were to submit completely, as all the other troops had to do, to the orders of the Commander-in-Chief at the front, and should abstain from every undesirable and illegal act.
2. The flying columns are never under any circumstances to recruit reinforcements for their forces, and they are to immediately stop the activity of people who have been appointed to undertake this. In the

same manner as the other troops, the need of reinforcements should be supplied by order of the commander-in- chief at the front.
3. The flying columns are not to undertake steps for the arrest of deserters, who shall be followed and arrested by the chief in command at the front, as is the practice in the other parts of the Army.
4. The Government is to be informed of all particulars about the liaison officers serving with the flying columns in certain places, in order that the families of the officers and men belonging to the flying columns shall be cared for. A copy of the code-key used by these liaison officers is to be given to us.

If these conditions are fulfilled, the flying columns will be permitted to continue their services as before within certain limits.

Celal Bey, Kılıç Ali Bey, Eyüp Sabri Bey and Vehbi Bey, together with Reşit Bey, left Ankara at noon on 23 December and arrived at Kütahya at 4.45 p. m. on 24 December.

I learned that Ethem Bey and Tevfik Bey, without the knowledge of the commander at the front, and without asking for his consent, had distributed regular troops that were in their zone at the front and had later on concentrated the flying columns in Gediz and the detachment of Pehlivan Ağa in Kütahya. In an open telegram that I sent to Celal Bey and his comrades in Kütahya on 25 December 1920, I said:

"I want to know urgently what this means. I am waiting at the telegraph set for your reply."

I sent a copy of this telegram to İsmet Pasha, Refet Pasha and Fahrettin Pasha and directed their attention to it.

They sent the following short reply which was signed by them jointly:

"Do not be uneasy. There is nothing to be anxious about. Tevfik Bey will arrive here tomorrow. We shall then have a general discussion about it; we shall let you know the result in detail."

From this reply I came to the conclusion that our comrades there had either been deceived or ill-informed about the situation, or, on the other hand, that they had been arrested and were compelled to write what they were told to. Pretending that I had not understood the situation, I wanted to give the impression that I was satisfied with the assurances they had given me in their short message.

Consequently, I replied that I had no doubt as to their having come to an agreement with Tevfik Bey after their meeting concerning the principles which would secure the greatest benefit to the country and the nation, and that I would succeed in clearly proving that the communications which had reached me were nothing but gossip, of which fact I was convinced myself; that it was unnecessary for the Government to do anything in the matter; that I was only waiting for the news that the question that affected the good understanding had been settled, and that I finally demanded from them not to disturb me any more.

Our troops who were following Ethem Bey's forces occupied Gediz on 5 January 1921 and consolidated themselves in this district. Ethem Bey and his brothers with their force occupied the most suitable position for them, namely in the ranks of the enemy. The "Affair of Ethem" no longer existed. This latter enemy who was born in the bosom of our own Army was expelled from it and had been pressed back into the enemy's front.

A day later, on 6 January 1921, the whole of the Greek Army delivered an attack on the whole of our line.

Imagine a line running from İznik via Gediz to Uşak. The portion of this line north of Gediz is two hundred kilometres long; that part of it between Gediz and Uşak is about thirty kilometres. The enemy advanced with three divisions from the northern point in this line in the direction of Eskişehir.

The main body of our troops at Gediz had to go by Eskişehir to meet the enemy.

They met him and defeated him. Our revolution had won the first Victory of İnönü.

I explained the position to the Assembly in a public sitting on Saturday, 8 January 1921. On this occasion everybody recognised the truth. Even those who had held the opinion that we ought to show a conciliatory spirit towards Ethem and his brothers were now in a state of indignation against them. Protests were heard when, in the course of my statements, I referred to them as "Ethem Bey, Tevfik Bey, Reşit Bey." I heard somebody remark: "Your Excellency, do not call them 'beys' but 'traitors'." To this I replied: "I would very much have preferred to have called them 'traitor Ethem' and 'traitor Tevfik,' but then I would have had to apply this expression also to Reşit Bey, who is still a member of the Grand National Assembly. My respect for you will not allow me to venture to apply it to him. I must first request you to deprive Reşit Bey of his position as representative."

The President then said: "Will those who wish to deprive Reşit Bey, Representative for Manisa, who is working with the enemy and who has turned his arms against the country and the nation, of his position as a representative, hold up their hands?"

The hands of everybody present were held up and the motion was therefore carried.

In this offensive undertaken by the Greek Army Ethem Bey and his brothers did not fail to do what was expected of them. They marched again towards Kütahya and opened an attack on the weak force we had left there. The skilful leadership and decisiveness on the part of İzzettin Pasha and the splendid heroic courage of the Turkish soldiers under his command overcame the treacherous force that was advancing to attack them under Ethem Bey and his brothers and compelled them to retire.

The rebels had dismounted. Facing a commander who hesitated to advance against them when they, as cavalry, would have had to fight on foot, which would have been especially disadvantageous for them, they remounted. Meanwhile our troops retired, which gave the rebels courage. Our commander was still hesitating as to how and where he should attack the enemy.

If troops following the sound of rifle and gunfire arrived on the field — even if they only had a single rifle themselves — wait for the defeat of that part of the army to which they belonged and which was still fighting, and thought that they would be only then useful, such an idea, it seems to me, must appear to be illogical not only to military experts but even to the most simple-minded person. Duty and courage of sacrifice demand that the attempt should be made to obtain success before part of the fighting force is beaten and retires.

All of Ethem's men were eventually taken prisoners and the brothers Ethem, Reşit and Tevfik alone were able to escape to the enemy's headquarters and were appointed to take up new duties there.

I am sure that every opportunity was given to us to show many an interesting thing to our guests who came from Istanbul and who were now in Ankara during their sojourn with us, which lasted five or six weeks. The forces of Ethem and his brothers were annihilated.

In three days, we defeated the Greeks at İnönü. A new phase, which could satisfy and at the same time disturb the Grand National Assembly, had been entered upon. İzzet Pasha and Salih Pasha, however, did not seem to be at all satisfied with it and wanted at any price to leave for the capital, as though they were homesick. We also observed that their colleagues in İstanbul were equally upset.

Tevfik Pasha and his Government say that they have been working for unity between Istanbul and Anatolia. That is perfectly true. We have also been working for this, but with the one difference that Tevfik Pasha and his colleagues — as has been happening hitherto — intended to annex Anatolia to Istanbul and make it subservient to Istanbul which was occupied by the enemy's troops. Tevfik Pasha and his colleagues were endeavouring to unite Anatolia with the Istanbul Government —a government that had the peculiar characteristic that if no objection to its existence was raised by the world it owed this fact to its capability of facilitating the realisation of the enemy's designs.

According to Tevfik Pasha and his colleagues, Anatolia's struggle had had a great share in creating the present favourable state of affairs; but it is by no means due to this struggle alone on the part of Anatolia that the present situation has been created. Perhaps this old diplomatist attributed the whole merit in this affair to the fact that he had come into power.

I sent this reply to Tevfik Pasha:

Ankara, 30 January 1921.

To His Highness Tevfik Pasha, Istanbul.
I will point out to you verbatim the fundamental provisions of the Constitution Act.

THE CONSTITUTION ACT
Fundamental Provisions.

1. Sovereignty is vested in the nation, without reservation and condition. The system of administration is based on the principle that the people guide their own destiny.
2. Executive power and legislative power are vested in the Grand National Assembly, the one and only representative body of the nation.
3. The Turkish State is governed by the Grand National Assembly, and its Government bears the name of the Grand National Assembly of Turkey.
4. The Grand National Assembly consists of members elected by the population of the Provinces.
5. Elections for the Grand National Assembly are held every two years. The term of office of elected members lasts two years, but they are eligible for re-election. The retiring Assembly exercises its functions until the new Assembly meets. If anything occurs to prevent new elections taking place, the legislative term may be prolonged for one year. Each member of the Grand National Assembly is not the special representative of the province which has elected

him. The combined body of representatives constitutes the representation of the whole nation.

6. The Grand National Assembly meets in the beginning of November in a full sitting without summons.
7. Fundamental rights, such as the execution of decisions regarding religion, the promulgation of all laws, their amendment and repeal, the conclusion of peace and the signing of treaties, the proclamation of a state of emergency in our country, are all vested in the Grand National Assembly. Provisions concerning religious rights and those legal provisions that conform most appropriately to the relations between private individuals or to the exigencies of the time, as well as customary usage,
8. constitute the basis upon which the laws and stipulations are drafted. The rights and responsibilities of the Council of Ministers are defined by special enactments.
8. The Grand National Assembly administers the different departments of the Government by Ministers elected according to a special law. The necessary lines of direction, which may be altered if it should become necessary, for the affairs of the executive power are indicated to the Ministers by the Assembly.
9. The President elected by the Grand National Assembly in a full sitting is President of the Assembly for the duration of the legislative term. In this capacity he is competent to sign on behalf of the Assembly and to sanction the resolutions of the Council of Ministers.

The Council of Ministers elects the President from among themselves, the President of the Grand National Assembly is, however, at the same time, by right. President of the Council of Ministers.

II. The provisions of the Constitution which are not in contradiction to the above clauses still remain in force. I call Your Highness's attention especially to the fact that it is impossible for us to act in a manner that is contradictory to the fundamental provisions I have just quoted, for we have no authority to do so. The Council of Ministers has been authorised to consider the question referred to in correspondence with the President of the Assembly.

Mustafa Kemal,
President of the Grand National Assembly of Turkey.

This is the first Act that describes and defines the position, rights, constitution and character of the Assembly and the National Government. The Assembly commenced its sittings on 23 April 1920, and about nine months elapsed before the Assembly was able to pass this fundamental Act. Let me tell you briefly why this was necessary.

At last, after four months had elapsed, this committee submitted eight clauses of the Bill under the title of "Legal provisions concerning the constitution and character of the Grand National Assembly." These clauses, the discussion of which had begun on 18 August 1920, on an urgent motion, contained at the same time a long covering memorandum.

The first clause of the Bill was drafted to this effect:

"Legislative and executive power is vested in the Grand National Assembly, which is actually, and in an independent form, above the administration and the State Government."

As the law stands, it is evident that the full power vested in the Assembly by this clause was only of a provisional nature. The authority of the Assembly as a provisional institution could similarly only be of a temporary character.

The conceptions and opinions of the committee on the Constitution Act were expressed to the same effect in the Assembly. There were even some representatives who, in order to define the intention in a clearer way, put forward proposals which were contrary to the draft of the committee. They said: "At the beginning of the first article there must be especially added the words: 'Until the liberation of the Caliphate and the Sultanate and the attainment of the independence of the country and the nation.'"

It was demanded that instead of the words appearing in the second article "until the realisation of the aim," the same long formula should be employed. This question produced long discussions. Some representatives were of opinion that only the word "Caliphate" should be used, because it included the "Sultanate".

Some of the Hodjas did not agree, and maintained that the Caliphate was a purely spiritual matter. This gave rise to the objection that the Caliphate had no sacerdotal character, to which the Hodja Efendis replied by saying: 'The Monarchy comprises only the land over which it rules; but the Caliphate embraces Islam, which exists all over the world."

These discussions lasted for many days. One of the ideas which met with opposition was: The Caliph and The Sultan exists and will continue to exist. As long as he exists, the present regime is only provisional. When the Caliphate and Monarchy have the oppor- tunity of again exercising their functions, we shall know what the appearance of the Constitution and the political organisation will be like.

Thirty-seven days later, on 25 September, I considered it necessary to make certain explanations to the Assembly at a secret sitting. After I had satisfied the prevailing conceptions, I developed the following ideas:

"It is not necessary that the Turkish Nation and the High Assembly should occupy themselves so minutely with the Caliphate and the Monarchy, with the Caliph and the Sultan, while we are struggling to secure the existence and independence of our country. Our higher interests demand that we should not discuss this at all at the present moment. If the question should arise as to whether we ought to remain loyal and true to the present Caliph and Sultan — well, this man is a traitor, he is a tool of the enemy employed against our country and our nation. If the nation considers him in the light of Caliph and Sultan, it will be obliged to obey his orders and thereby realise the enemy's plans and designs. Moreover, a personage who would be a traitor and could be prevented from exercising his authority and making use of the power bestowed upon him by his position, could not hold the exalted title of Caliph or Sultan. If you want to say: 'Let us depose him and choose someone else in his place,' this would not lead to a way out of the difficulty, because the present state of affairs and the conditions prevailing at this hour would not allow of it being done. For the person who must be dethroned is not in the midst of his nation but in the hands of the enemy, and if we intended to ignore his existence and recognise someone in his stead, the present Caliph and Sultan would not surrender his rights, but would retain the seat he occupies today with his Ministry in Istanbul and would continue to carry on his office. Will the nation and the High Assembly in such an event abandon their high aims and throw themselves into a fight for a Caliph? Shall we then once more witness the times of Ali and Muaviya?* In short, this question is of far- reaching importance and difficulty. Its solution is not one which we are struggling to find today.

If we would undertake the task of finally settling this problem, we would not succeed in this at the present moment; but the hour for that will come later.

The legal foundations that we want to lay today will establish and guarantee the necessary authority for the purpose of strengthening the National Assembly and the National Government which will save our existence and secure our independence."

The London Conference lasted from 23 February to 12 March 1921. It did not produce any positive results. The Entente Powers wanted us to promise that we would accept the result of an inquiry which they proposed to make regarding the population in İzmir and in Thrace. At first our delegation had agreed to this, but, after receiving a hint that came from Ankara, they proposed that this inquiry should be made dependent on the abolition of the Greek administration. We had become clear about the fact that the Entente Powers intended to guarantee the sincere execution of the other stipulations of the Treaty of Sevres without any opposition from our side. The proposals made to this effect had been replied to by our delegation in a way that was tantamount to a refusal. As for the Greek delegation, they had declined to accept an inquiry on principle. Thereupon the delegates of the Entente Powers had presented to both delegations —the Turkish and the Greek— a draft which contained certain suggestions and had asked them to give the Conference the replies that they would receive from their Governments to these proposals.

The draft handed to our delegation concerning the alterations in the Treaty of Sevres contained these points:

Increase of the actual strength of the special troops and gendarmerie which had been allowed to us to a very slight extent; a slight decrease in the number of foreign officers who were to remain in the country; a slight reduction of the zone of the Straits; a slight alleviation of the restrictions which had been imposed on our Budget and of our right to impose a tax on concessions in the sphere of public works...; and, finally, some indistinct promises which could raise somenhope of alterations being made in the Treaty of Sevres regarding the Capitulations, judicial affairs, foreign postal matters, Kurdistan, etc.

The delimitation of the frontiers of Armenia according to this draft were to be entrusted to a Commission appointed by the League of Nations. A special administration was to be established in the district of İzmir. The province of İzmir was nominally to be restored to us, but Greek troops were to remain in the town of İzmir; order in the Province was to be secured by Entente officers, and the gendarmerie force in this Province was to be composed of different elements in proportion to the composition of the population. A Christian governor was to be appointed over the province of İzmir, which was to pay an annual tribute to Turkey and which would be liable to be increased in proportion to the augmentation of the revenues.

This proposed *modus vivendi* for the province of İzmir was put forward in such a way that it could be altered by the League of Nations after the lapse of five years on application from either side.

Without waiting for the reply which the Entente Powers would receive concerning the proposal they had made through the delegation and while our delegation was still en route, the Greeks opened their offensive with all their troops and on all the fronts.

You see that the Greek offensive compels us to leave our description of the London Conference.

A strong part of the Greek army was in Bursa and to the east of this town; another part was in Uşak and to the east of Uşak.

On the evening of 26 March the enemy approached the advanced positions which İsmet Pasha had ordered to be taken up on the right flank. On the next day, we made contact with the enemy along the whole line of the front. On the 28th the enemy began to attack our right. On the 29th they attacked both flanks. They gained important local successes. 30 March was a day of violent fighting. These battles ended in favour of the enemy.

Now it was our turn. On 31 March, İsmet Pasha began a counter- attack, defeated the enemy on the same night and forced them to retreat. This victory was the second in İnönü recorded in the history of the revolution.

As we had gained the victory at İnönü, there was no doubt that nothing was left to do but to secure their retreat as soon as possible to save them from danger.

It was probable that our troops which had been victorious at İnönü would advance on Dumlupınar via Eskişehir and Altıntaş and, being able for a great part of the distance to make use of the railway, they would intercept the line of retreat of the Greek army which was east of Afyon Karahisar and would inflict upon it an annihilat- ing defeat. Indeed, no time was lost in carrying this out. The first divisions that were disengaged were immediately placed at the disposal of Refet Pasha, commanding the southern front, and were sent forward.

The Uşak troops of the Greek army began to retreat immediately after the battle of İnönü had come to an end. On 7 April 1921 Refet Pasha had his headquarters in Çöğürler; the 4th and 11th Divisions were in the Altıntaş zone; the 5th Caucasian Division and the battalion of Guards of the Assembly to the strength of one regiment, south of Çöğürler; the Ist and 2nd Cavalry Divisions in the district of Kütahya.

While Fahrettin Pasha pursued and harassed the enemy who had retired from Çal and Afyon, Refet Pasha, with the troops I have just mentioned, namely, three divisions and a battalion of infantry, attacked an enemy regiment which was in the district of Aslıhanlar, whilst two other divisions, the 24th and 8th, were sent southwards. The Greek regiment at Aslıhanlar held back Refet Pasha's attack, by which it gained much time while it was reinforced by about two divisions which came up from the rear. The troops retiring from Afyon succeeded in joining them.

One fact misled Refet Pasha as to the issue of the battle. Thanks to a turn which had taken place in the firing line during the battle and on account of the impossibility of our troops to beat and put out of action a regiment which the enemy east of Afyon Karahisar had left at Dumlupınar, the advanced part of the Greek army had retired to their main position which they intended to hold after their retreat to Dumlupınar.

Whilst Refet Pasha was actually defeated himself, he thought that the enemy was beaten and in retreat, and he reported this to us in a telegram, in which he said that after the battle of Dumlupınar had been going on for five days he had given the enemy his deathblow.

Our delegation which had gone to London returned to Ankara after the second victory of İnönü. You are aware that the Conference had not led to any results. Bekir Sami Bey, Foreign Minister, who had been at the head of the delegation, had, however, entered on his own account into contact and discussion with the statesmen of England, France and Italy and had signed a number of special agreements with each of them.

According to one of the agreements between Bekir Sami Bey and England, we were to release all the English prisoners of war who were in our hands. England in exchange was to return ours, with the exception of those of the Turkish prisoners who it was alleged had brutally or badly treated English prisoners or Armenians.

Our Government could naturally neither approve nor ratify such an agreement, because this would have meant that they would recognise a kind of right of jurisdiction on the part of a foreign Government over the acts of a Turkish subject in the interior of Turkey itself.

As, however, the English released some of the prisoners, although we had not ratified the agreement, we on our part released some of the English prisoners.

Later on, following an arrangement which took place on 23 October 1921 between Hamit Bey, Vice-president of the Red Crescent, and the English Comissioner in Istanbul, the exchange of all the Turkish prisoners in Malta and all the English prisoners in Turkey was decided upon, a decision which was duly carried out.

It appears that Bekir Sami Bey, besides his official negotiations and discussions, had had an interview of a strictly private nature with Lloyd George . . . The actual words that passed between them had been taken down in shorthand

... A protocol had been signed ... I do not remember that I had been informed of the contents of the copy which was in the possession of Bekir Sami Bey. Although I have recently asked him through the intermediary of the Foreign Office for a copy of it, Bekir Sami Bey has informed the Minister by letter that translations of this copy had been put before me at that time and that the original as well as the translations had remained among the documents to which they belonged when he left the Ministry of Foreign Affairs. This document, however, could not be found among the others. Nobody in the Ministry of Foreign Affairs knows anything about it or what it contained. As far as I am concerned, I do not remember ever having been informed of the existence of this document.

Another agreement was also signed on 11 March 1921 between Bekir Sami Bey and M. Briand, President of the French Council of Ministers. According to this agreement the hostilities between France and the National Government were considered to be at an end . . . The French were to disarm the bands and we on our part the armed volunteers . . . French officers were to be employed in our gendarmerie. The gendarmerie organised by the French was to be retained . . . The French were to have preference in enterprises for the economic development of the districts evacuated by France, as well as the provinces of Elazığ, Diyarbakır and Sivas, and, in addition, were to be granted mining concessions in Ergani, etc.

Last of all, Bekir Sami Bey had signed another agreement with Count Sforza, the Italian Foreign Minister, on 12 March 1921. According to it, Italy undertook to support our claims at the Conference for the restitution of Thrace and İzmir in exchange for which we were to cede to them a prior right for economic enterprises in the Sandjaks of Antalya, Burdur, Muğla, Isparta and in parts of the Sandjaks of Afyon Karahisar, Kütahya, Aydın and Konya, which were to be specified at a later date.

In this agreement it was agreed also to cede to Italian capitalists all those economic enterprises which would not be carried out by the Turkish Government or by Turkish capital, and to transfer the mines of Ereğli to a Turco-Italian company.

It is perfectly evident that the terms of these agreements which the Entente Powers had induced Bekir Sami Bey, the leader of the delegation which we had sent to Europe to conclude Peace, to sign, had no other aim than to cause our national Government to accept the Treaty which the same Powers had concluded among themselves, under the name of the "Tripartite Agreement", after the Sevres plan, and which divided Anatolia into three spheres of interest. The statesmen of the Entente had also succeeded in inducing Bekir Sami Bey to accept these plans. As you can see, Bekir Sami Bey was taken up in London more with these three individual agreements than with the discussions at the Conference. The contradiction between the principles of the National Government and the system followed by the personage who was Foreign Minister can unfortunately not be explained.

I must admit that when Bekir Sami Bey returned to Ankara with these agreements I was very much astonished, and my attention was aroused. He expressed his conviction that the contents of the agreements he had signed were in accord with the higher interests of the country, and maintained that he was able to support this conviction and defend and prove it before the Assembly. But there is no doubt that his opinion was wrong and his ideas illogical. It was not only certain that they could not be approved of by the Assembly but also that he would be overthrown as Minister of Foreign Affairs. As however, under the conditions prevailing at that time, I did not believe it necessary to involve the Assembly in long discussions and dissertations on political questions, I pointed out his error to Bekir Sami Bey personally and proposed that he should resign his office as Foreign Minister. Bekir Sami Bey consented to my proposal and resigned.

Nevertheless, influenced by the impression which the different conversations he had had during his journey in Europe as leader of the delegation had made on him, Bekir Sami Bey was persistent in his conviction that it was possible to come to an understanding with the Entente Powers within the scope of our principles. He maintained that it would be a good thing to arrive at such an understanding. Subsequently Bekir Sami Bey made a second journey to Europe, but this also had no positive results.

However, the Government considered it necessary after it had been discovered that the negotiations carried on with M. Franklin Bouillon at Ankara had been complicated by certain steps that Bekir Sami Bey had taken in Paris, to make known through their agency that Bekir Sami Bey had not been entrusted with any official mission.

During his second visit to Europe Bekir Sami Bey also sent me some communications, and after his return he sent a report to me. Certain considerations contained in these communications and his report were unfortunately not calculated to remove all doubt and hesitation on the question as to whether Bekir Sami Bey had completely grasped the ideal of the Turkish nation we were striving to reach and whether he had acted in the spirit of this ideal.

Bekir Sami Bey expressed his opinion in conformity with the influences and opinions that had affected him in Europe. After having criticised our policy, he said in a telegram in code on 12 August 1921: "While the opportunity is still given to us, prudent policy might save the country from the abyss into which it has fallen. Studying events carefully, an attitude must be assumed that is necessitated by the anxiety for the salvation of our country. If this is not done. none of us will be able to withdraw from the responsibility imposed upon him before history and the nation. I beg you in the name of the prosperity of our nation and of the salvation of Islam to adopt a fitting attitude and to tell me immediately that you have done so."

In all his suggestions Bekir Sami Bey advised us to put an end to the national fight so as to escape from slavery and humiliation on the lines of the agreements which he himself had concluded in London.

These considerations of Bekir Sami Bey's made no positive impression on me. The ideas he developed and his manner of thinking had brought me to the conviction that there would be no advantage or object to be gained by discussing or arguing with him.

You are aware that the committees of the Union for the Defence of the Rights of Anatolia and Rumelia were among the electors of the second class during the elections for the first National Assembly. In these circumstances, it might be said that the Assembly, taken as a whole, had the character of a political party which had developed from the Union for the Defence of the Rights of Anatolia and Rumelia, and this actually was so at first. The chief aim of the

Assembly as a whole served as the basis of the chief aim of the union. You know that the principles put forward at the Erzurum and Sivas Congresses, after having received the approval of the last Chamber of Representatives in Istanbul, had been combined and united into a whole under the title of the "National Pact." These principles having also been adopted by the Grand National Assembly, we were now working within its scope to achieve a peace which would secure the integrity of the country and the independence of the nation. In proportion, however, as time advanced, difficulties began to crop up regarding the organisation and aim of the common struggle. Votes were divided, even on the simplest questions, and the work of the Assembly was condemned to futility. To remedy this state of affairs some people took the initiative in the middle of the year 1920 in forming certain organisations. All these efforts were made to render regular debates possible and to reach positive results by firmly uniting the votes on questions which formed the subject of the discussion.

I have had an opportunity to explain to you that on 13 September 1920 I laid before the Assembly the programme that forms the foundation of our first Constitution Act. Part of this programme was read in the Assembly during the sitting on 18 September. Together with this part I had a motion printed and circulated which I had laid before the Assembly which served as a basis for this programme and which contained everything under the title of "Programme of a Popular Policy." This motion, which was read when the Assembly was opened and passed by them, defined the essential character of the Grand National Assembly and developed the policy of our administrative system. The organisations of which I have spoken, influenced by my programme, began to adopt a number of titles and to formulate their programmes. To give you an idea of this, I will mention the most important titles of these organisations:

A. The "Union" Party (Tesanüt).
B. The "Independence" Party (İstiklal).
C. The "Union for the Defence of the Rights" Party.
D. The "People's" Party (Halk Zümresi).
E. The "Reform" Party (Islahat Grubu).

Besides these parties, there were still some minor ones which had no name and had been formed for personal agenda. All the parties whose names I have just mentioned, although formed for the purpose of maintaining discipline and securing unanimity of voting during the debates, brought about contrary results through their existence.

As a matter of fact, these parties, whose number was considerable and whose adherents were in rivalry with one another, and the fact that they declined to listen to each other, had actually led to disturbances in the Assembly.

When the Assembly had passed the Constitution Act, that is to say, at about the end of January 1921, the fact became especially evident that it was very much more difficult to secure unity and co- operation among the members and parties in the Assembly in a general way on any question. This was to be attributed to the circumstance that the ideas and desires which had been united unconditionally and unrestrictedly concerning the principles of the National Pact, were far from presenting the same appearance when the question of the various points of view involved in the Constitution Act arose.

I was hard at work indirectly trying to bring forward a union between the parties in existence by strengthening one or the other of them, in order to be able at last to get on with some actual work. But after I had found out that the results attained in this way had no lasting effect, I felt myself compelled personally to interfere.

Eventually I took recourse to forming a party myself under the name of the "Party for the Defence of the Rights of Anatolia and Rumelia."

At the head of the programme which I prepared for this party I put a fundamental article, the meaning of which I summarised in two points. The first was this: "The party will secure the integrity of the country and the independence of the nation on the principles laid down in the National Pact. It will employ all the material and moral forces of the nation to guide them to this end and to obtain peace and tranquility. It will press all the organisations and institutions in the country, public and private, into the service of this aim." Secondly: "The party will henceforward exert all its efforts within the compass of the Constitution Act for the purpose of preparing and defining as far as possible the organisation of the State and Nation."

After having called together all the parties and most of the members of the Assembly, I succeeded in establishing a union on these two principles. The fundamental article which I have just quoted, as well as the other clauses that were drawn up relating to the inner regulations of the party, were agreed to at the sitting on the 10th May, 1921. I took over the chairmanship of the party, to which I was appointed at a general meeting.

In the same way as there was already in the country a "Union for the Defence of the Rights of Anatolia and Rumelia", the Assembly now had a party bearing a similar name which had its origin in this union. What the Chamber of

Representatives in Istanbul had failed to do was only realised in Ankara fourteen months after that Chamber was abolished.

This party allowed the Government to exercise its functions during the whole of the first legislative period. However, there were some people who believed the second point in the main article regulating the party to be significant. People of this type, who by no means expressed their feelings, were, nevertheless, immediately active in trying to prevent me from fulfilling the aim which this point expressed. Efforts of this description, to which we might give the name of negative activity, became evident in two forms.

It was first of all displayed within the party itself for the purpose of confusing their minds and prejudicing them against me, and the same thing happened all over the country and in the circles of our own organisation. The most striking example in support of this assertion is shown in the attempt undertaken by Raif Efendi, a man of religion and representative for Erzurum, together with some of his colleagues, after the Constitution Act was passed and before the party had been formed. With your permission, I will give you some further details about this. Raif Efendi and his colleagues changed the title of the local organisation at Erzurum from the "Union for the Defence of the Rights of Anatolia and Rumelia" into the "Union for the Salvation of the Sanctuaries." Besides this, Raif Efendi added at the head of the principles containing the chief ideas of the union some clauses which aimed at the maintenance of the Caliphate and Sultanate and the form of the Government. He also intended to extend his efforts to other Provinces — especially to the Eastern Provinces— by sending all kinds of proclamations into these districts.

As soon as I was informed of this, I called the attention of Kazım Karabekir Pasha who commanded the eastern front to it, and asked him to bring Raif Efendi, the man of religion, as well as his comrades to reason and convince them to abandon their plans. After some correspondence passed between Kazım Karabekir Pasha, who was at Sarıkamış, and Raif Efendi, who was at that time at Erzurum, Raif Hodja went personally to the headquarters of the Pasha. Raif Efendi told him of the reasons that had led him to use the title "Union for the Salvation of the Sanctuaries" and declared that his aim was to preserve the Caliphate and Sultanate and to prevent, at all costs, the establishment of a Republican Government, which, according to him, would be in the present and future life of the country and the Muslim world a source of great trouble and internal dissension. After having expressed his opinion that from certain symptoms he had come to the conclusion that the party for the "Defence of the Rights" formed in the Assembly had the intention of replacing the Government of the Caliph and Sultan by a Republican Government, he said that it would be unpardonable not to recognise the lawfulness of his activities.

In his telegram in code of 11 July 1921, in which Kazım Karabekir Pasha sent me this news he also mentioned, among other matters, the following: "We observe that the Constitution Act passed by the Grand National Assembly has also sanctioned the principles concerning the form of government. Anticipating difficulties in the carrying out of the provisions of this Act, I conceive it to be more advantageous if these provisions adopted the form of the programme of a political party.

"I would like to explain this idea from the point of view of general sentiment and of the opinions prevailing in my district and about the tendency of which I am well informed.

"Most of the adherents of the party which has been formed in the Assembly with the programme in favour of the Constitution Act are those who are apparently driven by ambition to play a role in the destiny of the country in favour of a political change; but among the people there is only an infinitesimal minority who support the new conceptions of the organisation. If the representatives are supporters of the Constitution Act this is only a matter of their personal opinion. In these enterprises, which mean nothing less than a radical change in the form of Government and which must mark an epoch in history, I am convinced of the necessity of consulting our military and civil authorities as well as the local committees of the 'Union for the Defence of the Rights' in the proper way, because all of them bear their share of responsibility for the destiny of our country. In the same way, the question ought also to be submitted to the investigation of an extraordinary Assembly; only after this has been done shall we be able to come to a decision."

After the decisive victory and the proclamation of the Republic by the second Grand National Assembly, Kazım Karabekir Pasha summarised the feelings and objections which he had given vent to long before in the statement he made in the Istanbul Press in the following form:

"We have not been consulted with regard to the proclamation of the Republic."

In his observations Kazım Karabekir Pasha seemed to have forgotten that the Grand National Assembly was just such an extraordinary Assembly consisting of representatives who had been endowed with extraordinary full powers by the nation. He simultaneously gives us to understand that he disapproves of the Act passed by this Assembly as well as the Constitution Act.

It is still more remarkable when he says that he was convinced of the necessity of consulting the military and civil authorities and the local committees of the "Union for the Defence of the Rights of Anatolia and Rumelia" in cases where the question arises of adopting resolutions which could lead to an alteration of the State system.

Kazım Karabekir Pasha also raises objections to the fact that I am connected with the party for the "Defence of the Rights." He said: "I have always considered that Your Excellency should hold yourself aloof from . . . political parties of this description," and he advises me to maintain a neutral attitude towards all parties. I replied to this telegram on 20 July 1921. I shall content myself with quoting here a few sentences of the somewhat lengthy reply which might throw light on certain points. I said: "The party of the 'Defence of the Rights' has been formed with a clear and precise aim before it, which consists in securing the complete independence of the country. The passing of the Constitution Act is also included in these aims. The Constitution Act is neither a complete statute nor one that enters into details regarding the whole legal position of the Turkish State and the subsidiary question relating to administration. The Act is confined to introducing the principle of democracy into our civil and administrative organisation as demanded by the exigencies of the time. There is nothing in this Act that expresses the idea of a Republic. Raif Efendi's opinion that it indicates the speedy substitution of the monarchical regime by a republican one is founded on mere imagination. Regarding the assertion that among the persons entrusted with the central administration there are some whose personalities and past lives give rise to criticism, these assertions must be supported by more concrete evidence.

"The idea of entrusting administrative duties only to men who are trained and who are thoroughly educated, as well as being in possession of administrative qualifications and all personal advantages, is at best an alluring dream.

"It is not only impossible for us, but for all the progressive nations in the world, to discover men in sufficient numbers who enjoy public esteem in all of the professions, circles and districts.

"The endeavour to weaken the combined and unified organisations which must support the country under the influence of deceptive and vague thoughts and claims could only be regarded as an act of insanity, if not even of treason.

"Your Excellency is well aware of the fact that every important enterprise leading to progress must inevitably be connected with serious difficulties according to circumstances. The important point is that nothing should be lacking in the selection of the means and the measures to be adopted which are most suitable to reduce these difficulties to a minimum."

Then I explained my ideas regarding the proposal for consulting the military and civil authorities and the organisations for the "Defence of the Rights" in drafting the Constitution Act, as follows:

"As Your Excellency is aware we have a constituted Government and we must adopt all the conceptions that result from this condition. You will probably agree with me that it is not possible, under the effect of ideas that come from a distance, to exercise any influence on the form which the Constitution Act has finally agreed upon after having discussed it in Committee and at the full sitting."

Kazım Karabekir Pasha had also asked to be informed of the reasons which had caused the haste in which, in his opinion, the Constitution Act had been drafted. In addition, he had also asked about the eventual difficulties of the application of the Act as well as our opinions on the question of the Caliphate and the Sultanate.

Referring to these points, I had said in my reply: "The reason for the attitude which had appeared to Your Excellency to have been hasty, is only the anxiety to guide the democratic current which reveals itself today in our country, as well as everywhere else, into a sound course and to prevent further complications which might arise on this question of the preservation of national rights, which have been misinterpreted and injured for centuries by incapable men. Also to secure the opportunity for the nation, which is the real possessor of these rights, to make its voice heard and, finally, to make the most of the extraordinary events of the moment which are so favourable for the development of this noble idea.

"For the purpose of carefully considering the possibility of putting this law into force, we ought to take into account the degree of administrative energy and the capability of those who will have occasion to preside over its application. The question of the Caliphate and the Sultanate is not to be treated as a priority. The principal question is to define the rights of the sovereign, in the settlement of the determination and limitation of which rights we must be guided by the experience of past centuries and the exact limitation of the rights of the nation included in the conception of the State. We do not yet possess a clearly defined formula grounded on this basis."

In my reply to Kazım Karabekir Pasha's proposal that I should remain neutral instead of being chairman of the party, I said:

"I am not the President of an Assembly like the Chamber of Representatives; but even if I were, it would be natural for me to be a member of a political party. As the Grand National Assembly exercises at the same time the executive power, it means that I am the President of an Assembly which has, in effect, the character of a Government.

"The head of the executive power must necessarily be a member of the majority party. There is nothing to prevent me under these conditions from being chairman of a political party which has thrown itself into the conflict with a programme that enters into details. Just as it is impossible for me to withdraw from the union with which I have identified myself with my whole being, in the same way it is absolutely necessary that I should take my place in the ranks of the party which this union has produced. In truth, the party has a crushing majority, comprising nearly all the members of the Assembly. Those who have held themselves aloof from the party are Celalettin Arif Bey and Hüseyin Avni Efendi, representatives for Erzurum, with others like them, and some who were anxious to preserve their freedom of action."

İzzet Pasha and Salih Pasha, who were at that time still in Ankara, did not feel at home there. They continually appealed to us, directly and indirectly, begging to be released and to be allowed to return to their families in Istanbul.

They assured us, over and over again, that they would keep entirely aloof from political life when they returned there.

At the beginning of March' 1921, while İsmet Pasha was in Ankara where he had arrived with the intention of attending to certain affairs, the Pashas renewed their appeals.

One day while the Council of Ministers were holding a sitting, Ahmet İzzet Pasha came to the Government building and asked to see İsmet Pasha who was attending the meeting of the Council. İsmet Pasha had an interview with him. İzzet Pasha assured him in a long explanation regarding the proposal made by us that he would give his word of honour that he would not accept an official position in İstanbul, and he renewed his request to be allowed to return to his family. He added that Salih Pasha, for his part, also pledged his word of honour and begged that he might be allowed to go.

İsmet Pasha informed the Council of these declarations and requests. The Council of Ministers were of the opinion that the presence of these two Pashas in Ankara had not been of any advantage to us in our work, but that they were rather a useless burden and that, moreover, they offered a pretext for certain antagonistic feelings towards us; consequently there was no objection to the return of the Pashas to İstanbul.

I pointed out, however, that I did not think that the pledge given by them was straightforward and sincere and that I was convinced beyond doubt that they would resume their duties in the Government when they returned to İstanbul and in this way cause us further annoyance. They pointed out the fact that the Pasha had given his word of honour. I held that permission should only be granted to them if they consented to give an undertaking in writing;

for hitherto they had only expressed themselves verbally. İsmet Pasha told İzzet Pasha, who was in the adjoining room, what I had proposed. He immediately picked up a pen and wrote out an undertaking to hand in his resignation to the Cabinet and signed it. If my memory does not deceive me, he made Salih Pasha also sign the document.

But this short undertaking did not seem sufficient to me. It had not the same meaning as the pledge he had given verbally. I called the attention of my colleagues to the fact that there was some trickery and that İzzet Pasha ought to draw up and sign the same declaration that he had given verbally to İsmet Pasha. But they would not admit that after so many assurances and declarations İzzet Pasha could have given his undertaking with any other intentions in his mind; therefore, they pleaded that this document should be accepted as sufficient. Through this deception, İzzet Pasha and Salih Pasha succeeded in obtaining permission to return to İstanbul.

When they returned, the two Pashas actually handed in their resignations; but a very short time afterwards they accepted other ministerial appointments in the same Cabinet and informed us by telegram that they had done so. İzzet Pasha, who had become Foreign Minister in the İstanbul Government, told us that he had only taken up this office to guard against the misfortune threatening the nation and the country, and then he gave us a great deal of advice.

Ahmet İzzet Pasha had preferred rather to make himself a servant of Vahdettin than to remain in the midst of the Turkish people, who had fed him and reared him, and come to their aid in the days of the darkest despair. He bowed to the Fetva of Dürrizade Esseyit Abdullah and took care not to disobey the Sultan's orders and lay himself open to the sentence of excommunication by the Sharia. Ahmet İzzet Pasha also involved himself in some other deceptions, about which I shall also speak to you.

By a strange coincidence, on the same day on which we had forced the enemy to retire by our counter-attack on the Sakarya, I was shown for official reasons a letter which had originated from this brain affected by megalomania, in which it was maintained that my behaviour would lead to our breakdown. This letter had caused us great astonishment.

After having witnessed the retreat of the Greek army, first from the Sakarya and afterwards from İzmir, and after having read the Treaty of Lausanne, İzzet Pasha quoted this sentence in his telegram of 6 July 1921, once more in which he said: "Far from admitting the credulity which is attributed to me, I am strengthened in the confidence in my own personality and my opinions by the collection of evidence that I had correctly judged the political situation in all its details then as I do now".

I am tempted to believe that this was so! Nearly three months passed between the second battle of İnönü and the general attack which the Greeks began on 10 July 1921.

Since the enemy's attack began in July, the progress made till then in the activity of the National Government and the command at the front did not seem sufficient to justify us in giving the order for a general mobilisation on our part, and thereby to oppose the enemy with all the auxiliary reserves and means which were at the disposal of the nation without allowing ourselves to be influenced by other considerations. In this fact you must seek the most evident reason of the disparity which existed in so many respects between the two armies facing each other. As we had not yet succeeded in procuring for our army the necessary means of transport which was so vital, the mobility of our troops was practically impossible. The main task we had taken upon ourselves from the military point of view against this attack which the Greek people, gathering all their forces, had begun against us, still remained the same as had been decided upon at the beginning of the national struggle. It can be summarised thus: To render assistance whenever the Greeks attacked, to hold them back, to meet them with adequate military tactics and to gain time while the new army was being formed. This main plan had not to be lost sight of, especially after the enemy's last attack. This consideration induced me after the visit I paid to İsmet Pasha at his headquarters at Karacahisar, south-west of Eskişehir, where I had carefully studied the position to indicate the general course to be followed:

"After the army has been concentrated in the north and south of Eskişehir, we must establish a large area between it and the enemy's forces so that we shall be able to carry on our reconstitution, reorganisation and reinforcement. For this purpose we would be able to retire even to the north of the Sakarya. If the enemy should pursue us without coming to a halt he would be getting farther away from his base of operations and would be obliged to take up new positions.

In any case, he would find that there were many difficulties in front of him which he would have to provide for. Taking this into account, our army will be able to rally and meet the enemy under more favourable conditions. The disadvantage of such tactics would be the moral shock which might be produced in public opinion by the fact that a wide territory and places so important as Eskişehir would be abandoned to the enemy. But these disadvantages will automatically disappear in a short time as the result of the successes which we shall achieve.

"Let us carry out without hesitation what the exigencies and the strategy of the moment demand from us. As for the disadvantages, we know how to overcome them."

The disadvantages of a moral kind foreseen by me, soon began to take shape.

The first excitement became apparent in the Assembly. Above all, the representatives of the opposition immediately began to make pessimistic speeches and express themselves in all possible tones: Where is this army going to? Where are the people being led? There must surely be somebody who is responsible for what is being done! Where is the person? He is invisible. We would like to see at the head of the army the actual originator of the sad and deplorable position in which we are today. There was no doubt that the person to whom these people were alluding was none other than me.

Finally, Selahattin Bey, representative for Mersin, mentioned my name from the tribune and asked me to take over command. The number of those who shared his opinion grew, while there were others who opposed them. We must now consider in a few words the reasons for this difference of opinion. Those who proposed to entrust me with the actual supreme command may be divided under two heads: From what I knew personally and the impressions of many others, some had come to the conviction that the army had been completely defeated, that there was no longer any hope of saving the situation and that the national cause which we were defending was irretrievably lost. Imbued with this conviction they wanted to relieve themselves by pouring out all their wrath upon me; they wanted me to perish at the head of the army which, as they thought, was in danger of dissolution and could not be saved. On the other hand, there were others — I might well say the majority — guided by their feelings of confidence and gratitude, who wanted to see me at the head of the army.

Those who held a contrary opinion had doubts about my taking over the supreme command and expressed their opinion in this way: It is not probable that the army will be capable of gaining success in any later fighting and that it will be compelled to retire still further. If in such an event the President of the Grand National Assembly were actually in supreme command himself, it might happen, judging from the prevailing public opinion, that the idea would spread that the situation was hopelessly lost. The general position, however, is not such that we should be called on to sacrifice our last strength, forces and resources. Consequently, the moment has not yet arrived for him to lead the military operations personally if we desire still to support a last hope in the opinion of the public.

With all the possible care that the case demanded, I studied the opinions which had been formed during the course of these discussions. Those who thought as I have just now explained, advanced important arguments. The clamour of those who brought forward insincere demands influenced in a considerably disturbing way those who proposed in good faith that I should take over the chief command. The entire Assembly came to the conclusion that my taking actual charge of the supreme command was to be regarded as the last step and the last resource left to us.

The point of view expressed by the Assembly about the situation also rapidly spread outside the Assembly. My silence and the fact that I showed no disposition to take over the actual supreme command in a hurry turned the fear of an inevitable and impending catastrophe into a positive conviction. As soon as I observed this, I mounted the tribune.

My proposal offered an opportunity for the disclosure of the secret designs of those who tried to conceal their real intentions, and objections were soon put forward. For instance, they began to say: "We cannot confer the title of Commander-in-Chief, for that is an office that is morally inherent to the Assembly itself. We ought to say, 'Representative Commander-in-Chief.'" The opinion was also expressed that there was no question of endowing me with such comprehensive privileges as to employ the full powers of the Assembly. I insisted on my point of view by maintaining that I could not accept an obsolete title which had once been bestowed by the Sultans and Caliphs, all the more so because I could not see why they should refuse me the corresponding title if I actually exercised these functions. We were passing through extraordinary conditions, of which fact the Assembly was well aware and as had been explained by its members. Consequently, my actions and the decisions I had to make had also to be of an extraordinary nature. It would be absolutely necessary for me to be in the position to carry out my plans and decisions energetically and rapidly. Cases might occur where the situation would not admit of any delay, which would necessarily be caused by an appeal to the Council of Ministers or by demanding the authority from the Assembly.

If I would have to ask every Minister or the Council of Ministers for their opinions or consent in every communication I had to make or with respect to every command I had to give, particularly when it was a question of communications and orders referring to the country and the employment of its resources, it would destroy all the advantages everybody was hoping for and which were expected to accrue from my personally taking over the supreme command. For these various reasons it would be necessary for me to be in the position to give orders unconditionally, which I only could do if the full powers of the Assembly were transferred to me personally. Consequently, I persisted all the more strenuously in making this demand, because I believed that their consent was absolutely necessary to enable me to succeed.

Some representatives, like Selahattin Bey and Hulusi Bey, maintained that the Assembly would be condemned to inactivity if they were to transfer their powers to somebody else, that they had no right to do so, that above all it could not be thought of that the full powers of the Assembly should be transferred to the man who commanded the army, and that from every point of view this was superfluous.

Some of the representatives went so far as to maintain that members of the Assembly would feel doubtful about their own personal safety towards any person who could dispose of the full powers of the Assembly.

I did not attempt to refute any of these opinions. I declared that I found all of them to be quite justified. I merely said that the Assembly must attribute great importance to the examination of this question and study it with the utmost care. I added that those who were afraid for their own safety were quite wrong. As the question had not been decided on 4 August, the debate was continued on the following day. It was found on this day that the reasons that had led some representatives to hesitate revolved around two points: Firstly, the question whether the Assembly would not be reduced to impotence and inactivity in some way or another, and, secondly, whether any of the members of the Assembly would be liable to be treated in an arbitrary manner.

After I had given them assurances to dispel these fears, I declared that it appeared to be necessary to add reservations and restrictions to the law which had to be passed.

I altered my motion, therefore, into the draft of a Bill, which I laid before the Assembly. Based on the discussions which had taken place on this draft, the Act conferring the functions of Commander-in-Chief on me was passed on 5 August 1921. Clause 2 of this Act defined the full powers given to me with the following terms: "In order to develop the forces of the army materially and morally to the fullest extent, so as to secure and consolidate the leadership and administra- tion of these forces, the Commander-in-Chief will be authorised to exercise full powers on behalf of the Assembly in these matters." This clause gave lawful authority to my command.

Following this appointment being conferred on me, I declared to the Assembly that "I shall prove myself worthy in a short time of the confidence which you have reposed in me," and I laid before them some requests, among them being the separation of the duties of the Chief of the General Staff from that of the Minister of National Defence, which were still combined in the person of His Excellency Fevzi Pasha, so that he would be able to devote himself exclusively to the affairs of the General Staff. I also requested that Refet Pasha, Minister of the Interior, should be appointed Minister of National Defence, and that someone else should be selected to fill the office that would thus fall vacant.

I took special care to explain to the Assembly that it would be very important for them and for the Council of Ministers to preserve a calm and firm attitude towards the country itself and foreign countries, and that it would be wrong to shake the position of the Ministers by trifling suggestions.

The draft of the Bill was read to a public sitting on the same day, and was hurriedly discussed and put to the vote. It was passed unanimously.

Having taken over the supreme command, I still worked for several days in Ankara. I formed my headquarters by uniting the official offices of the General Staff with the Ministry of National Defence. I installed a small office for my personal use in view of the effort to secure the unification and co-ordination in the common work of these two departments, as well as to settle with the aid of the authority of other departments issues relating to the army and the intervention of the Commander-in-Chief.

On 12 August, Gentlemen, accompanied by His Excellency Fevzi Pasha, Chief of the General Staff, I left for Polatli, where the headquarters at the front were. We had arrived at the opinion that the enemy, as soon as he came into touch with our front, would attempt an enveloping movement on our left flank. In view of this possibility, I courageously took all the necessary steps. Events proved that we were right. On 23 August 1921, the enemy's army came into serious contact with our front and opened an attack on it. Many bloody and critical phases, advances and retreats, took place on both sides. The enemy, superior in number, broke through our line of defence in several places, but each time they did so, we succeeded in throwing our forces against him.

The battle took place on a front of a hundred kilometres. Our left wing had withdrawn to a distance of fifty kilometres south of Ankara. Our front, which was facing westward, turned to the south. The rear part of the army leaning on Ankara was pushed to the north. Thereby we changed the direction of our front, but this was not to our disadvantage. Our lines of defence were broken through, one section after another, but every place where it was pierced was immediately reinforced in as short a time as possible.

The Greek army was beaten and was forced to retire. On 13 September 1921, no trace of the enemy was to be found on the east of the Sakarya.

The great battle of the Sakarya, which lasted from 23 August to 13 September, both days included, continued without interruption for twenty-two days and twenty-two nights and constitutes a unique example of a battle of the widest extent, not alone in the historical records of the new Turkish State but also in the pages of the world's history.

You are well aware that speaking of war does not mean two armies fighting against one another, but two nations who are both risking their existence and who summon for the fight all their resources, all their possessions and all their material and moral forces.

For this reason, I had to interest the Turkish nation in the war in all their actions, their sentiments and their conceptions, in the same way as the army at the front. Not only those who were facing the enemy, but every single individual in the village, in his home, in the fields, had to consider himself in the same manner as those fighting at the front as being entrusted with a special mission to dedicate himself with his whole heart to the conflict.

Nations that fail to sacrifice their material and moral possessions to their fullest extent in the defence of their country, or that even do this reluctantly, cannot be looked upon as being determined to carry on a war or as being convinced that they will bring it to a successful issue. In future wars also, the decisive element of victory will be found in this conception. The great military nations of Europe have already officially begun to adopt this principle.

When we took over the supreme command we did not demand from the Assembly a "Law for the Defence of the Country," but we tried to achieve the same aim by issuing commands which, supported by the full powers bestowed on us by the Assembly, had legal force.

In a more extensive, more positive and more definite manner, the nation will establish the means and conditions in future which are adapted to render our dearly beloved country unconquerable by studying the experiences we have made today and allowing themselves to be guided by them.

But I had yet another duty to fulfil, namely, to take part personally in the fight, to join the ranks of the army and carry on the fight myself. I consider that I also fulfilled this duty well within the limits of possibilities, although accidentally I broke one of my ribs. I held no military rank until after the battle on the Sakarya. After it was over the Grand National Assembly promoted me to the rank of Marshal, with the title of the 'Gazi'. You are aware that the military rank conferred on me by the Ottoman Government had been taken away from me by the same Government.

The Agreement of Ankara after the battle on the Sakarya signifies the satisfactory redemption of our relations with the West. This agreement was signed in Ankara on 20 October 1921. I will now give you a short account so that you may have an idea of the situation. You know that after the London Conference in which a special deputation of ours, under the leadership of Bekir Sami Bey had taken part, the Greek offensive had been repulsed ending in our second victory at İnönü.

Then followed a lull in the military situation for some time. We had concluded the Treaty of Moscow with Russia by which the position in the East had been made clearer. We thought it desirable to come to an understanding with the Entente countries who seemed to be inclined to respect our national principles. We attached special importance to the liberation of the districts of Adana and Antep from foreign occupation.

We noticed that the French, who occupied these Turkish provinces as well as Syria, were also inclined for various reasons to come to an understanding with us. Although the agreement made between Bekir Sami Bey and M. Briand — an agreement that was found to be unacceptable by the National Government — had been rejected, neither the French nor ourselves showed any desire to continue the hostilities. The attempt was made, therefore, on both sides to get into touch with one another.

The French Government had at first unofficially sent M. Franklin Bouillon, the former Minister, to Ankara. For about two weeks I negotiated with him myself in the presence of Fevzi Pasha and Yusuf Kemal Bey, the Foreign Minister, after M. Franklin Bouillon had arrived at Ankara on 9 June 1921.

After a private conversation for the purpose of making our mutual acquaintance, we had our first meeting in my quarters near the railway station in Ankara on Monday, 13 June 1921. After we had begun to exchange our views at this meeting, the question before us was to define what the starting of our negotiations should be like. I suggested that on our side it should be the National Pact. M. Bouillon pointed out the difficulties that would arise from a discussion about this and suggested the Treaty of Sevres. Then he remarked, as though it were a foregone conclusion, that it would be advisable if we took the agreement that had been made in London between Bekir Sami Bey and M. Briand as the basis of our negotiations, reserving discussion on the points which were in contradiction to the Pact. To support this proposal, he asserted that our plenipotentiaries had not spoken about the National Pact in London, and, moreover, that nobody in Europe or even in İstanbul had yet sufficiently grasped the sense and real bearing of the Pact and the national movement. In my reply, I remarked that a New Turkish State had arisen from the old Ottoman Empire, that it must be recognised, and that this New Turkey would, in any case, secure for herself the recognition of her rights in the same manner as the rights of any independent nation. "The Sevres Treaty," I said, "is such a death sentence for the Turkish nation that we demand that its very name shall not be mentioned by anybody who calls himself our friend. Its name must not be referred to in the course of these negotiations. We cannot enter into confidential relations with countries that have not banished the Sevres Treaty from their minds. In our eyes, this Treaty does not exist. If the leader of the Turkish Delegation which went to London has not spoken to this effect, it signifies that he has not acted in accordance with the instructions and within the compass of the full powers which were given to him. He has made himself guilty of a mistake. We are well aware that this mistake has led to unfavourable impressions in Europe and particularly in the public opinion of France. If we were to follow the same course as Bekir Sami Bey, we would be committing a similar error. It is impossible that Europe is ignorant about our National Pact. It must have been brought to its attention. Europe and the whole world, however, witnessing how we have been shedding our blood for years, must surely have reflected on the causes of these bloody struggles. There is no truth in the assertion that Istanbul knows nothing about the National Pact and the national struggles. The population of Istanbul, together with the whole of the Turkish nation, are fully informed and entirely approve of the National Struggle. The persons who seem not to support it, and all those who allow themselves to be influenced by them, are only a small group and are known to the nation.

In reply to my statement that Bekir Sami Bey had exceeded his instructions, M. Franklin Bouillon asked whether he might speak about this subject. I told him that he could do so to whomsoever he wished. Then he tried to make excuses so as not to be obliged to depart from the agreement made with Bekir Sami Bey and maintained that the latter had never spoken of the existence of the Pact, nor that he had been instructed to keep within the limits of this Pact. If he had done so, they could have discussed and acted as the necessities of the situation demanded, but considering the present state of affairs the question had become a much more difficult one. He added that public opinion would inquire: "Why have these Turks never had this question put forward by their representative? Now they are trying continually to raise new questions."

After long negotiations, M. Franklin Bouillon finally proposed that the discussion should be adjourned so that he could read the Pact and grasp its meaning. Then the Articles of the Pact were read one after the other from the beginning to the end, and after that been done the negotiations were resumed. The Article that delayed us most was the one that referred to the abolition of the Capitulations and our complete independence. M. Franklin Bouillon remarked that these questions required more thorough study and deeper consideration. My explanations on this point may be condensed thus: "The attainment of our full and complete independence is the very essence of the mission we have taken upon ourselves. It is the duty we have undertaken before the nation and before history. It is certain that before undertaking this obligation we have thought a great deal about the prospects for its fulfilment. But in the end we are convinced that we shall succeed in our enterprise. We are people who have learned how to be practical and to face things in a proper manner. As a result of the faults committed by our predecessors, our nation, nominally independent, found itself in reality subject to numberless restrictions in its actions.

"Everything invented hitherto with the object of depicting Turkey in the eyes of the civilised world as bristling with faults has its origin in this false impression and the consequences produced by it. To be governed by this error can only result in the country and the nation being deprived of their dignity and their vitality. We are a nation that wants to live, and desires to do so in full possession of our dignity and honour. We cannot be content to see ourselves deprived of these attributes, because we succumb to an error. All the individuals constituting our nation, whether ignorant or educated, have without exception rallied around one principle, perhaps even without being conscious of the difficulties lying before them, and they have resolved to shed the last drop of their blood to carry out what they have to do in order to defend it. This principle is the attainment and maintenance of our full independence. Whoever speaks of complete and full independence means thereby unlimited independence: political, economic, legal, military, cultural, and the rest. If in any of these spheres of independence there should be something lacking, it would be equivalent to saying that the country has not yet gained its independence in the fullest meaning of the word. We do not believe that we can enjoy peace and tranquility until we have achieved this aim. We may conclude peace and enter into purely formal agreements; but our nation will never be at rest nor mistress of her own existence under a peace or an agreement which does not bestow complete independence on her. It could never happen that the nation would have given up the material struggle and consented to their destruction. But if they would have been inclined to be satisfied with such conditions as these why would they have gone on fighting for two years?

"On the day of the Armistice they could have taken refuge behind a condition of inactivity and passivity."

M. Franklin Bouillon's observations in reply to my explanations showed his seriousness and sincerity. In the end, he expressed his conviction that, after all, it was only a question of time.

For many a long day, we carried on an exchange of views with M. Franklin Bouillon on a number of questions, some important and others of a minor character. I believe that at length we arrived at the stage of knowing one another as we really were in regard to our thoughts, sentiments and characters. But some time had to elapse before we could settle the points for a final understanding between the National Government and the French Government. What was to be expected? Perhaps, that the national existence ought to be confirmed by something still more impressive than the two battles at İnönü?

The Agreement of Ankara signed by M. Franklin Bouillon after he had obtained the final consent of his Government is a document which, as I have already pointed out, actually came into force on 20 October 1921, thirty-seven days after the great battle on the Sakarya. Thanks to this agreement, valuable parts of our country were freed from occupation without the slightest measure of our independence in political, economic, military or any other regard being sacrificed. Through this agreement our national efforts were for the first time admitted and formulated by a Western Power. M. Franklin Bouillon came to Turkey again several times later, and each time took an opportunity to express the friendly feelings which had been established between us from the very beginning in Ankara.

In the introduction to my general statements I spoke about the Pontus question. Everybody can read the requisite information about it in the relevant documents. As, however, this question has done us a great deal of harm. I will refer once more to several points which I consider it necessary to mention.

Since the year 1840, that is to say, nearly three-quarters of a century ago, there were some Greeks who were engaged in reviving the old forms of Hellenism on the Black Sea, between Rize and the Bosphorus. A Greek monk named Klematios, who had immigrated to the United States and returned, founded the first institution on a hill that is today called Manastır (convent) in İnebolu, which served as a meeting place of the adherents of the Pontus persuasion. The members of this institution appeared from time to time in the form of separate bands of brigands. During the general war the Greek villages in the neighbourhood of Samsun, Çarşamba, Bafra, and Erbaa had nearly all been turned into arsenals containing rifles, ammunition, bombs and machine-guns, which had been sent from foreign countries and distributed among them.

After the Armistice had been concluded, the Greeks, impelled by the Hellenistic ideal, assumed an arrogant and provocative attitude nearly everywhere.

Prepared morally by the propaganda of the "Ethniki Hetairia" and the American institutions in Merzifon, and encouraged materially by the foreign countries who supplied them with arms, the mass of the Greeks, on the other hand, began to cast amorous glances in the direction of an independent Pontic State. Led by this idea, the Greeks organised a general revolt, seized the mountain heights and began to carry on a regular programme under the leadership of Yermanos in the Greek Metropolitan of Amasya, Samsun and the surrounding country.

On the one hand, Tokomanidis, the leader of the Greek Comitasjis of Samsun, who was manager of the Tobacco Regie in that town, began to get into touch with Central Anatolia. Certain foreign Powers promised to aid in the erection of a Pontic State and collected the Armenians and the Greeks living in Russia at Batum with the intention of sending them into the district of Samsun to reinforce the ranks of the Greek population. After equipping these individuals with the arms taken from Turkish troops in the Caucasus, which had been stored in Batum, they proceeded to land them on our shores. In this manner several thousand Greeks were collected in Sohum with the intention of committing robberies, and a certain Charalambos was put at the head of them. Those who had been assembled in Batum were taken to Charalambros to reinforce his band.

In a leading article on 4 March 1919, the newspaper "Pontus," which made its appearance in İstanbul, announced that the aim of their endeavours was the erection of a Greek Republic in the Province of Trabzon. On the 7th April, 1919, the anniversary of Greek independence, meetings were organised to be held everywhere in the country and especially in Samsun. The insolent intrigues of Yermanos completely revealed the Greek plans. The Greeks living in the district of Bafra and Samsun continued to hold meetings in their churches, augmented their organisations and supplemented their equipment. On 23 October 1919, Istanbul was proclaimed to be the centre of the movement for "Eastern Thrace and the Pontus." Venizelos, postponing the settlement of the question of Istanbul, held that all efforts should be directed to the foundation of a Pontic State and had given instructions to this effect to the Ecumenical Patriarch.

Simultaneously Alexandros Simbrakakis, who was commissioned with the organisation of the secret Greek police in Istanbul, had sent a Greek corps of officers to Samsun on board the Greek torpedo-boat Eiffel with instructions to organise the gendarmerie at Pontus. At the time that this was taking place in Turkey, a Greek Government under the name of the "Greek Pontic Government" was formed on 18 December 1919 at Batum which, on its side, also undertook the formation of organisations. A congress of the Greeks of the Black Sea, the Caucasus and Southern Russia took place on 19 July 1919 at Batum to discuss the Pontic

Question. The memorandum drafted at that congress was sent by a member of it to the Ecumenical Patriarch in Istanbul. Towards the end of the year 1919, the members of the Pontic organisation redoubled their activities and began to work quite openly, thereby compelling us to take decisive steps.

The Pontic organisation which had been formed in the mountains was composed of:

A. Bands of armed men under the command of a number of leaders.
B. Elements capable of production among the Pontic population, whose occupation was to provision them.
C. Administrative and police organisations and transport columns, whose duty was to transport provisions from the towns and villages.

On 4 January 1922 the secret sitting of the Assembly was taken up with the following question: The Chief Command and the Administration of the General Staff had taken up their quarters in Ankara. This led to the conclusion that difficulties must have arisen in connection with the presidency of the Assembly and the chief command. It was stated that on account of this fact, military affairs were not progressing well and that the Assembly would have to appoint a War Council to study the military situation.

I had the opportunity to tell you that the Party of the Defence of the Rights which we had formed in the Assembly, had consistently helped to secure the regular course of the debates in the Assembly and to prevent any interruption in the work of the Council of Ministers. On the other hand, those who fostered sentiments and ideas that were contrary to our own hampered the work of the party in proportion as they obtained new adherents. The origin of the idea of an opposition lay in the second paragraph of the fundamental article of the regulations of the Party for the Defence of the Rights, namely, in the organisation of the State on the basis of the Constitution Act.

The last paragraph of the first article of the programme constituted a permanent obstacle to a complete reconciliation of the thoughts and feelings. The difference of opinion and the lack of discipline within the party itself was due to it. Many persons withdrew from it. Those who left made common cause with those who remained outside the party and were energetically trying to destroy it. But the steps taken hampered it. In the end, another party was formed under the name of the "Second Party."

The representatives of this "Second Party" were in the habit of rejecting my candidates and preferred to vote for members whom they put up on behalf of their own party, disregarding the letter of the law, and thereby interfering with the formation of the Government.

A movement hostile to the army had also been created in the Assembly. "Why," they said, "does the army not attack after months have gone by since the battle on the Sakarya? The army must go over to the attack at all costs. An attack on one part of the front, at least, must be undertaken, so that we may get an idea of its offensive strength."

We shattered this movement. We could not consent to the idea of a partial attack. As our well-defined plan consisted of carrying out a general attack which would lead to decisive results and as this plan could only be fulfilled when all our preparations were complete, we could not approve of the idea of a partial attack; besides, this would be of no use. The conviction which had been formed in the ranks of the opposition could be summarised to the effect that our army would not succeed in being strong enough to carry out an attack.

In this way the opposition impeded the movement which aimed at an attack and, changing their tactics, they advanced another theory. They said: "Our real enemy is neither Greece nor the Greek army. Even if we were to succeed in completely defeating them, our cause would not have been improved. We have yet to beat the Entente Powers—especially England. For this purpose, we must leave a screen in front of the Greek army, concentrate our main forces in Eastern Iraq and attack the English. This is the only thing left for us to do if we uphold the theory of achieving the success of our cause by force of arms."

These ideas, as senseless as they were illogical, were not favourably received. Then the leaders of the opposition began new propaganda: "Where are we going to?" they demanded. "Who is leading us and whither are we being led? Towards the unknown? Is it right to drive the whole nation recklessly towards dark and uncertain goals?" This propaganda emanated from the body of the Assembly itself and from Ankara circles and penetrated into the ranks of the army.

The army is determined to attack, but we are still postponing the moment for it because we still require time fully to complete our preparations. To depend upon half measures and only to be partially prepared for an attack is worse than not to attack at all. It is not advisable to explain ouy waiting attitude by saying that we had abandoned our determination to attack or that we were doubtful whether we would be able to launch our attack.

After explaining this, I made the following remarks:

"The Ottomans (the Turks under the regime of former times) have seen themselves forced to retire after they had reached the gates of Vienna, because they did not understand how to show wisdom and precaution to the extent that the magnitude of their enterprises demanded, but allowed themselves to be led by their sentiments and their ambition. Consequently, they could not maintain their position in Budapest. They retired further, were defeated in Belgrad and were forced to retreat from there also. They abandoned the Balkans. They were driven out of Rumelia. They left us this country invaded by the enemy as a heritage. Let us put aside our sentiments and passions; let us show ourselves to be at least cautious in defending what remains to be saved of our country's territory. To safeguard our salvation and our independence, there can, first and last, be only one single way, one single resolution, and that is to defeat the enemy and dedicate the entire strength of our souls to this object.

"No faith nor any importance should be attached to words or advice that could produce a destructive influence on our nerve. The mental attitude which has developed under the governmental system and under the policy of the Ottoman regime is deplorable. The independence of a country can never be secured by following advice that is tendered by foreign countries with the intention of raising the belief that an enterprise such as ours cannot be crowned with success by the army, by war, or by pertinacity. History has not recorded a single instance of this kind. There is no doubt that those who allow themselves to be guided by contrary opinions will find themselves face to face with fatal consequences. In this way Turkey in each century, each day and each hour has declined and degenerated more and more, because there were men who permitted themselves to be misled by erroneous ideas of this description.

"If this decline had only been felt materially, it would have been of no importance. But, unfortunately, we can observe moral consequences also. There is no doubt that this was the main factor that brought this great country and this great nation to their downfall."

At the time of which I am speaking those members of the Assembly who were most troublesome and showed the greatest pessimism were exactly those, as you are aware, who had formerly held the opinion that the Turkish people could not obtain their independence by their own power.

These were the people who had insisted on demanding a mandate from this or that country. This is what moved me to continue my remarks as follows:

"We must rescue Turkey from the hands of those who lead her to her destruction and her downfall by chosing the wrong path. There is only one truth that can help this aim, a truth that has already been discovered and that consists of inspiring the thinking mind in Turkey with a new faith and impressing on them a more elevated moral. It only remains for me now to explain to you what the military means we have to prepare or reinforce before we can carry out our final determination of attacking the enemy are.

I want to see our preparations assured in three directions. The first of them, the principal and most important one, is the nation itself; it is the steadfastness of the endeavours firmly rooted in the spirit and soul of the nation for a free and independent existence. In proportion as the nation expresses these endeavours by increased strength, they also give proof of a stronger will and faith in their fulfilment, and I am convinced that I possess the means to deal with the enemy. The second consists of the will and the courage which the Assembly, the representative of the nation, show in the manifestation of their national efforts and the decisive execution of the measures resulting therefrom. We dispose of a superiority in means compared with the enemy, which becomes more apparent in the extent to which the Assembly develops the national efforts in a pronounced spirit of decision and unity. The third is our army, comprising the armed sons of a nation confronting the enemy. We can imagine the front which these three causes present against the enemy in two ways. To make my thoughts easier for you to appreciate, I shall speak separately of the inward front and the outward front. The more essential one is the inward front. This is the front which is formed by the whole country and the entire nation.

The outward front is the armed front of the army which opposes the enemy directly. This front may waver and undergo change; it may be broken through. But such a possibility can never result in the annihilation of a country or a nation. The factor which is of vital importance is the destruction of the inward front which leads to the crumbling of the country to its very foundations and which may reduce the nation to slavery. Enemies who know this truth better than we do have been working for centuries and are still working for the purpose of destroying this front. So far they have been successful. It is, indeed, much easier to take a fortress by attacking it from the inside than to assault it from outside.

It is barely possible, or probable, that our inward and outward front can be shaken so long as the mentality, the actions and attitude of the Assembly are not such as to encourage the enemy. We cannot be in any doubt about the fact that they will even seek means to utilise the pessimistic speeches which have been made by one or more members in the Assembly. Among the documents in the Foreign Ministry there are many which give evidence of this. I emphatically maintain that as long as any hope, even involuntarily, is given to the enemy the national cause will suffer delay thereby."

Then I listened to the statements of the representatives belonging to the opposition.

I will not detain you too long with the speeches of the opposition, for they were nothing but an echo of the twaddle of misguided and ignorant brains. On the whole, the Assembly had received my explanations favourably.

Official and non-official relations with different Powers took place during the course of the year 1921. Turco-Russian relations developed very favourably.

In addition to the French, we entered into contact with the Italians and the English. Let me mention a matter here which led to a misunderstanding in June 1921. On 13 June 1921, two officers, Major Henry and Major Sturton, who, according to their assertion belonged to the suite of General Harington, Commander-in-Chief of the Allied forces, arrived on board a motor-boat. They requested me on behalf of the General to go on board a torpedo-boat from İnebolu to General Harington's Yalı* on the Bosphorus and come to an agreement with him about the foundation of peace. They said that England had recognised our complete independence and that the Greeks would be removed from our territory, and added that it would be possible to discuss other issues as well.

I replied to these officers that I would not go to Istanbul and that it would be more appropriate if General Harington came to İnebolu to have an interview with Refet Pasha, who was there at that moment.

On 18 June 1921 a telegram came from Hamit Bey in İstanbul. It ran as follows:

"An Englishman who holds an official position here has appealed to me in the name of the highest English authority in İstanbul and has asked me to inform his Excellency Mustafa Kemal Pasha that the English are willing to enter into negotiations for a speedy peace, and that they are desirous with this aim in view to enter into communication with his Excellency, and that they were expecting an immediate reply."

Hamit Bey answered that we were prepared to enter into negotiations.

On 5 July 1921 an English torpedo-boat arrived in Zonguldak bringing me a letter from General Harington. This letter, the translation of which was wired to me in Ankara, was worded thus:

"According to Major Henry's communication, your Excellency desires to have an interview with me and to make certain statements to me in conversation as one soldier to another.

"That being so, I have been authorised by the English Government to leave on board the English cruiser Ajax to meet your Excellency at İnebolu or İzmit on a day that it will be convenient for you to arrange.

"If you desire it, I am perfectly ready to have a completely clear and frank exchange of views with you about the situation. I am authorised to listen to your considerations and lay them before the English Government for examination. But I have no official authority either to negotiate with you or to discuss matters in their name.

"The meeting will have to take place on board the English cruiser. Your Excellency will be received with the honours due to your rank and will enjoy complete freedom until you return to land.

"If you agree to this, will you please inform me of the date and hour which would suit you?"

Judging from the contents of this letter, it would appear that it was I who had expressed the desire of getting into touch with General Harington and to speak to him. In reality, this was not at all the case.

This was the prelude to the direct correspondence which has been carried on between us.

"Your Excellency is cognisant of our national demands. I declare myself ready to enter into negotiations, provided that the deliverance of our national territory from the presence of its enemies and the recognition of our complete independence in political, financial, economic, military, legal and cultural respects will be agreed to.

For reasons explained by Major Henry we believe it appropriate that the negotiations should take place at İnebolu and on land, where the most agreeable reception will be prepared for your Excellency.

I await your reply, which I hope will state whether we are in agreement on the opinions mentioned above.

If your Excellency has no other purpose in view than to exchange opinions about the situation, I shall send my comrades for the interview."

No reply was sent to this letter. On 7 July, Mr. Rattigan, the English charge d'affaires, told Hamit Bey, whom he had seen in Istanbul, that General Harington had advised Major Henry, who had come to Anatolia as a merchant, to inquire about the health of the English prisoners and, if possible, to learn from me, Mustafa Kemal Pasha, whether the efforts in Istanbul would still continue, but that Major Henry had no authority to undertake any other steps.

Until August 1922 we had no serious relations with the Western Powers in a concrete form. We had the permanent and firm conviction that we could not flatter ourselves that there was any hope of success in a diplomatic way until we had driven the enemy out of our territory by force of arms and had given evidence of our national existence and our national strength by deeds.

The world is an arena of trials. After so many centuries, the Turkish nation finds itself again subject to trials, and this time they are of an especially hard description. Were we permitted to reckon on benevolent treatment without any hope of being successful? While preparing ourselves seriously for this kind of trial which we had to undergo before the whole world, we thought it well not to lose sight of the position and mentality of the spectators. We had, as you know, first sent Yusuf Kemal Bey, who was Foreign Minister at that time, for this purpose to Europe and later on Fethi Bey, Minister of the Interior.

We entrusted Yusuf Kemal Bey, who was to go to Europe via Istanbul, with some private affairs which he was to settle in that city.

One thing, for instance, was that he should have a conversation with İzzet Pasha and his colleagues, and with Vahdettin also if he considered that this was really necessary.

He was to propose to the latter that he should recognise the National Assembly and impress upon İzzet Pasha and his colleagues the necessity of proceeding in a way that was indicated by the aim we had in view.

Yusuf Kemal Bey acted in İstanbul within the limits of his instructions, but, unfortunately, he was misled by İzzet Pasha and his colleagues, who took him to the Sovereign as a petitioner.

But not satisfied with this, the Cabinet, for the purpose of confusing and rendering more difficult Yusuf Kemal Bey's work in Paris and London, sent İzzet Pasha before his own departure (Yusuf Kemal Bey's) to these cities, enabling him to travel through the territory occupied by the Greeks.

İzzet Pasha kept his journey a secret till the last moment.

Yusuf Kemal Bey's interviews in Paris and London were of no avail. It was only stated that the Foreign Ministers of the Entente would meet at a Conference in a short time and that they would make us peace proposals. Although the evacuation of Anatolia had been agreed to in principle, it was apparently necessary that we should conclude an armistice with the Greeks, because the steps for the conclusion of peace would be doomed to failure if war were resumed during the negotiations at the Conference. Yusuf Kemal Bey, who was informed of this by Lord Curzon, replied that a resolution of the Conference prescribing the evacuation of Anatolia beforehand, which would be communicated to both the interested parties, would be more effective than the armistice. But Lord Curzon insisted on the necessity of the armistice and asked Yusuf Kemal Bey to move the Government to this effect and to inform him of the answer that he would get.

Before Yusuf Kemal Bey's return on 22 March 1922 the Conference of the Foreign Ministers of the Entente proposed an armistice to the Turkish and Greek Governments.

At the time, I was at the front. I was informed of this proposal by Celal Bey, acting Minister for Foreign Affairs. The outlines of the proposed armistice were these: A demilitarised zone of ten kilometres was to be established between the forces of both sides. The troops were not to be reinforced by men or ammunition.

No alteration was to be made in the position of the troops. War material also was not to be transported from one place to another. Our army and our military position was to be under the control and inspection of the Military Commissions of the Entente. We were loyally to accept the decisions of these Commissions.

The Greeks immediately accepted the armistice. The Greek army had been both materially and morally defeated on the Sakarya. It was difficult for this army to tempt fortune again and undertake an attack on a wide scale. It was surely easy for everybody to realise the fact that it was impossible to employ the Greek army in operations with the idea that they could lead to a decisive result. It was a very serious matter for us to agree that our army, which we had been working for nearly a year to prepare, should be placed in a state of inactivity and that the National Government should be left in a state of suspense after their hopes had been raised to such a pitch, and thereby run the risk that during the intervening time the National Government and our army night become demoralised.

Consequently, we studied the conditions of the armistice which the Entente Powers proposed for the evacuation of Anatolia and the solution of the Eastern question with the greatest care.

The first thing we did was to put ourselves into direct communication at the telegraph set with the Council of Ministers in Ankara for the purpose of exchanging views. The first reply which we considered it expedient to give to the representatives of the Entente through our representative in Istanbul on behalf of the Ministry for Foreign Affairs, was as follows:

"I have received today, 24 March 1922, at ... o'clock the Note containing the proposal of the armistice, which is in continuation of your telegram of 23 March 1922. I have communicated its contents concerning the position at the front to the Commander-in-Chief at the front and have requested him to inform us of his views before I lay it before the Council of Ministers or, if necessary, before the National Assembly.

"Will you inform the representatives of the Entente Powers of this, and tell them that in conformity with their wish I will send them the reply of the Government of the Grand National Assembly of Turkey as soon as possible?"

On 24 March 1922 I informed the President of the Cabinet of my opinion by telegram, as follows:

"In the first place it would be inadvisable to answer by a refusal or in a manner that betrays disinclination or distrust of the proposed armistice which the Foreign Ministers have jointly suggested. On the contrary, we must favourably consider the proposal of an armistice. Consequently, our answer must be in the affirmative and not in the negative. If the Entente Powers have no good intentions, it is for them later on to take up a negative attitude.

"If we cannot consent to the conditions proposed, we will make counter-proposals."

On the following day, the agencies and telegrams referring to the Note from different sources gave the following items of news:

"It is declared in Government circles that the Government of the Grand National Assembly of Turkey has favourably received this proposal, which it is assumed has been made for the purpose of restoring peace in the Near East and of leading to the evacuation of Anatolia without further bloodshed and devastation. It is firmly hoped that the Government, confident of the goodwill and the impartiality of the Allied Powers, will give a favourable reply.

"We hope that the proposal in question contains reasonable and practicable conditions and that the period of time foreseen for the conclusion of peace will be as short as possible."

The Council of Ministers were inclined to postpone our reply till the return of our Foreign Minister, who was in Europe. Replying that this was not necessary, I drew up my decision regarding the reply to be given to this effect:

"We agree to the armistice in principle. However, we shall not desist for a single moment from pushing forward our preparations of the army and its improvement. We do not consent to foreign control commissions being established over our army. We shall make conditions which can be fulfilled, provided that the armistice which we shall agree to will include the evacuation. The most essential condition is that this evacuation shall commence immediately once the armistice is concluded."

On 24 March I personally sent at the telegraph set to the Council of Ministers the reply to be given to the Note. The Council on their part had sent me a copy of the reply prepared in Ankara. I noticed certain differences between the two drafts of the reply Note. At last, we resolved to have a meeting with the Council of Ministers during the night of 24 March at Sivrihisar and to draft the text of the reply Note.

According to a telegram in code which our special agent in Istanbul had sent on 25 March to the Ministry of Foreign Affairs, he had had a conversation with Tevfik Pasha and the latter had told him that the High Commissioners had handed a similar Note to the Government of the Sultan, with the request that it should be sent to Ankara and that they were to be informed of the reply they received.

Our agent asked Tevfik Pasha whether the right conceded to Ankara of expressing their opinion referred only to the proposal of an armistice or whether it embraced all other questions. Tevfik Pasha did not reply. To the question asked by our agent as to what news had arrived from İzzet Pasha, Tevfik Pasha replied: "İzzet Pasha announces that the Conference will soon meet, and remarked that matters ought not to be driven to extremes."

The Council of Ministers returned to Ankara after having decided at Sivrihisar upon the text of the Note to be sent in reply to the proposal of the armistice. But before they had had time to send it off, a second Note arrived from the Conference of Ministers in Paris on 26 March 1922. This Note contained the proposals of the Entente Powers regarding the foundation of peace. The main points were the following:

"Participation in the League of Nations to protect the minority rights in Turkey as in Greece, as well as the application of the conditions laid down on this question; the creation of a home in the East for the Armenians and participation of the League of Nations in this undertaking; the establishment of a demilitarised zone in the districts of the Gelibolu Peninsula and of the Straits to safeguard the freedom of the Straits; the settlement of the frontiers of Thrace in such a way that Tekirdağ will be surrendered to Turkey, Kırklareli, Babaeski and Edirne to the Greeks; the acceptance of a system guaranteeing to the Greeks in İzmir, which remained in our possession, and the Turks of Edirne, which came under Greek sovereignty, the possibility of taking part in a fair manner in the administration of these two towns.

Evacuation of Istanbul by the Allies after the conclusion of Peace.

Increase of the strength of the Turkish army, which had been fixed at 50,000 men by the Sevres Treaty, by 35,000 men, so that it would amount altogether to 85,000 men, and the transformation of the Turkish army into a volunteer army, as provided for by the Sevres Treaty.

Abolition of the Financial Commission as provided for in the draft of the Sevres Treaty and the introduction of a system reconcilable with Turkish sovereignty for the protection of the economic interests of the Entente Powers and for securing the payment of interest to the Public Debt, as well as the war indemnity which would be imposed upon us.

Appointment of a Commission for the modification of the legal and economic Capitulations.

Having examined the text of the first Note of the Allied Powers for the proposal of an armistice and having heard of the conditions set out in the second detailed Note, we had naturally come to the conclusion that these Powers who were supported by the Government of İstanbul had introduced a new phase in their destructive enterprise against us. In face of this fact, the situation had to be regarded as very serious and a terrific fight was anticipated. The first thing was to explain to the nation and to the public opinion of the world the nature of the conditions which had been proposed to us. I wrote to the Council of Ministers to this effect.

We agreed in principle to the armistice; but we considered it to be an indispensable and essential condition that the evacuation should commence after the armistice had been concluded. We proposed to fix the duration of the armistice and the evacuation of Anatolia at four months and agreed that the term of the armistice should be automatically extended for three months if the preliminary Peace negotiations should not have led to any result when the evacuation was complete.

We received an answer to our Note on 15 April 1922. This answer was, naturally, negative.

We replied on the 22nd of the same month. At the end of our reply we stated that even in case no agreement could be reached on the question of the armistice, it would not be desirable to postpone the Peace negotiations.

We proposed that a Conference be held at İzmit; but this, also, produced no result. A Conference to meet at Beykoz or Venice was mentioned several times, but none of these suggestions was carried out up to the moment of our decisive victory.

The Act of 5 August 1921 relating to our appointment as Commander-in-Chief has a special history. If you like, I will give you some particulars about it.

This Act was renewed for the first time on 31 October 1921, for the second time on 4 February 1922, and for the third time on 6 May 1922.

Each time these renewals were accompanied by criticisms of every description from the side of the opposition.

The third renewal, in particular, took the character of rather an important incident.

During the period before 6 May 1922 the question of renewing this Act, which was approaching expiration, was raised in the Assembly. On account of illness I was unable personally to be present in the Assembly. The Council of Ministers, who came to my house on the evening of 5 May, explained the position to me and said that the representatives of the opposition did not wish that I should continue to hold the post of Commander-in-Chief.

After a long debate, the question was put to the vote. The neces- sary majority was not obtained, consequently the renewal of the Act was not agreed to. The Council of Ministers and especially the admini- stration of the General Staff, as well as the Ministry of National Defence, were quite taken aback.

On account of the attitude of the Assembly, the Ministers asserted that they could no longer see what use there was in carrying on their duties, and that they considered that they ought to resign.

From the moment of the vote in the Assembly the army was without a leader.

If the Chief of the General Staff and the Ministry resigned, the outbreak of a great crisis in the general administration would be inevitable. For this reason, I requested the Chief of the General Staff and the Ministers to be patient for another twenty-four hours. For my part, I determined to continue to hold my position as Commander-in-Chief in the best interests of the country and the common cause, and informed the Council of Ministers of this resolve.

On the next day, 6 May, I announced that I would give some explanations at a secret sitting in the Assembly. I had previously sent for the protocols of the Assembly and the arguments put forward by the speakers who had opposed the chief command, and had examined them one after the other.

During this secret sitting violent discussions and even quarrels took place on other questions which the representatives of the opposition were putting forward with, the object of bringing about the overthrow of the Government and the dissolution of the army. Finally, the Assembly having been duly informed, gave their decision to the effect that they agreed to the renewal of the Act relating to the chief command by 177 votes to 11, with 15 abstentions.

Three months later, on 20 July 1922, the Act relating to the chief command was again brought up for discussion according to the provisions of the Act. Let me quote some of the general remarks I made on this occasion:

"The moral and material forces of the army have reached a degree of perfection that allows me to feel that the national efforts will certainly be realised without it being necessary to take any extraordinary steps. Therefore, I feel convinced that it is no longer necessary to maintain the extraordinary full powers. I hope that in the future no other occasion will arise when this would be considered necessary, which we can happily state today has disappeared. The duties of the commander-in-chief can at the utmost continue till the day when we have attained a decisive result corresponding to the spirit of the National Pact. There is no doubt that we shall achieve this happy result. On that day our precious city of İzmir, our beautiful Bursa, our Istanbul and our Thrace will all be rejoined to our mother-country. On that day, together with the nation, we shall live to experience the greatest happiness, and I, for my part, will also realise another joy, namely, that I shall take up the place again which I occupied on the day we began to defend our sacred cause. Is there a nobler joy than to be a free man among a free people? For those who are taking part in the great truths, for those who know no other joys than the moral and sacred delights of the heart and conscience, material dignities, high as they may be, have no value."

These conferences ended with my being entrusted for an unlimited period with the supreme command.

The activity shown by the opposition party in the Assembly will have to engage our attention for a little while longer.

The party known under the name of the "Second Party" still tested their strength for a long time by passive resistance. Through the Act of 8 July 1922 relating to the election of Ministers, they secured that the Ministers and the President of the Council were elected directly by the Assembly by secret ballot. I was thus actually removed from the presidency of the Council of Ministers and the provision that the Ministers were to be elected from among the candidates which I had selected was abolished.

After the opposition party began their attack, they undertook to make Rauf Bey President of the Council and succeeded in doing this. I understood the secret designs of the opposition; nevertheless, I asked Rauf Bey to come to see me. I told him that the majority of the Assembly was inclined to elect him President of the Council and that I was myself of the same opinion. Rauf Bey gave the impression as though he hesitated. "The Presidency of the Council of Ministers," he said, "is not connected with privileges." He intended to point out thereby that the President of the Grand National Assembly was actually President of the Council of Ministers and that the decisions of the latter could not be carried out before the consent of the former had been obtained, and that, consequently, the President of the Council had neither any special authority nor freedom of action.

As a matter of fact, this was so according to the Constitution Act. Notwithstanding this, Rauf Bey accepted the presidency of the Council, and held it from 12 July 1922 to 4 August 1923.

Another point must also be brought to your attention. From the very first day Kara Vasıf Bey and Rauf Bey were working hand in hand in the organisation of the opposition party, leading it and strengthening it. But Rauf Bey did not join the "Second Party" publicly, but prefered to remain with us. This state of affairs lasted for three years. In the end, Rauf Bey saw himself obliged to reveal his dissenting opinion, when —according to his own words— he said: "There is no possibility left of keeping up the appearance of being on our side."

The movement provoked in the Assembly against the army was carried on by the opposition. The members of it constantly spoke emphatically and violently of the incapability of the army to begin the attack and the necessity of settling the question by political means.

In reality, our army was on the point of completing its equipment and filling out its gaps. Already, in the middle of June, I had decided to open the attack. The commander at the front as well as the chief of the General Staff and the Minister of National Defence were the only persons who were aware of my decision. At this time I had to make a journey in the direction of İzmit —Adapazarı, and before I left Ankara I had a conversation with His Excellency Fevzi Pasha, Chief of the General Staff. Then I talked to His Excellency Kazım Pasha, who was Minister of National Defence at that time and whom I had taken with me as far as the station of Sarıköy, where his Excellency İsmet Pasha, who commanded the front, had arrived at my request. We decided what was to be done to rapidly complete our preparations for the attack.

The moment has now come to speak about the great attack. You know that the enemy's army after the great battle on the Sakarya had a very strong force between Afyon Karahisar and Dumlupınar. There was another strong force also in the district of Eskişehir. The reserves were concentrated between these two forces. The right wing was protected by some divisions which were lying in the district of the Menderes, and the left wing by others that were south of the lake of İznik. It may be said that the enemy's front extended from the Sea of Marmara to the Menderes.

Our idea was to fight a decisive battle by concentrating our main forces on one flank, if possible the outer wing of the enemy's force. The arrangement which we had considered to be the right one was to concentrate the main body of our force to the south of the enemy's right wing which was in the neighbourhood of Afyon Karahisar and the district reaching from Akarçay to the line of Dumlupınar. This was the most important and vulnerable position of the enemy. Attacking him from this side offered the prospect of bringing about a rapid and decisive result.

İsmet Pasha, who commanded the Western front, and Fevzi Pasha, Chief of the General Staff, had personally made the necessary inquiries and had examined the position from this point of view. Our plan of maneuver and attack had been decided upon for a long time.

On the pretext of meeting General Townshend, who after his arrival in Konya, had expressed a desire to see me. I left on the evening of 23 July 1922 for Akşehir, which was the headquarters of the Western front. We believed it appropriate to discuss the operations in the presence of the General Staff. I went on 24 July to Konya and returned to Akşehir on the 27th. His Excellency, Fevzi Pasha had also arrived there on the 25th. When the discussions, which took place on the night of 27 July, were over we decided to do everything to complete our preparations before 15 August and, according to our plan, to begin the general attack.

After I had given the order to carry out these preparations and to hasten on the attack, I returned to Ankara. On 6 August 1922 the commander of the Western front gave his armies the secret command to be ready for the attack.

At 4 o'clock on the afternoon of 20 August 1922, I was at the headquarters of the Western front, namely at Akşehir. After a short consultation, I ordered the commander of the front to open the attack in the forenoon of 26 August 1922.

During the night of 20 August 1922 I also invited the commanders of the Ist and the IInd Armies to come to the headquarters of this front.

In the presence of the Chief of the General Staff and the commander of the front I explained my point of view concerning the details of the attack, illustrating them on a map in the manner of a war-game. Then I renewed the order I had given on the same day to the commander of the front.

The commanders set to work at once. Our attack was intended to develop, both strategically and actually, in the nature of a surprise. For the purpose of bringing it to a successful issue, the greatest attention had to be paid to the secrecy of the concentration of our troops and our dispositions. For this reason all the movements were to be made at night and our troops had to rest by day in the villages and under the shade of trees. So that we should not attract the enemy's attention by road-making and similar work, we had to deceive them by pretending to carry out similar work in other districts.

On the morning of the 26th we were in Kocatepe. Our attack was opened by the artillery at 5.30 in the morning.

I do not think it is necessary to describe the battle of Afyon Karahisar and Dumlupınar and the operations which resulted in the Greek army being destroyed and their remnants being driven into the Mediterranean and the Marmara Sea. These operations, that had been developing for a long period of time, that were prepared in all their details and carried out in such a way that they were crowned with success, constituted a sublime action which once again in history proves and confirms the strength and the heroism of the Turkish army, Turkish officers and their commanders. This action is an immortal monument to the spirit of freedom and independence of the Turkish Nation. I am proud and happy to be the son of a nation and the commander of an army that can perform such deeds.

Now, we can revert to the realm of diplomacy. It is a fact that I had imposed a long period of waiting upon those, who, despairing of a military victory, had been fostering for a long time the hope and conviction of reaching a settlement by way of diplomacy. They ought, in any case, at last to have been satisfied when they saw me working seriously in support of the efforts they displayed in the sphere of diplomacy. We shall see whether this was so or not.

When, after the reconquest of İzmir and Bursa, our armies continued their march to İstanbul and the Dardanelles with the object, also, of delivering Thrace from the hands of the Greek army, Lloyd George, who was Prime Minister at that time, had adopted a determined attitude in favour of war and had appealed to the Dominions for reinforcements. To judge from events that followed, we can assume that this appeal was unsuccessful.

Meanwhile General Pelle, the High Commissioner of France, came to İzmir for the purpose of interviewing me. He advised me not to allow our armies to enter the zones which he described as neutral. I declared that the National Government did not recognise the existence of any such zone and that it was impossible to hold our armies back before they had delivered Thrace. General Pelle showed me a private telegram which he had received from M. Franklin Bouillon in which he expressed the desire of having an interview with me. I told him that I would receive him in İzmir. M. Franklin Bouillon arrived at that time on board a French warship. He stated that he had been sent by the French Government, with the acquiescence of the English and Italian Governments. During the course of our interview with M. Franklin Bouillon, a Note came from the Foreign Ministers of the Entente, dated 23 September 1922. It related specially to two essential points. One referred to the cessation of hostilities and the other to the Peace Conference.

We could not abandon our operations before we had reconquered the whole of Eastern Thrace as far as our national frontiers. If, however, the enemy's troops could be induced to evacuate these parts of our territory, further operations would automatically come to an end.

Asking in the above Note whether we would agree to send delegates to a conference which was to take place in Venice, or elsewhere, and to which Great Britain, France, Japan, Romania, Yugoslavia and Greece would be invited. They declared that our desire for the restitution of Thrace as far as the Maritza, including Edirne, would be taken into consideration, on condition, however, that we would not send troops against the neutral zones of the Straits whilst the negotiations were still pending.

In addition, the Note touched upon the questions of the Straits, the minorities and our inclusion in the League of Nations. We were promised in it that steps would be taken to compel the Greek troops to retire behind a line to be fixed by the commanders of the Entente armies before the conference met and the proposal was made to hold a meeting in Mudanya or İzmit for this purpose.

In a clear reply which I gave to this Note on 29 September 1922 I informed them that I agreed to the proposal of a conference in Mudanya. But I demanded that Thrace as far as the Maritza should be immediately restored to us. I added that I had chosen İsmet Pasha, Commander-in-Chief of the Western Armies, who was furnished with extraordinary powers to enable him to negotiate in the name of the Commander-in-Chief, to take part in the Conference in Mudanya, which, as I have said, was to meet on 3 October; the Go- vernment also sent a detailed reply, dated 4 October 1922 to the Note in question and proposed İzmir as the meeting place; in addition, they demanded that the Russo-Ukranian and the Georgian Republics should also be invited to attend the conference in connection with the question of the Straits. Our views regarding other questions were also put forward in detail.

The Conference, consisting of General Harington as the plenipotentiary for Great Britain, General Charpy, plenipotentiary for France, and General Monbelli, plenipotentiary for Italy, met in Mudanya under the chairmanship of İsmet Pasha. The Armistice of Mudanya, after violent discussions which lasted for a week, was signed on 11 October. In this way, Thrace was re-incorporated with the mother-country.

On my return to İzmir from Ankara, we were principally engaged in the negotiations at the Mudanya Conference. In the Council of Ministers, in the Assembly as well as in committee, the question of the composition of the delegation that was to be sent to the Peace Conference was discussed. Rauf Bey, President of the Ministerial Council, Yusuf Kemal Bey, Foreign Minister, and Rıza Nur Bey, Minister of Public Health, were regarded as men who would naturally be members of the delegation. For my part, I had not yet come to any decision about it. I could not persuade myself that a delegation under the leadership of Rauf Bey could have any success on a question that was vital to us. I had the impression that Rauf Bey himself did not feel equal to this task. He proposed to me that I should give him İsmet

Pasha as an advisor. I replied that I did not see what advantage it would be to send İsmet Pasha as an advisor, but that I was convinced that he would render the best services if we would make him the leader of the delegation. The matter remained thus. Rauf Bey continued to be busy with the combination he had suggested for the composition of our delegation. I did not pretend to place any importance on this. The Mudanya Conference had come to an end. İsmet Pasha and Fevzi Pasha, Chief of the General Staff, were in Bursa. I went there to meet them. Kazım Pasha, Minister of National Defence, was with me. I took Kazım Karabekir Pasha with me; on account of the hostile manifestations to which he had been subjected and which had made it impossible for him to continue in his office in the East, he had found himself compelled to come to Ankara. Refet Pasha, too, whom I had chosen for a mission to Istanbul, was with me. During my stay in Bursa, I sent him, as is well known, to that town. In spite of the numerous given facts I had before me, I re-examined the question as to whether İsmet Pasha would be able to fill the position of chairman of the delegation, and I took all the details into account concerning the way he had presided over the Conference at Mudanya. I did not say a word to İsmet Pasha himself about my plan. Finally, I came to a definite decision. I thought it would be best that he should first become Foreign Minister and then act as leader of the delegation. To carry out this idea I sent a personal and confidential telegram in code directly to Yusuf Kemal Bey, asking him to resign from his office as Foreign Minister and personally take steps to ensure the election of İsmet Pasha as his successor.

Before I left Ankara, Yusuf Kemal Bey had told me that İsmet Pasha was best qualified to occupy the position of chairman of the delegation. In his reply, Yusuf Kemal Bey told me that in obedience to my request he had done everything that was necessary. It was only then that I informed İsmet Pasha of an accomplished fact and that he would become Foreign Minister first and then go to the Peace Conference as chairman of the delegation. İsmet Pasha seemed to be surprised. He excused himself by pointing to his capacity as a military man. Finally, he gave in and accepted my proposal as an order. I returned to Ankara. Meanwhile, that is to say, on 28 October 1922, the Entente Powers had invited us to the Peace Conference which was to meet at Lausanne. These Powers insisted on recognising the existence of a Government in Istanbul and invited them also to come to the Conference with us.

The twofold invitation led to the final abolition of the personal monarchy. The Caliphate and the monarchy were actually separated from one another by the Act of I November 1922. The national sovereignty which had been exercised for the past two-and-a-half years was confirmed. Without any explicit rights, the Caliphate was still maintained for some time.

You know that the Sultanate and the Caliphate, taken separately or jointly, were regarded as questions of very great importance. To support this assertion, I will tell you something that I now remember. Some time before I November, the opposition abandoned themselves to a lively agitation among the representatives of the Assembly on the question of the proposal to abolish the Sultanate that was attributed to me. One day, Rauf Bey came to me in my room in the Assembly building and told me that he wanted to speak to me about some important matters, and that we could chat with greater ease if I would go to Refet Pasha in Keçiören. I fulfilled his request. I likewise agreed that Fuat Pasha should be present at the meeting. Consequently, we had a meeting of four at Refet Pasha's house. What I learned there from Rauf Bey can be summarised as follows: The Assembly is grieved to observe that the aim of abolishing the Throne and, perhaps, even the Caliphate is being pursued. They distrust you and the attitude you will adopt in future. I am, therefore, of the opinion that you ought to reassure the Assembly and thereby public national opinion.

I asked Rauf Bey to tell me what were his own convictions and views regarding the Sultanate and the Caliphate. In his reply he furnished me with the following precise statements:

"I am," he said, "devoted heart and soul to the Throne and Caliphate, because my father has received benefits from the Sultan and was one of the dignitaries of the Ottoman Empire. The recollection of these benefits is coursing through my veins. I am not an ungrateful man and could never become one.

"It is my duty to remain loyal to the Sultan. Regarding my attachment to the Caliphate, it is imposed upon me by my education. I might also mention considerations of a more general kind. It is difficult for us to make ourselves masters of the general situation; this can be secured by a higher office and the sublime dignity which everybody generally considers to be unapproachable. This office, this dignity, is the Throne and the Caliphate. The abolition of this dignity and the attempt to replace it by a body of a different character would lead to disappointment and disaster. This is unthinkable."

After Rauf Bey, I asked Refet Pasha, who sat opposite me, to give his opinion. His reply was: "I entirely share Rauf Bey's opinion. In fact, no other form of Government can come into question for us than that of the Sultanate and Caliphate."

After this, I was anxious to hear Fuat Pasha's opinion also. He declared that he had only recently returned from Moscow and that he had not had time as yet sufficiently to study public sentiment and opinion, and he apologised for being unable to express any concrete opinion about the question under discussion.

I gave the following laconic answer to my interlocutors:

"What we are talking about is not the question of the day. The alarm and excitement shown by some members of the Assembly are unjustified."

This reply did not seem to satisfy Rauf Bey. Nevertheless, he continued to expound this question from different aspects. Our conversation, which had begun towards evening, continued until the morning. I had the impression that Rauf Bey was trying to make sure of one thing, namely, that I would personally repeat in the Assembly from the tribune the words I had used regarding the Sultanate and the Caliphate, as well as the attitude I would adopt personally in future, words which they had considered reassuring.

I said that I had no hesitation to repeat my statements to the same effect before the Assembly. Besides this, I wrote down everything I had said on a piece of paper with a pencil and promised to seize an opportunity the following day in the Assembly to repeat it as a formal declaration. I carried out this promise.

In my declaration the opposition saw that Rauf Bey had been successful and expressed their satisfaction to him.

When I decided on the occasion of Tevfik Pasha's telegram to separate the Caliphate from the Sultanate and to abolish the latter, my first thought was immediately to ask Rauf Bey to come to my room in the Chamber. Standing erect before him and pretending not to know anything about his opinions and convictions which he took all night to explain at Refet Pasha's house, I made this demand to him:

"We shall separate the Caliphate from the Sultanate and abolish the latter. You will make a declaration from the tribune to the effect that you approve of this fact."

No other word was exchanged with Rauf Bey. Before he left my room, Kazım Karabekir Pasha, whom I had invited for the same purpose, arrived. I asked him also to express himself to the same effect.

As may be read in the protocols of that day, Rauf Bey made the declarations from the tribune that had been agreed upon, once or twice. He even proposed that day that the abolition of the Sultanate should be observed as a public holiday. One point might puzzle you here. Rauf Bey, who had regarded it to be his duty to remain loyal to the Sultan and had spoken of the fatal consequences which might follow an attempt to substitute the Sultanate by a body of quite another description — this same Rauf Bey had now succumbed to a new resolution after it had been brought to his knowledge and -what is still more remarkable— he even yielded to my proposal and my decision so far as to advocate the abolition of the Sultanate, without having expressed in any way his own opinion on the subject. How can such a proceeding be explained? Had Rauf Bey changed his mind? Or, rather, had he in principle been insincere when he had expressed his opinion? It is difficult to discern the truth and to come to a definite decision in favour of one or the other of these suppositions.

Instead of trying to throw light on this doubtful subject, I prefer to recall certain stages, certain incidents and discussions bearing on the situation and thereby facilitate your study of it.

I had previously explained that the abolition of the Sultanate had resulted from the fact that an invitation had been addressed also to Istanbul to send a delegation to the Lausanne Conference, and that this invitation had been accepted by Istanbul, that is to say, by Vahdettin, Tevfik Pasha and his colleagues, an acceptance which would serve as a pretext for lessening the advantages which the nation had gained at the price of so many efforts and sacrifices and which might even deprive them of any importance.

Tevfik Pasha at first sent a telegram addressed to me personally. In this telegram on 17 October 1922 he said that the victory that had been won had done away with any conflict and dualism between Istanbul and Ankara and that national unity had thereby been assured. Tevfik Pasha wanted to make us understand that there was no longer any enemy in the country, that the Sultan remained in his place with the Government at his side, and that the duty henceforward imposed upon the nation was to obey the orders emanating from these authorities. Under these conditions, no further obstacle stood in the way of national unity. Tevfik Pasha had employed special skill in rendering further services to Ankara. These services, considering the fact the Istanbul and Ankara were both invited to go together to the Lausanne Conference, were intended to assure the preliminary and most rapid despatch of a person furnished with secret instructions from my side to Istanbul (Document 260).

In a telegram which I sent to Hamit Bey in Istanbul to be communicated to Tevfik Pasha I informed him that "Tevfik Pasha and his colleagues, showing no hesitation to bring confusion into the policy of the State, were apparently taking a grave responsibility upon themselves".

Unfortunately, Hamit Bey hesitated about the necessity of communicating this telegram to Tevfik Pasha and looked upon it as an instruction addressed to himself. Within the course of three days, nevertheless, he sent us five communications composed in the sense of the above telegram.

He even sent to the newspapers and agencies the draft of a communique containing the essential points of the declarations which were made with the object of preventing Tevfik Pasha and his colleagues from sending delegates to the Conference.

It was easy to see that Vahdettin's gang, consisting of Tevfik Pasha and other Pashas of his type, this gang whose only interest consisted in clinging to the tottering feet of a sullied throne, did nothing else but make their secret plans to be agreed to at any price. After I had sent Tevfik Pasha a reply to the telegram sent to me which, however, he pretended never to have received, he appealed directly to the Presidency of the Assembly in a further telegram on 29 October 1922 in which he assumed the title of Grand Vizier.

The form given to the contents of this message was of the type peculiar to the Tevfik Pashas of the old regime. In this telegram Tevfik Pasha and his colleagues went so far in their impudence as to speak of the services which they had rendered in the attainment of the successes that had been achieved.

The discussion on the question about which we are speaking began on 30 October 1922. There were many speakers and they talked a great deal. They spoke about the different Cabinets which had followed one another in İstanbul, of the time of Ferit Pasha, which was succeeded by the comedy of Tevfik Pasha, of the types without conscience and without common sense who played a part in it and they demanded the application of the law in respect to them. "Persons of such mentality," they said, "persons who make us such idiotic proposals ... are in reality people who give their signatures to prove the historical character of the Sublime Porte, and are more devoted to it than anything else."

A motion was drafted describing the breakdown of the Ottoman Empire and the birth of a New Turkish State and confirming that, in accordance with the Constitution Act, sovereign rights belonged to the people. This motion, signed by more than eighty comrades, also bore my signature.

After this motion had been read, two of the representatives placed themselves at the head of those who had taken up an attitude of serious opposition. One of these was Colonel Selahattin Bey, representative for Mersin, and the other was Ziya Hurşit, who was subsequently hanged in Izmir. They openly declared that they were convinced that the Sultanate ought not to be abolished.

The Assembly did not sit on 31 October 1922; on that day a meeting of the Party for the Defence of the Rights took place. I made some statements there to prove the necessity for the abolition of the Sultanate. The same question formed the subject of long debates in the Assembly on 1 November 1922.

Speaking of the history of Islam and of Turkey, based on historical facts, I showed that the Caliphate and the Sultanate could be separated from one another and that the Grand National Assembly could possess national sovereignty. I asserted that the execution of the Caliph Mutassam by Hulagu had put an end to the Caliphate and that unless Yavuz, who conquered Egypt in the year 1517, had not attributed importance to a fugitive who held the title of Caliph, we could not have had the title handed down to our days.

Thereupon the motions concerning this questions were referred to three Committees, that of the Constitution Act, of the Sharia and of Justice.

It was certainly difficult for these committees to meet and solve the question in conformity with the aim we were pursuing. I had to follow these matters very closely in person.

These three committees met in one room. After the election of Hodja Müfit Efendi as chairman, they began to deliberate. The gentlemen of the Hodjas belonging to the Committee of the Sharia put forward the point of view that the Caliphate could not be separated from the Sultanate. They relied on well-known fallacies and absurdities. Those who spoke openly in opposition to these assertions did not venture to come forward themselves. We followed the debates from a corner of the crowded room. It is evident that it would have been of no avail to expect a settlement of the question in the direction at which we were aiming from such a debate at this. I was perfectly certain about that. Finally, I asked the chairman of the mixed Committee for permission to speak, and, standing on the bench in front of me, I made this statement in a loud voice: "Gentlemen," I declared, "neither the sovereignty nor the right to govern can be transferred by one person to anybody else by an academic debate. Sovereignty is acquired by force, by power and by violence. It was by violence that the sons of Osman acquired the power to rule over the Turkish nation and to maintain their rule for more than six centuries. It is now the nation that revolts against these usurpers, puts them in their place and actually carries on their sovereignty. This is an actual fact. It is no longer a question of knowing whether we want to leave this sovereignty in the hands of the nation or not. It is simply a question of stating a reality, something which is already an accomplished fact and which must be accepted unconditionally as such. And this must be done at any price. If those who are assembled here, the Assembly and everybody else would find this quite natural, it would be very appropriate from my point of view. Conversely, the reality will nevertheless be manifested in the necessary form, but in that event it is possible that some heads will be cut off.

In this way, the curtain fell on the last act of the overthrow and breakdown of the Ottoman Monarchy.

The first sentence of an official telegram on 17 November 1922 ran as follows: "Vahdettin left the Palace tonight." You must have read some other sentences of this telegram in the protocol of the sitting of the Assembly on 18 November 1922. The original of this telegram, however, contained another part, the end referring to those persons who could possibly intervene in facilitating his departure and of the steps to be taken for the preservation of the sacred relics.

We Turks are a people who during the whole of our historic existence have been the very embodiment of freedom and independence. Also, we have proved that we are capable of putting an end to the comedy played by the Caliph who exposed himself to humiliations of every description for the miserable object of dragging out an unworthy existence for a few days longer. Acting as we have done, we have confirmed the truth that individuals, and especially those who are base enough to think only of their personal positions and their own lives — even to the injury of the state and nation to which they belong — cannot be of any importance in the mutual relationship of states and nations.

The Grand National Assembly of Turkey proclaimed the fugitive Caliph to have been deposed, and in his stead Abdülmecit Efendi was elected as the last of the Caliphs.

Before the National Assembly proceeded to the election of a new Caliph, every possibility had to be excluded that the newly elected one would yield to the desire to rule and try to place himself for this purpose under any foreign protection. For this reason, I asked Refet Pasha, our delegate in Istanbul, to speak to Abdülmecit Efendi and to get him to sign a document in which he bound himself to complete subjection to the decisions respecting the Caliphate and Sultanate which had been arrived at by the National Assembly.

In the instructions which I sent to Refet Pasha on 18 November 1922 by telegraph in code to Istanbul, I had particularly emphasised the following points:

Abdülmecit Efendi shall bear the title of Caliph of all Muslims. No other title or quality should be added. He is first, through your mediation and first of all by telegram in code, to communicate to us the manifest to the Muslim world which he must prepare. When we have given our consent, the text will be returned to him, also through you and in a telegram in code, and not before then will it be published. The text of the manifesto is mainly to comprise the following points:

(a) He shall explicitly express his satisfaction at having been elected Caliph by the Grand National Assembly of Turkey.

(b) Vahdettin Efendi's conduct shall be submitted to thorough condemnation.

(c) The manifesto shall contain in an appropriate form the first ten Articles of the Constitution, and care shall be taken that their meaning and essential purpose are expressed in a precise form; it is also to emphasise the special character of the Turkish State, the Grand National Assembly and their Government and is to declare that their administrative system is the most appropriate and the most fitting one in the interests and desires of the population of Turkey, as well as of the whole Muslim world.

(d) It shall mention in a praiseworthy manner the services which the democratic national Government of Turkey has rendered, as well as the endeavours worthy of recognition that have been made.

(e) Beyond these points that have been mentioned, the manifesto is not to contain any reference that could be of a political character.

In an open telegram which I sent to Abdülmecit Efendi on 19 November 1922, I informed him that "The Grand National Assembly, being in the possession of the legislative and executive power bestowed upon it by the Constitution Act, according to the wording of which the sovereignty of the Turkish State belongs without reserve or restriction to the nation, and which is constituted by the only true representatives of the nation, had elected him Caliph at their sitting on 18 November 1922 in accord with the principles and for the reasons unanimously agreed to by them on I November of the same year" (Document 265).

Refet Pasha replied to our telegraphic communication in a telegram in code on 19 November 1922. He said that Abdülmecit Efendi had expressed his opinion that it would be possible and opportune for him to put above his signature the title of "Caliph of all Muslims and Servant of the Sacred Places," and that he should wear a cloak and turban, as worn by Mehmet II. the Conqueror, at the Selamlık.

Regarding the contents of the manifesto addressed to the Muslim world, he had excused himself for not being able to say anything with regard to Vahdettin, and he had proposed that the manifesto should be published in the Press of Istanbul in both the Turkish and Arabic languages.

In the answer which I sent to Refet Pasha at the instrument on 20 November 1922 I agreed that the title "Servant of the Sacred Places" should be added to that of Caliph. I regarded it abnormal that the costume of the conqueror should be worn at the Friday ceremonies. I insisted that a frock-coat or a "İstanbuline"* might be worn, but that a military uniform was quite out of the question. I also added that it would be necessary to characterise the moral personality of the late Caliph without mentioning his name, and to describe the decadence into which the nation had fallen under his rule.

In the first sentence of his telegram in code of 20 November 1922 Refet Pasha remarked that Abdülmecit Efendi, in his letter of 29 Rebiü'l-evvel* had used the title "Caliph of the Messenger of Allah, Servant of the two Holy Cities" and had signed the letter "Abdülmecit, Son of Abdülaziz Khan".

Abdülmecit, who had declared that he took our advice, had, therefore, been unable to resist the temptation of substituting the expression "Caliph of the Muslims" by the title "Caliph of the Messenger of Allah" and had used the title "Khan" because of his father's name. After having made some other remarks, he still added that he had abandoned the idea of declaring anything with regard to Vahdettin, because "for the reason of his character and his principles, it would be painful for him to make any such declarations, even if they only referred to despicable actions on the part of other people."

This was the second sentence. The third contained the reply to the telegram I had sent him in my capacity as President of the Assembly to announce to him his election to the Caliphate. His reply was addressed to me personally and was headed: "To His Excellency Marshal Gazi Mustafa Kemal Pasha, President of the Grand National Assembly of Turkey, Ankara."

The fourth paragraph contained a copy of the manifesto to be addressed to the Muslim world. It was carefully pointed out in it that it had been composed in Istanbul, the "High Seat of the Caliphate."

In a telegram we sent on 21 November 1922 we declared that the title "Caliph of the Messenger of Allah" must be altered to "Caliph of the Muslims", as previously communicated. We reminded him that the reply to our telegram informing him of his election as Caliph must be addressed to the Presidency of the Grand National Assembly and not to me personally.

We pointed out that his letter contained forms of expression which touched on questions of a political and general character and that he must abstain from that.

The essential point which I want to emphasise by these explanations, which can easily be regarded as unimportant details, is this:

With regard to myself, I was of the opinion that after the abolition of the monarchy the Caliphate, being only an authority of a similar description under another name, was also abolished. I found it quite natural to express this opinion at a favourable moment. It cannot be maintained that Abdülmecit, who was elected to be Caliph, was quite ignorant of this fact. As, above all, some people were still dreaming of finding the means to bring him into government under the title of Caliph, it was impossible to believe in the naivete of our correspondent and in that of his natural followers.

The plenary sitting of the Lausanne Conference took place on 21 November 1922. His Excellency İsmet Pasha represented Turkey. Hasan Bey, representative for Trabzon, and Rıza Nur Bey, representative for Sinop, constituted the delegation under the leadership of İsmet Pasha. The latter left Ankara for Lausanne in the first days of November.

The results of the Lausanne Conference, which lasted for eight months in two sessions, are known to the world at large.

For some time, I followed the negotiations of the Lausanne Conference from Ankara.

The debates were heated and animated. No positive results regarding the recognition of Turkish rights were noticeable. I found this quite natural, because the questions brought forward on the agenda did not exclusively concern the new regime, which was only three or four years old.

Centuries-old accounts were regulated. It was surely neither a simple nor convenient task to find our way through such a mass of old, confused and rubbishy accounts.

We know that the Ottoman Empire, whose successor was the new Turkish State, was fettered by the Capitulations which existed in the name of old Treaties. The Christian elements enjoyed numerous privileges and favours. The Ottoman Government could not exercise the administration of justice in regard to foreigners dwelling in the Ottoman Empire. It was forbidden to impose taxes on foreigners as were imposed on our own citizens. The Government was also prevented from taking steps against those elements in the interior that undermined the foundations of the State.

The Ottoman Government was also prohibited from securing the means of carrying on their existence in a manner worthy of human beings by the Turkish people, the original element from which they emanated. They could not restore the country, could not build railways and were not even free to establish schools. If we tried to do so the foreigners immediately interfered. In order to secure a luxurious existence for themselves, the Ottoman sovereigns and their Courts had not only placed all the revenues of the country and the nation at their disposal, but they had in addition floated numerous loans, thereby sacrificing not only all the resources of the nation, but even the honour and dignity of the State. And this was done to such an extent that the Empire had become incapable of paying the interest on these loans and was regarded in the eyes of the world as being in a state of bankruptcy.

The Ottoman Empire, whose heirs we were, had no value, no merit, no authority in the eyes of the world. It was regarded as being beyond the pale of international rights and was, as it were, under the tutelage and protection of somebody else.

The monarchy having been abolished and the Caliphate stripped of its powers, it had become very important to get into close touch with the people and once more to study their psychology and spiritual tendencies.

The Assembly had entered upon the last year of their legislative period. I had resolved when the elections took place to transform the Union for the Defence of the Rights of Anatolia and Rumelia into a political party. If peace should be restored, I considered it necessary that the organisations of our union should be converted into a political party and in this regard it also seemed advisable for me to study our army very carefully, for since the victory it had begun to devote itself to its training.

Such were the aims I had in view when I left Ankara on 14 January 1923 to travel through Western Anatolia.

I began at Eskişehir, İzmit, Bursa, İzmir and Balıkesir, collected the people in suitable buildings and had long conversations with those present. I requested that the population should freely ask questions on subjects that were near to their hearts. In order to answer them I delivered long speeches which often lasted for six or seven hours.

The main points on which the population everywhere wanted information were these:

The Lausanne Conference and its results; national sovereignty and the Caliphate, their position and mutual relations; and, further, the political party which they knew I intended to create.

Everywhere I gave a comprehensive idea of the negotiations at the Lausanne Conference, as they took place, and

I tried to calm the nation down by expressing my conviction that we should arrive at a positive result.

The people were justified in showing their curiosity and anxiety about the question of the position of national sovereignty and the Caliphate, as well as the character of their mutual relations, because, while the National Assembly, by their resolution of 1 November 1922 had proclaimed that the form of Government based on personal sovereignty had become part of history from 16 March 1920, the Hodjas — as for instance, Şükrü — had begun agitations pretending that the "public opinion of the Muslim world would be alarmed and perturbed." They said: "The Caliphate and the Government are the same thing, and no human being and no Assembly has the right to annul the rights and authority of the Caliphate." They dreamed of maintaining the personal monarchy abolished by the Assembly under the form of the Caliphate and to place the Caliph in the position of the Sultan.

In fact, a reactionary party published a pamphlet under the title of "The Islamic Caliphate and the Grand National Assembly," which was signed by Hodja Şükrü, representative for Afyon Karahisar. It was in İzmit that my attention was attracted to this pamphlet having been published at Ankara on 15 January 1923, and to its having been distributed among all the members of the Assembly. On its outside cover was simply "1923."

It was discovered, however, that the pamphlet, which had been prepared and printed while I was still at Ankara, had been distributed on the very day of my departure, namely, 15 January. Hodja Şükrü Efendi and his colleagues wanted to represent the national Assembly simply as an advisory council to the Caliph and the Caliph himself as President of this Assembly and thereby as the Head of the State. Their favourite absurdity was the statement that: "The Caliph is dependent on the Assembly which for their part are dependent on the Caliph."

On the other hand, the Caliph was the object of some signs of loyalty which could inspire him with a certain amount of hope.

I must call attention to the fact that Hodja Şükrü Efendi, as well as the politicians who pushed forward his person and signature, had intended to substitute the sovereign bearing the title of Sultan or Sultan by a monarch with the title of Caliph. The only difference was that, instead of speaking of a monarch of this or that country or nation, they now spoke of a monarch whose authority extended over a population of three hundred million souls belonging to manifold nations and dwelling in different continents of the world. Into the hands of this great monarch, whose authority was to extend over the whole of Islam, they placed as the only power that of the Turkish people, that is to say, only from 10 to 15 millions of these three hundred million subjects. The monarch designated under the title of Caliph was to guide the affairs of these Muslim peoples and to secure the execution of the religious prescriptions which would best correspond to their worldly interests. He was to defend the rights of all Muslims and concentrate all the affairs of the Muslim world in his hands with effective authority.

The sovereign entitled Caliph was to maintain justice among the three hundred million Muslims on the globe, to safeguard the rights of these peoples, to prevent any event that could encroach upon order and security, and confront every attack which the Muslims would encounter from the side of other nations. It was to be part of his attributes to preserve by all means the welfare and spiritual development of Islam.

So long as the sentiments and knowledge of mankind with regard to religious questions are not yet freed from myths and purified in the light of true science, we shall find historians everywhere who play a religious comedy. We must actually belong to those "beings who live wholly in Allah," like Şükrü Hodja, not to be enlightened about the absurdities of the illogical ideas and impracticable prescriptions which they sow in all directions.

If the Caliph and Caliphate, as they maintained, were to be invested with a dignity embracing the whole of Islam, ought they not to have realised in all justice that a crushing burden would be imposed on Turkey, on her existence; her entire resources and all her forces would be placed at the disposal of the Caliph?

According to their declarations, the Caliph-Monarch would have the right of jurisdiction over all Muslims and all Muslim countries, that is to say, over China, India, Afganistan, Persia, Iraq, Syria, Palestine, Hijaz, Yemen, Assyr, Egypt, Tripoli, Tunis, Algeria, Morocco, and the Sudan. It is well known that this Utopia has never been realised. The pamphlet itself signed by Hodja Şükrü emphasises that the Muslim communities have always been separated from one another under the influence of aims that were diametrically opposed to one another; that the Umayyids of Andalusia, the Alids of Morocco, the Fatimids of Egypt and the Abbassids of Bagdad have each created a Caliphate, that is to say, a monarchy of their own. In Andalusia, there were even communities embracing a thousand souls, each of which was "a Commander of the Faithful and a Torch of Faith." Would it have been logical or reasonable to pretend to be ignorant of this historic truth and to designate under the title of Caliph a ruler destined to govern all the Muslim States and nations, some of which were independent, while most of them were under a foreign protectorate? Particularly the fact that a mere handful of men consisting of the population of Turkey, burdened with the anxiety of supporting such a sovereign, would it not have been the surest means for strangling this people? Those who say: "The attributes of the Caliph are not of a spiritual kind," and "the basis of the Caliphate is material strength, the temporal power of the Government," proved thereby that for them the Caliphate was the State. And thereby it could easily be perceived that they pursued the aim of putting at the head of the Turkish Government some personality bearing the title of Caliph.

I made statements everywhere that were necessary to dispel the uncertainty and anxiety of the people concerning this question of the Caliphate. I formerly declared: "We cannot allow any person, whatever his title may be, to interfere in questions relating to the destiny, activity and independence of the new State which our nation has now erected. The nation itself watches over the preservation and independence of the State which they have created, and will continue to do so for all time." I gave the people to understand that neither Turkey nor the handful of men she possesses could be placed at the disposal of the Caliph so that he might fulfill the mission attributed to him, namely, to found a State comprising the whole of Islam. The Turkish nation is incapable of undertaking such an irrational mission.

For centuries our nation was guided under the influence of these erroneous ideas. But what has been the result of it? Everywhere they have lost millions of men. "Do you know," I asked, "how many sons of Anatolia have perished in the scorching deserts of the Yemen? Do you know the losses we have suffered in holding Syria and Iraq and Egypt and in maintaining our position in Africa? And do you see what has come out of it? Do you know?

"Those who favour the idea of placing the means at the disposal of the Caliph to brave the whole world and the power to administer the affairs of the whole of Islam must not appeal to the population of Anatolia alone but to the great Muslim communities which are eight or ten times as rich in men.

"The New Turkey, the people of the New Turkey, have no reason to think of anything else but their own existence and their own welfare. She has nothing more to give away to others."

To enlighten the people on still another point, I employed these expressions: "Let us accept for a moment that Turkey would take this mission upon herself and would devote herself to the aim of uniting and leading the whole Islamic world and that she would succeed in achieving this aim. Very good, but suppose these nations whom we want to subject and administer would say to us: 'You have rendered great services and assistance to us for which we are thankful to you, but we want to remain independent. We do not suffer anybody else to interfere in our independence and sovereignty. We are capable of leading and administering ourselves.'

"In such a case, will the efforts and sacrifices made by the people of Turkey result in anything more than earning thanks and a benediction?

"It is evident they intended that the people of Turkey should be sacrificed to a mere caprice, to a fancy, to a dream. To this effect the idea of attributing functions and authority to a Caliph and a Caliphate can be comprehended."

I asked the people: "Will Persia or Afganistan, which are Muslim States, recognise the authority of the Caliph in a single matter? Can they do so? No, and this is quite justifiable, because it would be in contradiction to the independence of the State, to the sovereignty of the people."

I also warned the people by saying that "the error of looking upon ourselves as masters of the world must cease."

I will by no means deny the beauty of the idea of the "United States of the World" the establishment of which would produce the result that the experience, knowledge and conceptions of mankind at large would be developed and uplifted, that mankind would abandon Christianity, Islam, Buddhism, and that a pure, spotless, simplified religion, understood by all and of a universal character, will be established, and that men will understand that they have lived hitherto in a place of misery amidst disputes and shame, their desires and gross appetites, and that they will decide to eradicate all infectious germs which have hitherto poisoned both body and soul".

In our midst also an idea similar to this plan has been formed for the purpose of satisfying the adherents of the Caliphate and a Pan Islam, on the condition, however, that it would not become a source of difficulties for Turkey.

The theory put forward was this:

"Muslim communities dwelling in Europe, Asia, Africa and in other regions, sooner or later in future will attain the liberty and ability of acting according to their will and carry out their wishes. And then, if they think it expedient and advantageous, they will find certain points of union and concord in accordance with the exigencies of the century.

Every State, every community undoubtedly has needs that could be satisfied and protected by other States and communities; States have reciprocal interests.

During the time we had been engaged with the question of the Caliphate and of religion we had become clear with regard to the fact that one point of the Constitution Act offered a problem to public opinion and especially to the intellectuals.

Article 7 of the Constitution Act of 20 January 1921 and Article 26 of the Constitution Act of 21 April 1924 refer to the authority of the Grand National Assembly. In the beginning of the Article we find it laid down as the first duty of the Assembly that "the prescriptions of the Sharia should be put into force."

But now there are people who cannot understand the nature of these prescriptions nor what is meant by the "prescriptions of the Sharia."

The authorities of the Grand National Assembly referred to and enumerated in the same Article, that is to say, relating to the publication, amendment and interpretation of the laws, their repeal and cancellation, etc. as clear and comprehensible in themselves that the existence of an independent formula, such as "the putting into force of the prescriptions of the Sharia," cannot and are not intended to express anything other than the "prescriptions of the law."

Any other interpretation would be incompatible with the conception of modern law; unless a totally different meaning were to be attached to the expression "prescriptions of the Sharia."

I was myself in the chair when the first Constitution Act was drafted. Many attempts were made to explain that the expression "prescriptions of the Sharia" had nothing whatever to do with the law which we were drafting. But it was impossible to convince those who, guided by a wrong conception, attached quite another interpretation to this expression.

The second point consists of the sentence at the beginning of Article 2 of the new Constitution Act: "The State religion of Turkey is Islam."

Long before this sentence was incorporated in the text of the Constitution Act, during the course of long meetings and consultations with journalists from İzmit and İstanbul, one of my interviewers at İzmit put the following question: "Will the new State have a religion?"

If a State having amongst its subjects elements professing different religions and being compelled to act justly and impartially towards all of them and allowing justice to prevail in its tribunals equally towards foreigners as well as its own subjects, it is obliged to respect freedom of opinion and conscience. It is surely not justified in making restrictions in this natural authority of the State by attributing other qualities to it which are capable of having an ambiguous meaning.

When we say that "the official language of the State is Turkish," everybody understands what this means; everybody understands that it is natural that the Turkish language should be used in official affairs. But will the sentence "The State religion of Turkey is Islam" be accepted and understood in the same way? It must naturally be criticised and explained.

I could not answer the question put to me by the journalist, my interviewer, with: "The State cannot have a religion." On the contrary, I answered: "It has one — Islam." I immediately felt the need of commenting on and qualifying my answer by the following sentence: "The Muslim religion includes the freedom of religious opinion." Thereby I wanted to express that the State is obliged to respect freedom of opinion and freedom of conscience. Undoubtedly my interviewer did not find my reply reasonable and repeated his question in the following form: "Did you mean to say that the State will identify itself with a particular religion?"

"I do not know," I said, "whether this will be the case or not." I wanted to end the debate, but this was not possible. "Then," they told me, "the State will prevent me from expressing an opinion that corresponds to my views and thoughts on any question. And if the case should arise I shall be punished for having done so."

"But will everybody discover a way to silence his conscience?"

At that time I was thinking of two things. The first was: Will not every grown up person in the new Turkish State be free to choose his own religion?

Then I recalled Hodja Şükrü's proposal which was: "Some of my colleagues among the Ulema (Religious Muslim Men) as well as myself, consider it to be our duty to publish our common thoughts, as well the prescriptions of Islam, which are confirmed and set forth in the books of the Sharia. . . to enlighten the minds of the Muslims, which have unfortunately been led astray."

I also recalled the following sentence: "The Caliphate of Islam has been entrusted by the Prophet to protect and perpetuate the religious prescriptions and to be the representative of the Prophet in the exercise of the Sharia."

But to quote the words of the Hodja would be equivalent to an attempt to abolish national sovereignty.

But, on the other hand, we did not have to consider the bulk of the knowledge of the Hodjas comprised in formulae which had been dictated in the time of Caliph Yezid and which had been appropriated to a regime of absolutism.

Consequently, who would be deceived if the expressions "State" and "Government" were enwrapped in the cloak of religion and the Sharia? Although the meaning of these expressions, as well as of the authorities of the Assembly, are now clear to everybody, what need is there for this deception?

This was the actual truth; but I did not wish to discuss this subject any longer with the journalist on that day at İzmit.

After the Republic was proclaimed and while the Constitution was being drafted a formula was added in the same way to Article 2 of the Act, which deprived this Article of any sense. And this was done with the intention of not playing into the hands of those who are only lying in wait for a pretext to give the expression "Government of laymen" the meaning of being hostile to religion.

The superfluous expressions which were incompatible with the modern character of the new Turkish State and our republican regime, contained in Articles 2 and 26 of the Act, constitute compromises to which the revolution and the Republic ought to have agreed, so as to satisfy the exigencies of the time.

When the first favourable opportunity arises, the nation must eliminate these superfluities from our Constitution Act.

I had long conversations everywhere with people on the formation of a political party.

On 7 December 1922, I declared, through the Press in Ankara, my intention of forming a new party on a democratic basis under the name of the "People's Party." I called upon all patriots and men of Art and Science for help and co-operation in drawing up the programme which should guide this party.

The views I received in writing from various people, as well, also, as the direct exchange of opinion with the people, were very helpful, indeed, to me.

At last, on 8 April 1923, I set down my views in the form of nine leading principles. This programme, which I had published during the elections for the Second Grand National Assembly, served as the foundation for the formation of our party.

This programme contained essentially all that we had carried through up to that day. There were, however, some important and vital questions which had not been included in this programme, such as, for instance, the proclamation of the Republic, the abolition of the Caliphate, the suppression of the Ministry of Education, and that of the Medreses and Tekkes and the introduction of the hat.

I held the opinion that it was not appropriate to give into the hands of ignorant men and reactionaries the means of poisoning the whole nation by introducing these questions into the programme be- fore the hour had come to do so, because I was absolutely sure that these questions would be settled at the proper time and that the people in the end would be satisfied.

There were some people who found that the programme which I had published was inadequate and too short for a political party. They said that the "People's Party" had no programme. The programme which is known by the name of "Principles" was actually no book of the kind that these slanderers had seen and were accustomed to, but it was full of substantial and practical matter.

The "Principles" sufficed for the foundation and activity of the People's Party; as is known to you, the title of the party was in course of time changed to the "Republican People's Party," by the addition of the word "Republican."

I shall now revert to the Lausanne Conference.

The Conference was interrupted on 4 February 1923. The delegations of the Entente Powers presented the draft of a Peace Treaty to our delegation. This contained nothing but the summary of the debates that had taken place during the course of two months. This draft contained provisos that were contrary to the spirit and sense of our independence. The judicial, financial and economic provisions were, above all others, unnacceptable. We were absolutely compelled to reject this draft. In reply, our delegation wrote a letter to the following effect: "We want to sign a peace on the points about which we have come to an agreement." In the letter it was also said:

"We shall examine the questions of second and third Orders. These proposals must be regarded as non-existant if they should be repudiated by the Entente Powers."

The proposal of our delegation was not taken into consideration; instead of a rupture, they spoke of a suspension in the negotiations. The delegations of the individual states returned home. Our delegation did the same. Regarding myself, I was just on my return journey from Western Anatolia. On 18 February 1923, I met İsmet Pasha at Eskişehir and we returned together to Ankara.

After having heard that İsmet Pasha's return to Ankara coincided with mine, a strange and inexplicable mentality had apparently been shown in Ankara ... It was regarded as a disadvantage that İsmet Pasha had met me and exchanged his views with me before he had come to Ankara and entered into communication with the Government and the Assembly ... It was asserted that there might be people who would interpret this meeting unfavourably . . . The one who wrote this to me was Rauf Bey, President of the Council of Ministers. I naturally placed no importance on this communication. On the contrary, I arranged my journey in a way that I should meet İsmet Pasha at Eskişehir, in order to be able to converse with him at the earliest possible moment. After our return to Ankara İsmet Pasha explained the situation in the Council of Ministers and asked for further instructions.

It was thought necessary to ask for the advice of the Assembly. The question was put before them. The debates and the discussions of the Assembly on this subject lasted for many long days.

We felt that the adherents of the opposition had become irreconcilable enemies to our delegation and İsmet Pasha . . . After peace had practically been made, he had not concluded it but had returned ... The delegation had acted contrary to the orders of the Council of Ministers.

The attacks which began in the secret sitting of 27 February 1923 were continued with the same violence and passion till 6 March 1923; I was obliged to take part in these debates from the beginning to the end. The opposition truly gave the impression that they did not know what they wanted. The result was that the Assembly was not capable of coming to any resolution, either for or against.

Finally, I declared that the delegation was responsible to the Council of Ministers, who on their part are responsible to the Assembly. The Assembly must give new instructions to the Cabinet. Based on these instructions, the latter must give special instructions to the delegation. It was neither useful nor possible for the Assembly to occupy themselves with details.

I also expressed my point of view regarding these instructions: "It would not be possible to begin a discussion of the temporary suspension of the Mosul question, but that it was most essential to enforce in certain and uncompromising form the independence and right of the nation and country in every administrative, political, economic, financial and other questions, and to obtain the complete evacuation of the recovered territories."

I added to my remarks the following: "Our delegation fully and completely fulfilled the duty entrusted to them. They have maintained the dignity of our nation and Assembly. If you are desirous of bringing the Peace question to a successful issue the Assembly must also morally support the delegation to enable them to continue their work. When you act in this manner we shall be able to hope that we might enter into an era of peace."

The Lausanne Conference met again on 23 April 1923. Whilst our delegation were endeavouring to restore peace at Lausanne I occupied myself with the new elections.

The representatives who accepted our point of view and wanted to become representatives, first of all told me that they accepted the "Principles" and shared our views. It was my task to present the list of candidates and to publish the names of those candidates at a given time in the name of the party.

The nation made the "Principles" which I have published completely their own. It became evident that it was impossible for those who were in opposition to the "Principles" and even to my own personality to be elected representatives by the nation.

The second legislative period of the Grand National Assembly of Turkey coincided with a happy transition period in the history of the New Turkey. Our four years' fight for independence was crowned by a peace worthy of our national past.

The Peace signed at Lausanne on 24 July 1923 was ratified by the Assembly on 24 August of the same year.

After the armistice of Mudros, the enemy Powers had four times made peace proposals to Turkey. The first one was the draft of Sevres. This draft had not been the result of any negotiation. It was drawn up by the Entente Powers with the participation of M. Venizelos, the Greek Prime Minister, and had been signed by Vahdettin's Government on 10 August 1920.

This draft was not even regarded as a basis for discussion by the Grand National Assembly of Turkey.

The second Peace proposition took place at the end of the London Conference which met after the battle of İnönü. This proposition actually contained some alterations of the Sevres Treaty, but it must be admitted that it included the maintenance of all stipulations in this treaty of those questions which were passed over in silence.

These proposals remained without result, and without giving rise to a discussion on our part, as meanwhile the second battle of İnönü had begun.

The third Peace proposal was made by the Foreign Ministers of the Entente Powers who had assembled in Paris on 22 March 1922, that is to say, after the victory of the Sakarya and after the agreement arrived at with the French at Ankara, at a time when a speedy offensive from our side was expected.

In these proposals the system of taking the Sevres Treaty as a basis was actually abandoned, but they were in substance far from satisfying our national claims.

The fourth proposal is constituted by the negotiations which led to the conclusion of the Lausanne Treaty.

The Treaty of Lausanne is the document which reveals in a decisive manner the failure of a vast plot which had been hatching for centuries against the Turkish nation, a plot which they believed they had carried to success through the Sevres Treaty. It is a political victory which was not matched in the whole of Ottoman history.

I wish to enlighten public opinion by speaking about a question which had arisen during the negotiations at Lausanne and about which rumours had been spread after the conclusion of peace. This question concerns the conflict which arose between İsmet Pasha, the leader of the Delegation, and Rauf Bey, President of the Council of Ministers.

Both Rauf Bey and İsmet Pasha were very obstinate in their opinions, and had both used very energetic language in expressing them. Rauf Bey found himself in a sphere of propaganda where it was easy for him to shine in the eyes of the Assembly and of public opinion. He defended the following thesis:

"After the brilliant victory, we cannot abandon our claim for reparations from the Greeks who have devastated our country. The Entente Powers might leave us alone and unimpeded facing the Greeks. We shall regulate our accounts with them."

İsmet Pasha, regarding the question of peace to its full extent and aiming at its realisation on its great lines, found himself during these days of conflict with the President of the Council of Ministers forced into a situation in which he had to propose sacrifices regarding the Greeks. It was naturally not very easy to explain to the public the justness of this point of view, and the necessity of its acceptance.

The attitude which I assumed in general towards both of the parties was nothing less than amiable. I made use of the system of agreeing with one party and imposing silence on the other.

So as to explain to you how I faced the situation and in what form I settled my point of view, I shall submit to you verbally the text of the communication which was addressed to İsmet Pasha after the sitting of the Council of Ministers on 25 May 1923.

Two telegrams in code were sent to İsmet Pasha. The one containing the decision of the Council of Ministers bore the signature of Rauf Bey; it was dictated by me to Kazım Pasha.

From the contents of the telegrams we sent to İsmet Pasha, it became clearly evident that in principle, we were willing to abandon our claims for reparations for the cession of Karaağaç.

We drew İsmet Pasha's attention, however, to the necessity of securing on the essential questions a favourable solution of those points which we regarded as being especially important and in need of settlement. This was in fact also the sense and the intention which İsmet Pasha himself derived from these communications.

We shall naturally constantly use the question of the Greek reparations as an argument for the solution of all questions in suspense. We have kept this option for ourselves.

The settlement of the Greek reparations question has not raised the hope that a satisfactory solution of other questions can be attained by threatening us.

On the contrary, the possibility of threats has been removed. The situation has become much calmer again. If it should sooner or later come to a rupture, the Greek army will either not march because they have no special reason to, or we shall prove that they are marching with the others and on their account.

Both these eventualities appear to us more advantageous, morally and materially, than that the Greek troops should open a campaign under the pretext of reparations.

There is no reason to fear that the Council of Ministers will have to face a *fait accompli*.

Our procedure can at most lead to differences with regard to the form which is due to our way of contemplating the situation as a whole.

At last the Conference came to an end in the middle of July.

After the execution of the protocol for the evacuation which forms an addition to the Lausanne Treaty, Turkey was completely freed from foreign occupation, and had thus realised the integrity of her territory. It was a question of the future to legally fix the seat of the Government of the New Turkey.

Considerations of all kinds categorically demanded the this seat could only be in Anatolia and in Ankara.

As the result of our meeting in Çankaya, the Council of Ministers sent in their resignations in the following letter which was signed by all of them.

"We are of the firm conviction that Turkey is absolutely in need of a very strong Cabinet, which possesses the absolute confidence of the Assembly, in order to bring the important and difficult task which she has to fulfil towards the interior as well as the exterior to a happy issue. We have therefore the honour of respectfully informing you that we send our resignations for the purpose of contributing to the formation of a Cabinet which in every respect enjoys the confidence of the High Assembly and is supported by their co-operation." In the afternoon of Saturday, 27 October 1923, this letter was communicated to the party in a full sitting which was held under my presidency and was read afterwards officially in the Assembly, which met on the same day at about 5 o'clock. As soon as the resignation of the Cabinet was made known, the representatives began to put up Ministerial lists, and met in groups either in the rooms of the Assembly or their private dwellings. This state of affairs lasted till the late hours of 28 October. No group was successful in putting up a list which would have been acceptable to the whole of the Assembly and suitable to be accepted favourably by the general opinion of the nation. Considering the respective candidates for each Ministry, they found themselves confronted by so many applicants that the difficulties in giving preference to one of the lists which contained certain names to another one, disheartened those who had charged themselves with making the lists and brought them to despair. It is true that certain Istanbul journals did not lose the opportunity of attracting attention by the reproduction of the pictures of some individuals who were mentioned as "notable and honourable persons" and who would be suitable in their opinion of being chosen as President of the Council.

At a late hour on 28 October I was asked by the leading Committee of the party to be present at their meeting which was then taking place. The President was Fethi Bey. He declared that the Comittee had put forward a list of the candidates and they had asked me, as President of the party, to come as they wanted to hear my opinion about it. I ran through the list and declared that I approved of it, but also that the persons who were mentioned on it ought to be asked for their opinions. Everybody agreed to my proposal. Thus, we asked, for example, Yusuf Kemal Bey, who came into question for the Foreign Ministry. He told us that he declined to accept this office. I concluded from this fact as well as from similar occurrences that the leading committee of the party also was not able to put forward a final and acceptable list. I left the members of the committee, advising them to produce a final list after further consultations with the persons who would come into question. It was already dark. At the moment, I left the building of the Assembly to return to Çankaya, I met Kemalettin Sami Pasha and Halit Pasha in the lobby waiting for me. I had read in the papers under the heading of "Farewell and Reception Ceremonies" that these Pashas had arrived in Ankara on the very day of Ali Fuat Pasha's departure. I had not seen them up to the hour of this meeting in the lobby. When I learned that they had waited till a late hour to see me, I asked them through Kazım Pasha to come and dine with me. I also told İsmet Pasha, Kazım Pasha as well as Fethi Bey to accompany me to Çankaya. When I arrived at Çankaya I found there Fuat Bey, Representative for Rize, and Ruşen Eşref Bey, Representative for Afyon Karahisar, who had also come to talk to me. I also asked them to stay to dinner. During the meal, I declared: "Tomorrow we shall proclaim the Republic." The Comrades present hastened to join in my opinion. We got up, and immediately afterwards I drafted a short programme of action containing the role which I assigned to each of the Comrades.

You have noticed that in order to decide on the proclamation of the Republic, it was neither necessary for me to call together all my Comrades nor to debate or discuss the question with them. I did not doubt that they were naturally and in principle, of the same opinion as I was.

Some persons, however, who were not in Ankara at the time and who, by the way, had nothing to say on this question, believed that they should use the fact that the Republic had been proclaimed, without previously asking them and getting their consent, as a pretext for dissatisfaction and contradiction.

The Comrades who were with me that night left early. Only İsmet Pasha was my guest at Çankaya. When we were left alone, we drafted a law. The articles of the Constitutional Law of 20 January 1921 referring to the State Constitution I had altered as follows: At the end of the first article I added the sentence: "The form of Government of the Turkish State is Republic." Article 3 was altered in the following way: "The Turkish State is administered by the Grand National Assembly. The latter directs the individual branches of the administration into which the Government is divided through the mediation of the Ministers."

We drafted in addition the following articles for the purpose of making Articles 8 and 9 of the Constitutional Law clearer:

"The President of the Turkish Republic will be elected in a full sitting of the Grand National Assembly by its members and for the time of a legislative period.

"The mandate of the President lasts till the election of a new President. The President is eligible for re-election.

"The President of the Republic is the head of State. In this capacity, he presides over the National Assembly as well as the Council of Ministers when he believes it necessary.

"The President of the Council is elected by the Chief of the State from the members of the Assembly, after which the other Ministers will be elected by the President of the Council from among the said members.

"Thereupon the President of the Republic submits the list of the entire Cabinet to the Assembly for approval. If the Assembly is not sitting, the approval will be postponed till the next sitting."

The Commission and the Assembly added to these articles the article which is known to you concerning religion and language.

I shall now describe to you what happened in Ankara on Monday, 29 October 1923:

On this day the group of the People's Party assembled at 10 o'clock in the morning under the Presidency of Fethi Bey, President of the leading Committee. A discussion was opened up with regard to the election of the Cabinet.

Eyüp Sabri Efendi (Representative for Konya) was of the following opinion:

"We have elected His Excellency the Gazi as arbitrator. To say that we are deprived of the right to alter the Constitutional Law would be equal to admitting our illegitimacy. It is quite evident that the Assembly is competent for the alteration of this law. It is necessary that the form of our Government should be Republic."

Then İsmet Pasha spoke and expressed the following: "It is absolutely necessary to accept the motion of the leader of the party. Everybody knows that we are discussing the form of Government to be adopted. If we do not succeed in coming to the end of these discussions and formulating the result, we shall perpetuate the crisis and the chaos. Allow me to tell you my experience. The European diplomats have drawn my attention to the following point: 'The State has no head,' they said; 'in the present form of your Government, the President of the Assembly is the head which means that you are waiting for another.'

"This is the point of view of Europe, but we ourselves do not see things in this light. The nation is actually mistress of her own destiny; it is sovereign. Why do we hesitate to give a legal expression to the real facts? The proposal of electing a Minister of the Council without there being a President of the Republic would undoubtedly be illegal. The motion of His Excellency the Gazi must receive legal force so that the election of the President of the Council can be made legal and possible. It is absurd to prolong this state of affairs which is causing the general weakness. The Party must act according to the requirements and the responsibilities which they have assumed towards the whole nation."

The sitting of the party was closed and the meeting of the Assembly immediately opened. It was six o'clock in the evening. Whilst the Commission of the Constitutional Law carefully examined the motion and prepared their report, the Assembly deliberated on certain other questions.

At last, İsmet Pasha, the Vice-President, who presided, declared:

"The Commission of the Constitutional Law urgently proposes to discuss the motion for the amendment of this law."

Shouts of approbation were heard; the report was read and put forward for discussion. Finally, the law was accepted after speeches by different representatives who were greeted with shouts of "Long live the Republic!"

Thereupon the election of the President was put to the vote. İsmet Pasha announced the result in the following words:

"One hundred and fifty-eight Representatives have participated in the election of the President of the Republic. By 158 votes they have unanimously elected His Excellency the Gazi Mustafa Kemal Pasha, Representative for Ankara, President."

As is known, the first Cabinet was formed by İsmet Pasha and Fethi Bey was elected President of the Assembly. The proclamation of the Republic was enthusiastically received by the nation. This enthusiasm was manifested everywhere by brilliant demonstrations.

Only two or three newspapers in Istanbul and a few persons who were still united in this town hesitated to participate in the sincere and general joy of the nation. They felt uneasy about it and began to criticise those who had intervened for the purpose of securing the Republic.

It is known that according to the wording of this Constitutional Law the President of the Assembly has the right to sign in the name of the Assembly. It has also been foreseen that the President is at the same time the natural President of the Council of Ministers, but it is not expressly stipulated that he is the Head of State.

Considering the conditions and conceptions which existed at the time when this Constitutional Law was elaborated, it is easily to be understood that at that time the necessity existed for omitting an important and essential point in the law.

This omission resulted, up to the day of the proclamation of the Republic, in nourishing the hope of those who, in spite of the existence of the National Assembly and their Government, persisted in the belief that, after the abolition of the monarchy, the Caliph was the Chief of the State. According to the system which Rauf Bey pointed out to be the most eligible, he undoubtedly regarded the Caliph as the Chief of the State. The real reason for the alarm of Rauf Bey and his supporters after the proclamation of the Republic was the fact that the President had been endowed with the dignity of the Head of State.

We must indeed admit that those who tried to attribute special qualities and authorities to the Caliphate, and who were happy to regard his benevolence as a "Divine Grace," had every reason to be sorry for the disappointment caused to them by the stipulation of the law: "The President of the Republic is the Head of State."

Rauf Bey did not confess his hostility against the Republic. But does not the fact of his speaking of the necessity for certain conditions for its maintenance on the very day of its proclamation clearly show that he did not believe that the happiness of the nation could be assured through the Republic?

The Republic had, undoubtedly, its supporters and its adversaries. Even if its supporters had tried to explain to the adversaries the considerations they had in view when they thought it time to proclaim the Republic and to prove to them that they had been right in thinking and acting in this manner, can it be expected that they would have succeeded in breaking their intentional stupidity? It is evident that the supporters would have realised their ideal one way or another, if they were capable of doing so, be it by way of insurrection, revolution or in a legal way. This is the duty of everybody who nourishes a revolutionary ideal.

On the other hand, the adversaries would naturally raise protests, sound alarms, undertake reactionary attempts, as Rauf Bey and his supporters had done when the Republic was proclaimed.

At the same time, our Army Inspectors in Istanbul expressed their views and feelings in interviews with journalists and in speeches which they delivered during banquets organised for different occasions.

After the proclamation of the Republic there were also persons and journalists in Istanbul who had the idea of making the Caliph play a role. The newspapers published all sorts of rumours and contradictions about the dismissal of the Caliph which had already taken place or was going to. Finally the following was written:

"We learn that the question is not limited to such a rumour and cannot be solved by a simple contradiction. It is a certain fact that the proclamation of the Republic has raised once more the question of the Caliphate."

It was written that the Caliph, "sitting at his writing desk," had made a statement to an editor of the newspaper "Vatan," that the Caliph enjoyed great popularity amongst all believers; that he received thousands of letters and telegrams from the Muslim world, even from the remotest corners of Asia; that numerous delegations from many places came to him; and the attempt was made of giving the people to understand that the authority of the Caliphate was not of a nature easily to be shaken. Then it was affirmed that the Caliph would not abdicate until Islam had declared itself against him. Simultaneously it was said:

"The Government being absorbed in numerous internal questions has not yet been able to occupy itself with the rights of the Caliphate. "The world of Islam undoubtedly knows that the Government is very much occupied with internal questions and naturally finds that it has not yet been able to dedicate itself to the question of defining the rights of the Caliphate."

Requesting us in such phrases to define the rights of the Caliphate, to a certain degree they threatened us by letting us know that the Muslim world, that had hitherto excused us, could act quite differently in future. On the other hand they tried to attract the attention of Islam for the purpose of inducing it to influence us on this question.

When we read the leading article of the "Tanin" on 11 November 1923 under the heading "And Now the Question of the Caliphate," we saw that those who could not have prevented the proclamation of the Republic were manoeuvring now in order to maintain the Caliphate at any cost. "Tanin" which tried to win the minds of the people for the dynasty by publishing letters from Ottoman princes, alleges in this article that the rights of the dynasty had been the target of a mean attack and that the aggressors belonged to the elite of our party. The article, after having rattled off all that was necessary to discredit the Republic in the eyes of the nation, passed on to the rumour of the Caliph's dismissal and continued as follows: "We find ourselves facing a resolution taken in an underhand way. It is indeed painful to state that the National Assembly is fettered to such a degree and is restricted to register the resolutions which are arrived at outside."

Their intention was to incite the Assembly against us and to assure the fact that after the proclamation of the Republic had been decided upon, the Assembly would abstain at least from carrying through the abolition of the Caliphate.

The chief editor of "Tanin" expressed his views and reflections concerning the Caliphate in the following lines:

"No great wisdom is necessary to understand that if we lose the Caliphate, the Turkish State, comprising between five and ten million souls, would no longer have any weight in the Muslim world, and that we would degrade ourselves, in addition, in the eyes of European diplomacy to the rank of a small state without any importance.

"Is this a national way of thinking? Every Turk who really possesses national feeling must support the Caliphate with all his strength."

As I have already explained my views concerning the Caliphate, I believe it unnecessary to submit these statements to another analysis. I shall restrict myself simply to saying that great sagacity is by no means required to understand that a form of government demanding an unconditional adherence to the Caliphate could not be a republic. I now draw your attention to some other passages of the leading article in the "Tanin."

"To endanger the Caliphate, the heritage of the Ottoman dynasty acquired forever by Turkey, would apparently be an action which could by no means be in accord with reason, patriotism or national sentiment."

The chief editor of "Tanin" had declared himself a republican, but a republican who wanted to see at the head of the republican government a member of the dynasty as Caliph. Without this, he said, the accomplished fact would not be in accord with reason, patriotism or national sentiment.

According to his opinion we were to protect the Caliphate in such a manner that would make it impossible for it ever to escape from us. The manoeuvres undertaken in this spirit had been wrecked . . .

The significance of these articles and the aim of these reasonings are easily explained today. Tomorrow they will be understood still better. Do not suppose that coming generations will be astonished that at the head of those who relentlessly attacked the Republic on the very day of its proclamation were exactly those who pretended to be republicans! On the contrary, the enlightened republican sons of Turkey will have no difficulty in analysing and penetrating into the real mentality of these pretended republicans.

They will easily understand that it was impossible to maintain a form of government which after having proclaimed itself a republic, would have undertaken the obligation of preserving under the title of Caliph at its head a rotten dynasty, and this in a manner which would never have made its removal possible.

In the newspapers of that time two other questions were also brought forward. The one was my illness and the other the services rendered in Turkestan by Enver Pasha, who, it pretended, was still alive ...

It appears that the latter during his stay in foreign countries worked for the cause of Pan-Islamism; he used the title of "Son-in- law of the Caliph," and had this title even engraved on one side of a seal that he had made for himself in Turkestan.

These questions were naturally not constantly discussed without a certain aim in view.

The articles which I have just now quoted, as well as the attitude of certain persons can briefly be defined as follows:

"National sovereignty constitutes the foundation. It is the developed form of the Republic. The Turkish people have realised national sovereignty. It is therefore unnecessary to proclaim the Republic. This is an error. In Turkey exists the most suitable form of government in a constitutional regime with a member of the Ottoman dynasty as Head of State, under the maintenance, how- ever, of the principle of national sovereignty, but without proclaiming a Republic.

"It is the same thing in England, where, in spite of national sovereignty, a king who is also Emperor of India stands at the head of the State."

Those who had rallied around this principle had nearly all revealed themselves through their speeches, their attitude and their writings. It was only to be expected that Rauf Bey would be elected President of this group.

This party, which consisted of elements of different factions, believed it had found in the person of Rauf Bey the most suitable defender for the assertion of their thoughts. They believed that they could found their greatest hopes on him.

Meanwhile Rauf Bey started for Ankara. According to the statements of the newspaper "Vatan," a great crowd accompanied him to the railway station, at the head of which were Kazım Karabekir Pasha, Refet Pasha, Ali Fuat Pasha and Adnan Bey. Speaking of this "Vatan" announced to the nation the political attitude which Rauf Bey would take up in Ankara, in the midst of the Assembly. In a very clear manner it was said that Rauf Bey's activity would not be personal and negative, but that he would have in view the welfare of the nation and respect for the law that he would defend in the Assembly salutary principles by creating an element of order and discipline.

Undoubtedly we ought not to concede the right to the proprietor of the newspaper "Vatan" of providing such information and assertions for himself.

Rauf Bey had been elected representative in the name of our party. He had to follow our programme, and could not adopt an independent position before resigning from our party. Up till now, however, he had not revealed his divergent opinion. In his persistency to remain attached to the party he had even stated that he had no intention of leaving it. There was no explanation for the personal policy he pursued in continuing to belong to the party but violating its discipline.

To pass from the monarchical to the republican system of government we have gone, as you know, through a transition period. During this time, two ideas and concepts constantly clashed against each other. One of them aimed at the maintenance of the monarchy. The supporters of this idea are known. The other idea wanted to put an end to the monarchy and carry the republican *regime* through. That idea was ours.

We hesitated clearly to announce our ideas. Consequently, we were forced to frustrate the application of the ideas professed by the monarchists while we reserved to ourselves the possibilities of application so as to arrive later at a suitable moment for their realisation.

At the promulgation of the new laws, and especially of the law of the Constitution, the Monarchists insisted on their demand to define the rights and prerogatives of the Sultan and Caliph, while we on our part believed it to be useful to pass this point in silence. We therefore said that the moment for it had not yet arrived and that there was no necessity to proceed to do this.

Without referring to the Republic, we began to organise the administration of the State according to the principles of national sovereignty and to give it a form that made its development into a republic possible. It was necessary to persistently to preach that there was no higher authority than the Grand National Assembly and to prove the possibility of the country being governed without the monarchy and without the Caliphate.

Without giving the Head of the State a name, we had practically entrusted the President of the Assembly with his authorities and he effectively exercised them.

The real President of the Assembly was actually its Vice-President. A government existed but it was called the "Government of the Grand National Assembly." We abstained from adopting the Cabinet system, because the monarchists would immediately have stood for the necessity of permitting the Sultan the use of his prerogatives.

During the phases of the struggles of the transition period, we were forced to adopt this form, this system of government of the Grand National Assembly.

Endeavouring to move us to call this form of government explicitly a constitutional *regime,* our adversaries were justified in finding that this form was imperfect, and they expressed their dissent in the following terms: "To whom and to which form of government does the one which you want to create resemble?" To such questions, which were put for the purpose of forcing us to explain ourselves, we had to give such answers as corresponded with the exigencies of the time for the purpose of reducing them to silence.

From the beginning to the end of his declarations, Rauf Bey seemed by his attitude and language to have counted on the generosity and friendly feelings of the members of the party. On the other hand, they were so incoherent and disconnected that it was not easy for everybody to immediately recognise to what extent his speeches were sincere and serious. We must admit that in addition to these reasons, a most important secret factor which had caused hesitation and half- heartedness in our feelings and thoughts was based on the hostile propaganda which was expressed in the words "accomplished fact," "irresponsible," "after the Republic."

It is quite certain that the frame of mind of those who attributed to the situation the importance of a conflict between İsmet Pasha and Rauf Bey, which had nothing to do with the question of the Republic, had promoted the adoption of a senseless decision.

This decision gave to Rauf Bey and his friends the opportunity of still working for some time in the party to accomplish its overthrow.

On the other hand, the articles which were directed against the highest interests of the country and the Republic, and which were continually appearing in certain newspapers in İstanbul, created such an atmosphere in İstanbul that the Assembly believed it necessary to send an Independence Court there.

I shall again discuss the question of the Caliphate and the Caliph which appeared on its own accord in all the problems which were raised and in each stage of our procedure.

In the beginning of the year 1924 it had been decided to carry out war games of some importance. They were to take place in İzmir. For this reason, I headed for İzmir at the beginning of January 1924, and I remained there for nearly two months.

During my stay, I believed that the moment for the abolition of the Caliphate had arrived. I will try to follow the course of this affair as it actually happened.

On 22 January 1924, I received from İsmet Pasha, President of the Council of Ministers, a telegram in code which I will read to you in full:

Telegram in code.

To His Excellency the President of the Turkish Republic.

The First Secretary of the Caliph sends me the following: For some time, there have been articles in the newspapers concerning the situation of the Caliphate and the person of the Caliph which give rise to misunderstandings. The Caliph is very much disturbed about the articles which seem to lower his authority without reason, and particularly the fact that the leaders of the Government coming from time to time to Istanbul, as well as the official bodies, avoid him. The Caliph had thought of making his feelings and wishes on this question known either by sending a Chamberlain to Ankara, or by requesting that a trustworthy person should be sent to him, but he declares that he has abandoned this idea, because he was afraid that this step might be misinterpreted.

The General Secretary writes at length about the question of allocations, and asks that the question should be examined and the necessary steps taken in this matter according to the communications of the Government of 15 April 1923 which stated that the Ministry of Finance would help if the expenses were beyond the means of the Treasury of the Caliphate or outside the obligations of the Caliphate. The question will be discussed in the Council of Ministers. I shall have the honour of informing Your Excellency of the result of the discussion.

(Signed) İsmet.

In reply to this telegram, being by the set, I sent the following reply to İsmet Pasha:

At the set. İzmir.

To His Excellency İsmet Pasha, President of the Council of Ministers, Ankara.

Reply to the telegram in code of 22 January 1924.

It is to the attitude and manner of acting of the Caliph himself that the origin of the misunderstandings and the unfavourable interpretations regarding the Caliphate and the Caliph himself must be attributed. In his private life and especially in his public appearances, the Caliph seems to follow the system of the Sultans, his ancestors. As proof: the Friday ceremonies, the relations of the Caliph to foreign representatives to whom he sends officials; his tours in great pomp; his private life in the Palace where he goes even so far as to receive dismissed officers to whose complaints he is listening, mixing his own tears with theirs. When the Caliph considers his situation, placing himself face to face with the Turkish Republic and the Turkish people, he must adopt as a measure of com- parison the situation of the Caliphate and the Caliph towards the British Empire and the Muslim population of India, of the Government of Afghanistan and the people of Afghanistan. The Caliph himself and the whole world must know in a categoric manner that the Caliph and the office of the Caliph as they are now maintained and exist, have in reality neither a religious nor a political meaning or any right to exist. The Turkish Republic cannot allow itself to be influenced by fallacies and cannot expose its independence and existence to danger.

To complete the analysis, the dignity of the Caliphate can have no other importance for us than that of a historical memory. The demand of the Caliph that the dignitaries of the Turkish Republic and the official bodies should have contact with him constitutes a flagrant violation of the independence of the Republic. The fact that he wants to send his First Chamberlain to Ankara or his demand to inform the Government of his feelings and his wishes through a trustworthy person sent to him, shows likewise that he is taking up a position antagonistic to the Government of the Republic. He has no authority to do this. It is also suggested that he should commission his First Secretary to act as mediator in the correspondence between him and the Government of the Republic. The First Secretary must be told that he must abstain from such impudence. Allocations inferior to those of the President of the Turkish Republic must suffice to secure the means of subsistence of the Caliph. Luxury and pomp are out of place. The question is only to secure a decent living for the Caliph. I do not understand what is meant by the "treasury of the Caliphate." The Caliphate has no treasury, and ought not to have any. If this should be an inheritance of his ancestors, I request you to make inquiries and to give me official and clear information about this question. What are the obligations which the Caliph cannot fulfil with the allocations he receives, and what promises and declarations have been made to him through the communication of the Government dated 15 April? I ask you to inform me of this. A duty which the Government ought to have fulfilled hitherto is to specify and fix the place of residence of the Caliph. There are a great number of palaces in Istanbul which have been built with the money raised from the bread of the people, and the furniture and valuable objects they contain; in short, all is given over to destruction, because the Government has not exactly defined the situation. Rumours are spread to the effect that persons who are attached to the Caliph are selling here and there in Beyoğlu the most precious objects of the palaces. The Government must take the treasures which still remain under its protection. If there is a reason for selling anything, it is for the Government to do so. It is necessary to submit the administrative functions of the Caliphate to a serious examination and reorganisation, for the fact that there are "First Chamberlains" and "First Secretaries" always sustains the dream of power in the mind of the Caliph.

If the French today, a hundred years after the Revolution, are still of the opinion that it would be dangerous for their independence and sovereignty to allow members of the royal family and their confidants to come to France, we, on our part, in the attitude which we have to adopt in view of a dynasty and its confidants who are eager to see on the horizon the sun of absolute power rise again, cannot sacrifice the Republic for considerations of courtesy and sophism. The Caliph must be told exactly who he is and what his office represents and must content himself with this situation. I ask you to proceed in such a manner that the Government takes fundamental and serious steps and to inform me of this.

(Signed) Gazi Mustafa Kemal,
President of the Turkish Republic.

After this exchange of correspondence, İsmet Pasha and Kazım Pasha, Minister of War, arrived in İzmir for the war games. Fevzi Pasha, Chief of the General Staff, was already there. We agreed about the necessity of suppressing the Caliphate. We had decided at the same time to suppress also the Ministry for Religious Affairs and the "Evkaf" and to unify public instruction.

On 1 March 1924 I had to open the Assembly.

The discussion about the Budget began in the Assembly. This afforded us an opportunity of occupying ourselves for a short time with the question of the allocations to the members of the dynasty and the Budget of the Ministry for Religious Affairs and the Evkaf. My comrades began to make remarks and criticisms aimed at attaining the proposed aid. The debate was intentionally prolonged. In the speech which I delivered on I March, the fifth anniversary of the opening of the Assembly, I especially emphasised the three following points:

1. The nation demands that now, in the future, for ever and unconditionally the Republic shall be protected from every assault. The will of the nation can be expressed through the fact that the Republic is founded immediately and completely on the whole of the positive principles which have been put to the test.

2. We declare that it is necessary without loss of time to apply the principle of unity of instruction and

education which has been decided by the vote of the nation.
3. We also recognise that it is indispensable, in order to secure the revival of the Islamic Faith, to disengage it from the condition of being a political instrument, which it has been for centuries through habit.

The group of the Party was invited to a sitting on 2 March. The three points I have just mentioned were brought forward and discussed. We were united in principle. Among other matters received, the following motions were read on 3 March during the first sitting of the Assembly:
1. Draft of the law of Sheikh Safvet Efendi and fifty of his colleagues concerning the abolition of the Caliphate and the expulsion of the Ottoman dynasty from Turkish territory.
2. Draft of the law of Halil Hulki Efendi, representative for Siirt, and fifty of his colleagues concerning the suppression of the Ministry for Religious Affairs, of the Evkaf and the Ministry of the General Staff.
3. Motion of Vasıf Bey, representative for Manisa, and fifty of his colleagues concerning the unification of instruction.

Fethi Bey, who presided, announced: "Gentlemen, there are proposals with numerous signatures,' demanding immediate discussion of these questions of law. I put this demand to the vote."

Without referring it to commissions, Fethi Bey immediately put the motions to the vote, and they were accepted.

The first objection was raised by Halit Bey, representative for Kastamonu. One or two joined him in the course of the discussion. Numerous important speakers ascended the platform and gave long explanations in favour of the propositions. Besides the signatories of the motions, the late Seyit Bey and İsmet Pasha made convincing speeches which were of a highly scientific nature and which will always be worthy of being studied and borne in mind. The discussion lasted for nearly five hours. When the discussion closed at 6.45 p.m. the Grand National Assembly had promulgated Laws No. 429, 430 and 431.

In virtue of these laws, the "Grand National Assembly of Turkey and the Government formed by it is authorised to give legal form to the stipulations which are in force in the Turkish Republic with reference to public affairs and to carry through their application," "The Ministry for Religious Affairs and the Evkaf has been abolished."

All scientific and educational institutions in Turkish territory, all religious schools, are transferred to the Ministry of Public Education.

The Caliph is declared deposed and the office abolished. All members of the deposed Ottoman dynasty are forever forbidden to reside within the frontiers of the territory of the Turkish Republic.

Certain persons who wrongly believed that it was necessary, for religious and political reasons, to maintain the Caliphate, proposed at the last moment when the decisions were to be taken, that I should assume the office of the Caliphate. I immediately gave a negative reply to these men.

When the Grand National Assembly had abolished the Caliphate, Rasih Efendi, a religious scholar and representative for Antalya, was president of the deputation of the Red Crescent which was in India. He came back to Ankara via Egypt. After soliciting an interview with me, he made statements to the effect that "the Muslims in the countries through which he had been travelling demanded that

I should become Caliph, and that the competent Muslim bodies had commissioned him to inform me of this desire."

In the reply which I gave to Rasih Efendi, I expressed my thanks for the benevolence and affection which the Muslims had shown me and said: "You are a religious scholar. You know that Caliph signifies Head of the State. How can I accept the proposals and desires of people who are governed by kings and emperors? If I should declare myself ready to accept this office, would the sovereigns of those people consent to it? The orders of the Caliph must be obeyed and his interdictions submitted to. Are those who want to make me Caliph in a position to execute my orders? Consequently, would it not be ridiculous to fix me up with an illusionary role which has neither sense nor the right to exist?"

I must frankly and categorically declare that those who continue to occupy themselves with the chimera of the Caliphate and thereby mislead the Muslim world, are nothing but enemies of the Muslim world, and especially of Turkey. They are only ignorant or blind men who could attach hopes to such illusions.

Is it from love of our faith that such people as Rauf Bey, Vehip Pasha, Çerkez Ethem and Reşit, all the "Hundred and Fifty"*, all members of the deposed dynasty of the Sultanate and the Caliphate with their adherents, all enemies of Turkey, are working with so much bitterness? Is the aim of those who are working so energetically against us, sheltering themselves under the words "holy revolution," but who use means such as murderous attempts, and gangs of brigands, and who maintain organisation centres at our frontiers, who have always made the destruction of Turkey their aim - is this aim actually a holy one? Indeed, to believe this would mean that we were possessed of unmitigated ignorance and boundless blindness.

From now onwards, it will not be so easy to suppose that the Muslim peoples and the Turkish nation would have fallen to such a low level as to continue in the abuse of the purity of the conscience and the tenderness of the sentiments of the Muslim world to criminal aims. Impudence has its limits.

Let's cast a glance at "Tanin." In a leading article in this paper under the heading of "Political Agitation" it is mentioned that it had come to their knowledge that "among the high personages worthy of esteem and confidence who have distinguished themselves in the national fight, a united action has been set to work; and that the Press which entertained sincere relations with the People's Party and the Government had received the news very badly and had explained matters in a very disagreeable manner," and that "they had begun to develop opinions of a nature to discredit the future party already."

Alluding to the question of the programme and having emphasised the point that the People's Party had no programme, the article continues: "We ourselves are by no means satisfied with the People's Party, but we are quite in favour of the things which they say and manifest in the name of the principles of the People's Party." After having explained the meaning of the principles of the People's Party, the question is put: "But in reality is it so?"

The editor himself answers this question in the negative and says: "For the reason that we wish with all our heart to see a party of renovation and reform before us, we imagine a People's Party in the form which we recommend." Then the editor continues as follows: "The programme of the People's Party is one thing, and the speeches they deliver and the way they pursue it is another. The democracy of the People's Party only consists of words."

In the first sentence the author of these opinions wants to say that the People's Party had neither adopted in their programme nor announced anywhere the principle of the proclamation of the Republic and the abolition of the Caliphate, but that they had actually accomplished this alteration. In this he is right. But what he interpolated to the People's Party in his second sentence was not exact.

To the profusion of words which he used, the writer added to the article the following in order to prove the legitimacy of the endeavours of the opposition to form a government: "Has the virtue of acting and being inspired by the anxiety of our country only been accorded by Divine grace to those who are in power?"

In a leading article of 4 November 1924, under the heading of "The Army and Politics," the chief editor of "Tanin" expresses the following opinions: "The form of the Government is the Republic. But there is no advantage in only changing the name. What must really be altered are the spirit and the principles. In America today, besides the United States, there are about twenty countries bearing the name of Republic. Even Haiti, which consists exclusively of negroes, is a Republic. But the difference between a Republic and absolutism is very small in these countries. We see there a little tyrant who has become President of the Republic by force and who takes the place of a hereditary monarch. That is all. The autocrat bearing the name of President of the Republic governs according to his pleasure. As absolute sovereign he knows no other law than that of his caprice."

After having made an exception to Chile, the editor of the "Tanin," referring to the other American Republics, says: "None of these countries is today worthy of bearing the name of a true republic. For they are not founded ...

on democracy. The military leaders are the cause of the absolute system governing under the name of republic."

I should like to dwell on this point for a moment. This article deals with the subject of the dismissal of the commanders who were representatives, and for this reason. But it was written at a moment when the commanders of our armies, having abandoned their corps, came into the Assembly in order to overthrow the Government. The editor in question had, the previous day, filled column after column with the creations of his mind to prove the legitimacy of their desire to come into power. The editor who quotes examples in order to prove that a Republic need not necessarily differ from an absolute government, and indicates as a reason for this fact that it is not founded on democracy, is the same person who, on the other hand, asserts that "the attachment of the Governmental party to democratic principles only exists in words." The individual who says that such things happen because there are military leaders existing in it is at the same time the editor who knows that the President of the Turkish Republic is one of the military leaders. And it is again this same person who is steadfastly working to oppose this or that military leader becoming the President of the Turkish Republic, also the Turkish Prime Minister who belongs likewise to the group of military leaders. To prove to the nation that the party he does not like must be overthrown, he quotes in addition examples which are presumably worthy of meditation and capable of serving for instruction. He says: "The general who can gather round himself the greatest number of revolters is the one who rises to the dignity of the President of the Republic," and by entering into the fight with the chiefs of the brigands, they usurp the position of President.

It is impossible, not to understand the reason why these and similar words have been written, and not to be enlightened about the regrettable effects which these articles were bound to exercise on the members of the Assembly and on public opinion.

Indeed, the effect produced unfortunately had further repercussions in the practical sphere.

The same Republican journalist who seems to be affected by the fact that Refet Pasha, Kazım Bekir Pasha and Ali Fuat Pasha had not been appointed to the Commission for National Defence disapproves this time of the fact that the commanders of the army had not been elected to a commission which will have an influence over the armies.

On this point, however, he cannot abstain from adapting himself to the democratic principles for which, as he wants us to believe that he felt so much sympathy for. Let us go together through the sentences in which these ideas are expressed.

Among the news which has been published in the political columns, the following sentence appears: "The Commission for National Defence constitutes a sphere of activity which is surely the least political one of the Assembly and which has even no relation to politics." The editor intends to ask thereby why and for what reason the Army Inspectors have not been given the opportunity of working in a sphere which has no relation to politics. We would answer this as follows:

It has not been done because, as surely as the Commission for National Defence is a sphere of activity which was to have no relation to politics, it would lead to disagreements to bring people into it who have entered the Cabinet with the very intention of occupying themselves with politics.

Then the editor continues:

"It is there where the laws are elaborated which will contribute to direct, improve, reorganise and ameliorate the Army which is called upon to defend the honour and independence of the nation. For those whose only thought is of our country without letting themselves be governed by political passions, it is a duty of loyalty to confide this care to the most capable of our military commanders."

I want to dwell on these sentences for a moment.

It is in fact one of the most important questions to direct, improve, reorganise and ameliorate the condition of the army. The authority entrusted with this task is the General Staff, to which our most prominent military leaders belong, as the editor himself points out.

Each time this great General Staff, which occupies itself with the administration, organisation and perfecting of the army judges it necessary, it informs the Government of its proposals.

The questions reported on after mature deliberations by the great General Staff and the Ministry of National Defence, the head of which is a member of the Cabinet, are examined and reviewed by the Supreme War Council which meets annually. This Council consists of the Chief of the General Staff, the Ministers of National Defence and of Marine and also the Army Inspectors.

After the questions have been examined by the Supreme War Council, those whose application is judged necessary are laid before the Government. Those which require the passing of a law the Government submits to the Assembly. After having passed in the regular way through the Commission of National Defence, and ithe subject requires it, also through other commissions, the questions are discussed in a full sitting of the Assembly and put into legal form. It is necessary that the members of the Commission for National Defence should be well informed in military art and science. But this is not sufficient. It is also necessary that the members of the Commission for National Defence should be *au fait* with regard to the finances and policy of the State and many other questions.

If the knowledge of military science could have sufficed for the elaboration of legislative projects relating to the army, it would not have been necessary to have them reexamined by one or several commissions, after they had been formulated by the General Staff and approved of by the Supreme War Council; for the persons who occupy themselves with politics, even if they should come from the army, could neither be more competent nor more authorised than those who have spent their lives in following the continual progress of military art and science and in studying its applications.

The Army Inspectors who believe they have sound judgment with regard to the administration and reorganisation of the army, who believe they have great experience, and who, according to the law, are members of the Supreme War Council, should find the most suitable field for their activities at the head of the armies and in the Supreme Council.

If the attempt were to be made to introduce into the Commission of National Defence commanders who, without appreciating the importance of their own functions, wanted to be taken seriously by finding fault with the Ministry of National Defence and the General Staff; who preferred to work in the political sphere and who regarded all those as incapable who did not appreciate their opinions and plans; if the attempt should be made, I say, to introduce these persons into the Commission for National Defence, it would mean nothing less than to satisfy their injurious inclinations consisting in the prevention of the application of propositions of all kinds regarding the army submitted by the Government to the Chamber and to use pretexts in order to overthrow the Government and to replace the Chief of the General Staff by another.

It is useless to suppose that the aim of the chief editor of "Tanin" had been anything else than this.

The editor who was annoyed that his aim has not been realised, writes:

"In the ancient Athenian Republic people were devoted so passionately to democratic principles that in no branch of administration could a sound principle be adopted even when experience and practical knowledge required it.

"In spite of this excess of democracy the military chiefs were kept away from the application of this principle."

For one who tries to make the nation understand that the democracy of the People's Party consists only of words, and that there was no difference between a republic and an autocracy, it is, according to my opinion, surely neither loyal nor correct to pretend, in the same days when these fallacies are read, that it appears indicated to exempt the generals whom he wanted to bring into power from the application of the rules of democracy.

Would you like to have an example of the language used by men when hatred and passion obscure their spirit and conscience? Listen to these words of the same editor:

"How disgusting is the sight which the People's Party and İsmet Pasha's Government present to the country!

"The leading personages who are to such a degree slaves of their passions cannot pretend that they want to form a National Party and to represent the nation.

"Young men full of enthusiasm and hope in the future have sacrificed their noble lives in the bloom of their lives to save the country, but not to surrender it as a toy for politicians who only think of their persons and of their interests!"

The author of these fallacies and arguments who finds pleasure in expressing the absolute contrary to truth, finds the sight of the party which we have formed disgusting and unsympathetic, and represents it as such; he says the same thing of îsmet Pasha and the Government which we had commissioned him to form.

Our face was always pure and will remain so. Those who have an ugly and repulsive physiognomy are rather those who, with an infamous soul and driven by low instincts, try to degrade and blacken our actions and attitude which are most patriotic, conscientious and honourable.

İsmet Pasha's Government received a vote of confidence by 148 voices against 19 and one abstention.

The journalist friends of those who had been defeated in Parliament were naturally not very satisfied with this result. They resumed their campaign with greater bitterness and more obstinacy.

The leading article of "Vatan" of 9 November is full of criticisms such as the following:

"The existing form of administration represents on paper the most advanced degree of national sovereignty; but making a somewhat more exhaustive study of the mentality of those who govern we can observe that in reality nothing has been changed."

The word 'reactionary' becomes fashionable again.

The leading article of "Vatan" of 10 November reminds me of the anecdote of Timurlenk's elephant and contains remarks such as the following, in which complaints are raised against the bad tactics of those who try to overthrow the Government:

"When the interpellation took place at Ankara there existed a majority ready to criticise." Those who criticised have not understood how to maintain this position; they have given themselves up to eriticise individually without having a common organisation; even the individual criticisms were not carried through in a serious form.

"When the interpellations took a general turn, nobody thought of consulting his notes of vacancies. Even the most embittered critics had not the courage to say what they thought." Considering the situation from the point of view of a politician, the author of this article says: "It is evident that the supporters of the Government have from beginning to end manoeuvred in mature consideration of a plan and the tactics of its application."

At this point, I feel inclined to ask the writer the following question:

If, after many months of preparation and long and secret con- ferences with their comrades of İstanbul, the persons to whom you suggested to confide the destiny of our country have lacked confidence in themselves to such a degree that they, as you say, did not venture to express that which they repeated over and over again; if nineteen persons at the utmost show themselves incapable of agreeing about their action in the Chamber, how could it be expected that they possessed the capability and high qualities for taking the direction of the State into their hands?

The editor, who fills this column with his prose, reflects in the eyes of the whole world the spectacle in Parliament and encourages its complaints when he says:

"Alas! he too has revealed himself similar to the others."

This editor, who also hides himself, listens to words others whisper in his ears such as the following:

"What can be expected from a building which has been constructed from old material?"

Did the one who wrote these lines really think so on that day? Or did he intentionally use these senseless words in order to raise the nation against us?

By whatever standard his conduct might be interpreted neither of these interpretations could be justified. Dirty fellows of this nature have done much harm to the Republic.

"Tevhidi Efkar" continued to publish a series of unnecessary and senseless articles under the heading of "The Useless and Worthless Victory."

In describing to you the question of the plot and depicting the scenes in Parliament, I have entered very much into details which may appear superfluous. I hope you will pardon me for this. An interpellation can take place under every government and at any time. Is it permissible to attribute such importance to an interpellation which I must add immediately had no normal character? It formed a special phase of the plot.

It was after this episode of the interpellation that the opposition was forced to unmask itself. As you know, it was at the time that the members of the opposition had founded a party under the name of "Republican Progressive Party" and published its programme which was drafted by an unknown hand.

Could seriousness and sincerity be attributed to the deeds and attitude of people who avoided pronouncing even the word Republic and who tried to suppress the Republic from the very beginning, but who called the party Republican and even Republican Progressive?

If the party founded by Rauf Bey and his comrades had introduced itself under the name of "Conservative" a reason might perhaps have been discovered for it. But naturally they could not be justified when they pretended to be more republican and more progressive than we were.

Could any sincerity be expected from people who had adopted the following principle: "The Party respects religious thoughts and religious doctrines"? Was not this principle the standard of all those who pursued personal aims whilst they allured and deceived the ignorant, fanatical and superstitious people? Has not the Turkish nation for centuries been dragged into endless suffering and into the pestilential swamps of obscurity under this banner, rescue only being possible through great sacrifices?

Did those who appeared under the same flag, but who wanted to be regarded as progressive Republicans, not follow the deep design of provoking the religious fanaticism of the nation, putting them thus completely against the Republic, progress and reform?

Under the mask of respect for religious ideas and dogmas the new Party addressed itself to the people in the following words:

"We want the re-establishment of the Caliphate; we do not want new laws; we are satisfied with the Mecelle (religious law); we shall protect the Medreses (religious schools), the Tekkes (Islamic lodges), the pious institutions, the Softahs, the Sheiks, and their disciples. Be on our side; the party of Mustafa Kemal, having abolished the Caliphate, is breaking Islam into ruins; they will make you into unbelievers, into infidels; they will make you wear hats."

Can anyone pretend that the style of propaganda used by the Party was not full of these reactionary appeals.

Read these sentences, Gentlemen, from a letter written by one of the adherents of this programme on 10 March 1923 to Cebranh Kurd Halit Bey, who was later on hanged:

"They are attacking the very principles which perpetuate the existence of the Muslim world ... I have also read your commentaries addressed to our comrades . . . They have contributed much to strengthen their zeal. . . Assimilation with the West means the destruction of our history, our civilisation.

"The idea of abolishing the Caliphate and founding a secular State can only lead to one result, namely to produce factors which endanger the future of Islam."

Facts and events have proved that the programme of the Republican Progressive Party has been the work emanating from the brains of traitors. This Party became the refuge and the point of support for reactionary and rebellious elements.

They worked in order to facilitate in our country the application of plans which had been hatched by our enemies for the annihilation of the new Turkish State, the young Turkish Republic. Trying to find out and studying the reasons for the insurrection in the East due to a concerted movement of a general and reactionary character, you will discover among the most effective and important causes the religious promises of the Republican Progressive Party as well as the organisations and activities of the "delegated secretaries," which the same Party sent into the Eastern provinces.

Did a "delegated secretary" who filled his notebook with prescriptions of the Prophet treating the virtues of prayer, of devotion, not try to apply the programme of his party when he occupied himself with religious manoeuvres in the Eastern Provinces?

When a politician, who perhaps never in his life has said a prayer, recommends the innocent population to recite night prayers in addition to the five required day prayers, should his aim remain enigmatical?

Had the fanatical and reactionary elements, who perceived the institutions and suspicions of former days crumbling bit by bit under the power and extension of our revolution, held tight with both hands to a party that proclaimed its respect for religious thought and religious doctrines and, especially, to men whose names had obtained a certain celebrity within this party?

Were those who had created the new party not fully aware of this truth? Unfolding the standard of religion, where did they intend to lead the country and nation? In the answer which this question requires words such as goodwill, distractedness or indifference are not of a nature to excuse the leaders of a party that makes publicity with the promise to lead the country towards progress.

The new party in its activity showed itself exactly the contrary to the meaning of the words "progress" and "republic."

The leaders of this party actually inspired the reactionaries with hope and strengthened them.

Let me quote an example:

In a letter written to Sheikh Sait by Kadri (who was subsequently hanged), whom the rebels of Ergani had recognised as the Governor, he said: "Kazım Karabekir Pasha's party in the Assembly is pious and respects religious rights. I do not doubt that they will give us their support. And even the 'delegated secretaries' who are with Sheikh Eyüp (one of the rebel leaders who was executed) have brought the regulations of the party."

At this time, Sheikh Eyüp declared: "The only party that could save religion is the one which Kazım Karabekir Pasha has formed; in the principles of this party it is mentioned that religious prescriptions will be esteemed."

Could anybody assume that people who, using the words "progress" and "republic," believed it to be wise to conceal the flag of religion from our sight as well as from that of the cultured elements of the country were not aware of the fact that there were people who in our own country as well as abroad made preparations of all kinds and devised all sorts of plots with the purpose of raising in the country a reaction to produce a general rebellion?

It must be admitted that even if not all the members belonging to this new party, in any case those who regarded the religious promises as a means of success and who had adopted the corresponding formulas as their guiding principles, would have been favourably disposed towards the country and ourselves, and not have known of the attacks which were being prepared.

Let us assume that they knew nothing of the secret meetings which had already been held months before the revolt in various parts of the country; of the organisations of the "Secret Islamic Society", of the promises of support for the prospective revolt which had been made in the course of a meeting in Istanbul to the Nakşibendi Sheikhs, and, finally, of the great hopes expressed by those who carried on a revolutionary agitation beyond the frontiers in their proclamations about the party of Kazım Karabekir Pasha*. When they were told directly through the mediation of Fethi Bey himself that the attitude of their party was harmful, and calculated to lead to indignation and reaction, must they then not have been obliged to examine the position in its true light? Must they not at least, after the Government's warning and my own, which were prompted by the most sincere feelings, have seen the truth and acted accordingly? On the contrary, even then they took the utmost trouble to interpret the formula of the "respect for religious thought and articles of belief" in quite a contrary sense, that is as though they intended therewith to give us to understand that they had shown the far-reaching liberalism in their respect for the ideas and articles of belief of any religion or its adherents.

One cannot describe this attitude as correct and sincere. On the political field one experiences many manoeuvres;

but if ignorance, fanaticism and agitation of all sorts oppose themselves to the Republican administration which is the incorporation of a holy ideal, and to the modern movement, then the place of the Progressives and Republicans is at the side of the true Progressives and the true Republicans, and not in the ranks from which reaction draws hope and energy.

What happened then? The Government and the Committee found themselves forced to take extraordinary measures. They caused the law regarding the restoration of order to be proclaimed, and the Independence Courts to take action. For a considerable time they kept eight or nine divisions of the army at war strength for the suppression of disorders, and put an end to the harmful organisation which bore the name "Republican Progressive Party."

The result was, of course, the success of the Republic. The insurgents were destroyed. But the enemies of the Republic did not consider this defeat the last phase of the controversy. In an unworthy manner they played their last card which took the form of the İzmir attack. The avenging hand of Republican justice again mastered the army of conspirators and saved the Republic.

When in consequence of serious necessity we became convinced for the first time that it would be useful for the Government to take extraordinary measures, there were people who disapproved of our action.

There were persons who disseminated and sought to gain credence to the thought that we were making use of the law for Restoration of Order and the Courts of Independence as tools of dictatorship or despotism.

There is no doubt that time and events will show to those who disseminated this opinion how mistaken they were, and put them to shame. We never used the exceptional measures, which all the same were legal, to set ourselves in any way above the law.

On the contrary, we applied them to restore peace and tranquility in the country. We made use of them to insure the existence and independence of the country. We made use of them with the object of contributing to the social development of the nation.

As soon as the necessity for the application of the exceptional measures no longer existed, we did not hesitate to renounce them. Thus, for instance, the Independence Courts ceased their activity at the given moment, just as the law regarding the Restoration of Order was re-submitted to the Assembly for examination as soon as its legislative term had ended. If the Assembly considered it necessary to prolong its application for some time this certainly happened because it saw therein the higher interest of the nation and of the Republic.

Can anyone be of the opinion that this decision of the High Assembly was intended to hand over to us the means for the carrying on of a dictatorship? Gentlemen, if you consider the work that has been carried out during the period in which the law for the Restoration of Order and the Courts of Independence were in practice, you will notice that the confidence and trust of the Assembly and the nation have not been abused. The peace and order that has been brought about as a result of the suppression of important rebellions and plots in the country has naturally met the approval of the nation. Gentlemen! It was necessary to abolish the fez, which sat on our heads as a sign of ignorance, of fanaticism, of hatred to progress and civilisation, and to adopt in its place the hat, the customary headdress of the whole civilised world, thus showing, among other things, that no difference existed in the manner of thought between the Turkish nation and the whole family of civilised mankind. We did that while the law for the Restoration of Order was still in force. If it had not been in force we should have done so all the same; but one can say with complete truth that the existence of this law made the thing much easier for us. As a matter of fact the application of the law for the Restoration of Order prevented the morale of the nation being poisoned to a great extent by reactionaries.

It is true that a representative of Bursa, who, during his whole time of being representative, had not once appeared on the speaker's rostrum, nor ever spoken a word in the Chamber in defence of the interests of the nation and the Republic, the representative of Bursa, I say, Nurettin Pasha, introduced a lengthy motion against wearing hats and mounted the rostrum to defend it.

He asserted that hat-wearing was a "contradiction of the fundamental rights of the national sovereignty, and of the principle of the integrity of personal freedom," and attempted "on no account to let this measure be forced upon the population." But the outbreak of fanaticism and reaction which Nurettin Pasha succeeded, from the tribune, in calling forth, merely led to the sentencing of a few reactionaries by the Courts of Independence.

While the law regarding the Restoration of Order was in force there took place also the closing of the Tekkes, of the convents, and of the mausoleums, as well as the abolition of all sects and all titles such as Sheikh, Derviş, "Guide," Çelebi, Fortune Teller, Magician, Mausoleum Guard, etc.

One will be able to imagine how necessary the carrying through of these measures was, in order to prove that our nation as a whole was no primitive nation, filled with superstitions and prejudices.

Could a civilised nation tolerate a mass of people who let themselves be led by the nose by a herd of Sheiks, Dedes, Seyyits, Çelebis, Babas and Emirs; who entrusted their destiny and their lives to palm readers, magicians, dice-throwers and amulet sellers? Ought one to preserve in the Turkish State, in the Turkish Republic, elements and institutions such as those which had for centuries given the nation the appearance of being other than it really was? Would one not therewith have committed the greatest, most irreparable error to the cause of progress and reawakening?

If we made use of the law for the Restoration of Order in this manner, it was in order to avoid such a historic error; to show the nation's brow pure and luminous, as it is; to prove that our people think neither in a fanatical nor a reactionary manner.

At the same time the new laws were worked out and decreed which promise the most fruitful results for the nation on the social and economic plane, and in general in all the forms of the expression of human activity ... the Civil Code, which ensures the liberty of women and stabilises the existence of the family.

Accordingly we made use of all circumstances only from one point of view, which consisted therein: to raise the nation on to that level on which it is justified in standing in the civilised world, to stabilise the Turkish Republic more and more on steadfast foundations . . . and in addition to destroy the spirit of despotism for ever.

I shall consider myself very happy if I have succeeded in the course of this report in expressing some truths which are calculated to rivet to the interest and attention of my nation and of future generations.

I have tried to show, in these accounts, how a great people, whose national course was considered as finished, reconquered its independence; how it created a national and modern State founded on the latest results of science.

The result we have attained to day is the fruit of teachings which arose from centuries of suffering, and the price of streams of blood which have drenched every foot of the ground of our beloved homeland.

This holy treasure I lay in the hands of the youth of Turkey.

Turkish Youth! Your primary duty is ever to preserve and defend the National independence of the Turkish Republic.

That is the sole foundation of your existence and your future. This foundation is your most precious treasure. In the future, too, there will be ill-will, both in the country itself and abroad, which will try to tear this treasure from you. If one day you are compelled to defend your independence and the Republic, then, in order to fulfil your duty, you will have to look beyond the possibilities and conditions in which you might find yourself. It may be that these conditions and possibilities are altogether unfavourable. It is possible that the enemies who desire to destroy your independence and your Republic represent the strongest force that the earth has ever seen; that they have, through craft and force, taken possession of all the fortresses and arsenals of the homeland; that all its armies are scattered and the country actually and completely occupied.

Assuming, in order to look still darker possibilities in the face, that those who hold the power of Government within the country have fallen into error, that they are fools or traitors, yes, even that these leading persons identify their personal interests with the enemy's political goals, it might happen that the nation came into complete privation, into the most extreme distress; that it found itself in a condition of ruin and complete exhaustion.

Even under those circumstances, Turkish child of future generations, it is your duty to save the independence of the Turkish Republic.

The strength that you will need for this is in the noble blood which flows in your veins.